With the
Imperial Camel Corps
in the Great War

With the Imperial Camel Corps in the Great War

The Story of a Serving Officer With the
British 2nd Battalion Against the Senussi
& During the Palestine Campaign

Geoffrey Inchbald

LEONAUR

With the Imperial Camel Corps in the Great War:
The Story of a Serving Officer With the British 2nd
Battalion Against the Senussi & During the Palestine Campaign.
Compiled from the published writings of Geoffrey Inchbald

Copyright © Geoffrey Inchbald

Published by Leonaur Ltd

Material original to this edition
copyright © 2005 Leonaur Ltd

ISBN (10 digit): 1-84677-012-2 (hardcover)
ISBN (13 digit): 978-1-84677-012-8 (hardcover)

ISBN (10 digit): 1-84677-007-6 (softcover)
ISBN (13 digit): 978-1-84677-007-4 (softcover)

http://www.leonaur.com

Contents

List of Illustrations & Maps

The publishers wish to thank the **Imperial War Museum** for its assistance in providing and allowing the use of many of the photographs used in the book. **Imperial War Museum** reference numbers are listed below with the relevant descriptions.

Between pages 124 - 140

(1) The author on 'Mick' after inspection by General Allenby.
(2) Lt Merlin Huth, Abassia, January 1917. (I.W.M. Q03787)
(3) Lt Inchbald, Abassia, January 1917. (I.W.M. Q163786)
(4) Captain C.W. Mason-Macfarlane. (O.C. No. 8 Company). Killed at the Baharia Oasis in September 1916.
(5) Captain J.J. Paterson.
(6) Camels being exercised.
(7) No. 10 Company on the march.
(8) Bikanir Camel Corps.
(9) No. 8 Company section.
(10) Trekking.
(11) Lt. Huth, No. 8 Company, Western Desert, 1916. (I.W.M. Q104019)
(12) Lt Alan F.J Baron de Rutzen (O.C. No. 6 Company). Killed at Romani in August 1916.
(13) Major F.C. Gregory, M.C. (O.C. No. 7 Company). Killed near Jaffa in November 1917.
(14) Captain A.F. Newsom. (O.C. No. 8 Company). Killed at Amman in March 1918.
(15) Captain J.A. Lyall, M.C. (O.C. No. 10 Company, 1918).
(16)Lieutenant Geoffrey Inchbald of No. 8 Company feeding his camel in the Western Desert, 1916. (I.W.M. Q103976)
(17) "Signalling by heliograph on the summit of Gobel Libni", Sinai, summer 1917. Patrol commanded by Lieutenant Inchbald (seated right). (I.W.M. 103793)

Maps

Foreward

Written at the time of the publication of
'The Imperial Camel Corps'

Following the publication of *Camels and Others** I had the good fortune to establish contact with Mr Laurence (Rory) Moore, M.B.E. of Leeds, who not only served with the Imperial Camel Corps throughout the whole of its existence and for most of the time as N.C.O. i/c Signals with 2nd Battalion H.Q. (this Battalion comprised the whole of the British as distinct from the Australian and New Zealand contingents) but also took an active part in the Hejaz operations, and he has very kindly supplied me with an account of the latter which is based on a series of lectures which he has given to various Rotary Clubs over the last two or three years. And this is not all. Mr Moore has played the chief part in maintaining in Yorkshire and the North Midlands an Imperial Camel Corps old Comrades Association of which he is the Honorary Secretary, and from time to time he publishes a newsletter which he distributes to the various survivors, and it is surprising how many there still are, with whom he has retained or established contact over the years.

One of these survivors is Wing Commander C. H. N. Ashlin of Chiddingfold, who was wounded at Romani, and to whose kindness I am indebted for permission also to include an account of the operations based on one which he wrote some years ago, and I think I am justified in saying that the material which has been provided from these and other sources, when added to the account which I have already given in Camels and Others, makes up a fairly complete history of the Imperial Camel Corps from its inception in the early part of 1916 to its disbandment

*Inchbald's first book.

11

in 1919 a few months after the final surrender of the Turkish armies. I am, of course, referring to the 2nd Battalion. The 'Deeds and Misdeeds', to quote the author, of the Australian and New Zealand contingents were described in a book called The Cameliers by Oliver Hogue (who wrote under the nom de plume of Trooper Bluegum) which was published in London in 1919 by Andrew Melrose Ltd.

1. Childhood

I was born in 1896 in a bungalow high up on the Peak at Hong Kong. This not particularly interesting event occurred in the middle of an unusually severe typhoon and my mother's confinement cannot have been assisted when the fireplace was blown into her bedroom with a resounding crash. I believe it was on this occasion that my father, on his way home from his office in the town, spent several hours crouched in a ditch to avoid being blown away. By morning there was not a single movable object left outside the house. Not only the chickens but even the henhouse itself had completely disappeared.

My father was a banker with relatively slender means but in those days a little went a long way and we had a house full of Chinese servants. My parents were devoted to them, a sentiment which they apparently returned. They were honest, clean, cheerful and willing and they had a tremendous sense of humour and fun, two quite different things. Until my fifth year I was looked after by amahs whom I adored, and I can remember them now with their cafe-au-lait complexions, faces criss-crossed with hundreds of little lines, and black hair pulled tightly back. One of them accompanied the family when it made one of its periodical visits to England a year or so after I was born, and another returned with us when we left China for good and I was nearly four years old. My father was taking up an appointment in London after serving more than twenty years in Hong Kong, Shanghai and other parts of China.

From what he told me it must have been a wonderful life. A couple of hours work at the bank in the early morning followed by a game of racquets, a glass or two of champagne and lunch at the club, siesta and a little more work in the afternoon. He either owned, or knew several people who owned, a string of ponies and he was in the saddle pretty well every evening. In his earlier years out there he had several adventures. On one occasion he went on a shooting expedition with a friend of his, somewhere in the interior of China, and was fortunate enough to kill a wild boar. He had very little experience of shooting but a lot of courage and common sense. The animal suddenly emerged from a thicket about two hundred yards away and promptly put its head down and charged him. His coolies took refuge in the nearest tree but he held his ground until the boar was almost on him when he side-stepped and fired at it at point-blank range as it passed. Nothing happened and the boar carried straight on until it was out of sight. However, after the party had returned to camp that night, the boar was brought in by some villagers. The bullet had gone through both its lungs but it had carried on for another mile before it dropped dead. But the real point of this story is that it weighed 438 pounds, which was a world record at that time, and for all I know still is, with the result that although I believe that my father never fired another shot from a rifle he became a celebrity in the sporting world, and appeared in nearly every book which was written on the subject of big game shooting. The head was preserved and mounted with a suitable inscription and we still have it in the family.

On another occasion he had to take a consignment of gold bullion up the Yangtse-kiang during the Boxer rebellion and he was pursued and shot at by hordes of Chinese on either bank. Things looked pretty nasty but at a critical moment one of their leaders who was waving his rifle about and screaming imprecations missed his footing and fell head over heels into a ditch, which so convulsed his companions that they gave up the chase and made gestures towards the launch of the utmost friendship and good humour, pointing at their luckless colleague and roaring with laughter. I think that this incident is typical of the sense of fun which I have already mentioned and which is, or rather was, always just underneath the surface.

In the island of Hong Kong it seems that the occupational hazards included both bandits and snakes. There was the day when a cobra got into the bungalow, and on another occasion my father had to make a considerable detour on his way home to avoid a colony of rattlesnakes which showed unmistakably aggressive intentions.

I had two elder brothers, one of whom was born in Shanghai and the other in Plymouth during one of the family visits to England. This might be a convenient place to say a brief word about them. Peter, born in 1890, was destined for the army and after spending five years at Cheltenham and two at Woolwich, he was commissioned to the Royal Field Artillery in 1912 and went to France with the first expeditionary force in August 1914. A month or two later he was one of the first four officers to be awarded the Military Cross, a new decoration, the announcement of which was actually made on the same day that the first awards were published. My brother's battery had been heavily engaged during the whole of the battle of Mons and was in fact the last to retreat after inflicting very severe damage on the enemy. In the event it was very nearly cut off as the German armies had advanced several miles on either side, and by the time the battery galloped through to safety the gap had very nearly closed.

The havoc wrought by artillery on the massed German infantry during the earlier years of the war must have been appalling and I can vividly recall my brother's description of a day when, as F.O.O. to the battery, he watched from a front-line trench for literally hours on end as the Germans advanced shoulder to shoulder in a solid mass of field grey and every shell exploded with deadly effect on a target which it was impossible to miss.

Although he fought for three years almost without a break except for a very occasional few days leave in England, Peter somehow survived the war unharmed, although blown up on more than one occasion and suffering severely from shell shock and battle fatigue, which brought an end to his active service at the end of 1917. Later on he became an instructor at Woolwich, but finally retired from the army a year or two after the war and became a stockbroker. He was recalled for the second world war but soon after that was over he retired for good and went to live in a beautiful Elizabethan manor house, which he and his wife had acquired in Dorset and where he died a few years ago.

My second brother, Jack, who was born in 1894, was one of the most brilliant young men of his ill-fated generation. He was a scholar at Winchester and New College, Oxford, where he had only spent a year when the war broke out. He joined up immediately, being commissioned and posted to the 9th Battalion of the Devonshire Regiment towards the end of 1914. The battalion crossed to France in the following year and was soon involved in heavy and continuous fighting. In April 1917, while leading his company in an attack on the German trenches somewhere near Bapaume, he was killed together with his four subalterns, and they were all buried together in the corner of a small cemetery not far from the scene of the action. After the war my father and mother put up a stained-glass window in his memory in the parish church of Thurlestone in Devon, and the inscription, which was composed by Montague Rendall, the Headmaster of Winchester, reads as follows:

IN MEM DILECTI FILII
JOHN CHANTREY ELLIOT INCHBALD
UTRIUSQUE COLLEGII DE
WYKEHAM SSHOLARIS COHORTIS
DEVON CAPITANI QUI AD BAPAUME
ANNOVITAE SUAE XXIII
SALUTIS MCMXVII BELLANDO OCCIDIT
FENESTRAM HANC POSUERUNT PARENTES

Soon after our return to England we went to live for a short time at Gipsy Hill, near the Crystal Palace. The only incident there which remains in my mind was the death of Queen Victoria and seeing my mother, dressed up in black from head to foot, go off to the funeral. In 1901 we moved to Harefield, which was the dower house of Nonesuch Park at Cheam in Surrey, and it was not until then that all the belongings which my parents had brought from China were finally removed from store and unpacked. These consisted almost entirely of Chinese furniture and furnishings including heavily carved blackwood tables, chairs and cupboards of various descriptions, dozens of beautiful porcelain vases, Chinese (and Japanese) prints, several kekemonas and some bronze dragons, of which I still have two. These were supplemented by modern furniture, which my father bought in London, and some very nice pieces of antique walnut and mahogany, which are all that remain today. Harefield was a large and comfortable house with a beautiful garden including a couple of grass tennis courts. There were also two large fields between the house and the road, which were separated by a double row of elms bordering the drive. Later on we constructed a nine-hole golf course in the fields and the trees presented a splendid natural hazard. To surmount them you had to use a mashie from the tee and, as at one hole the green was not very far away from the trees, you were liable to overshoot it if you succeeded in negotiating the trees. I remember a famous shot by Peter when the ball soared over the trees and green, hit the railway line which lay just beyond, bounced about fifty feet in the air and was found lying on the green two inches from the hole. Had it gone in I feel that it must have been the most distinguished hole in one on record.

One thing I used to love as a child was to watch from the landing when my parents were giving a dinner party. There never seemed to be less than seven or eight courses and the sight and smell of them as they were brought through the hall on their way to the dining room used to make my mouth water. Occasionally, after I got back to bed, my governess used to bring me up tit-bits which she had succeeded in extracting from the cook, and I thought to myself how wonderful it must be to be grown up and have delicacies like this every day. Another treat was to go down to my mother's bedroom before the guests arrived, or she went out to dinner, and see her dressed up in one of her gorgeous Edwardian evening gowns, which suited her so perfectly. Another adventure was Derby Day. The road was the main, or one of the main roads, from London to Epsom and during the morning there was an endless stream to watch of coaches, carriages, wagons, costermongers' carts and conveyances of every description and, what with the horns tooting away merrily for all they were worth and everybody shouting and singing and calling out ribald remarks to passers-by, the din and confusion was terrific. So was the dust. This was Edwardian England letting her hair down with a vengeance and it is sad to reflect that within a few years all this was to disappear for ever. At night the whole proceeding was repeated in the reverse direction and intensified by the large amount of liquid refreshment which had been consumed during the day, and I used to lie awake for hours and listen until at last the sound and fury died away.

Domestic servants presented no problem in those days and there was one occasion which made a deep impression on me though I cannot have been more than six years old. My mother wanted a kitchen maid and I accompanied her on a visit to Mrs Jones's establishment in Epsom where she had made an appointment to inspect any candidates for the vacancy. The name was probably not Mrs Jones, but this will serve. We were greeted at the door by the great lady herself, dressed in what I think must have been black bombazine. Anyway it was all shiny. She ushered us into a large room which had on one side a sort of throne placed on a platform above the level of the floor. My mother was deposited on this and I sat on a little chair by her side, while Mrs Jones took up her position, standing of course, on the other side. When everyone was settled Mrs Jones clapped her hands and there emerged from a hidden doorway a little girl, who could not have been much more than fourteen years old. She walked slowly across the room until she reached a spot exactly opposite the throne when she turned round and curtsied to my mother before resuming her walk and disappearing through an identical door on the other side. This proceeding was watched closely by my mother, but she made no comment, and Mrs Jones promptly clapped her hands again and a similar little girl went through the same performance with the same negative result. At last, when about the fifth little girl had been presented in this way, my mother got up, carefully returned her glasses to their case and said, 'I'll have that one.' And that indeed was that. The necessary formalities were completed without, so far as I can remember, any consent on the part of the little girl, who was engaged on the spot at a salary which I cannot recollect but probably did not exceed twelve pounds a year in addition, of course, to her bed and board. The former was probably comfortable enough though its surroundings would be icy in winter-time, and the latter was undoubtedly far superior to anything she had ever experienced before. My mother was the kindest of employers and did everything she could with, I think, complete success, to make her servants as comfortable, happy and well fed as possible. But I cannot help wondering what it must have been like for a girl who was virtually sold into domestic servitude in this way if she fell into the hands of an employer who, though perhaps neither callous nor cruel, made no real attempt to make any sort of home for these girls, who worked far longer hours and had far less time off than any self-respecting girl, even if one could be provided by the modern Mrs Jones, would dream of putting up with today, and at a salary which on any sort of comparison of values would have filled the Edwardian employer with horror.

2. Early Schooldays

In 1905 I went to a school in Warwickshire, where both my brothers had preceded me, Peter being now head of the school and Jack, although only eleven years old, being in the top form and showing unmistakable signs of scholarship. I must confess that I quite enjoyed my first term. I had the privileges usually accorded to the youngest boy in the school and I also had my brothers who kept an aloof but friendly eye on me. But both of them left at the end of the term, Peter to go to Cheltenham and Jack to Cheam School, where he was likely to get more intensive coaching for the Winchester scholarship on which my father had set his heart, with the result that my second term was horrible. While my brothers were there I must have been insufferable and I paid for it when they were gone.

It was during that second term that we celebrated the centenary of Trafalgar and I can remember that we all walked round the playing field waving little Union Jacks and pulling a very small cannon which we contrived, at considerable danger to ourselves, to fire in salute to Lord Nelson.

It was an extraordinary school in many ways. On the whole I was quite happy and, as so often happens, the fact that I was very fond of games helped a great deal. Arthur Bourchier, the actor, had a son, or nephew, there and I remember one summer term when we had a visit from Oscar Asche and his wife Lily Brayton. Oscar Asche was a keen cricketer and bowled to us at the nets. This was, of course, several years before Chu-Chin-Chow!

We used to play several other schools, the team being conveyed with one of the masters in a horse-drawn charabanc. If we were beaten the return journey was rather subdued, but if we won we started cheering as we approached the school gates, and the entire school turned out to join in. Talking of cricket, I remember the Easter holiday of 1907 when my father decided it would be good for us to have some professional coaching, and particularly Peter, who was nearly seventeen. So he purchased a net and we prepared quite a good pitch on one of the fairways of the golf course. He had already been in touch with the Surrey County Cricket Club to enquire whether they could send down a professional two days a week during the holidays. They said they had just the man for the job, a young professional who had been given his county cap the year before. We did not know his name but when he arrived he announced himself as Jack Hobbs. Little did we realise that we were going to be coached by someone who was to become the greatest batsman of all time and who was on the threshold of a career which, according to Mr Wisden, was to include, despite the interruption of the 1914-1918 war, one hundred and ninety-seven centuries in first-class cricket, and sixty-one Tests, which brought him fifteen centuries at an average of 56.94. He was also a very useful fast bowler and a magnificent cover point. Last but not least he was a gentle and charming man and my mother in particular was completely captivated by him! Although, in fact, all that my 'coaching' consisted of was to field (I was not permitted to bat or bowl) on my return to school I basked in a sort of reflected glory from the great man who was now beginning to hit the headlines, and from then on I was treated with the utmost respect, at any rate during the cricket season.

I think that one of the more unsatisfactory aspects of the school was due to the complete lack of psychology (was there such a word then?) on the part of the headmaster, who was basically a very decent sort of man. I can give one or two instances.

There was one occasion when a junior boy had been guilty of some anti-social but quite trifling offence and the headmaster, having addressed the assembled school on the subject, went on to say that he did not propose to punish the wretched culprit himself but would hand him over to the monitors, of which there were six, to deal with as they thought best. I witnessed the dealing. The boy was taken upstairs and told to kneel down by his bed as though he was saying his prayers. The monitors then put on their football boots and in turn ran across the dormitory and kicked him on his backside. This was repeated three times, eighteen kicks in all, at the end of which the boy, who was an epileptic, had a fit. It was not a pleasant spectacle. Even then I realised that it was the headmaster, and not the monitors aged about twelve, who was to blame.

We all of us at one time or another used to share in a less painful but more humiliating experience. Each term one or two whole holidays were given which were forfeited by those boys who had received more than a certain number of bad-conduct marks, and who had to stay in and work most of the day. They were not allowed to speak to anyone and nobody was allowed to speak to them. I suppose this was fair enough. What was so awful during the summer term was that after tea we were taken out and marched in single file for hours on end, still in complete silence, round and round the playing fields in front of all the assembled guests, which included various mothers and sisters who had come for the day. I can remember my shame and embarrassment when I had to take my part in one of those chain-gang exercises which culminated in my getting a blinding headache and being violently sick.

In 1908 my brother Jack got his scholarship at Winchester and the following term I was sent to Cheam School to see whether, with the help of some expert coaching, I could in due course repeat his performance.

The headmaster was Arthur Tabor, an old Etonian and a former Cambridge cricket blue. In addition to his scholastic abilities he was mad on games and on match days his temper in the evening depended to a great extent on whether we had succeeded in defeating our rivals, which included Sandroyd, Banstead, Rose Hill, Reigate, Shrewsbury House and a number of other well-known preparatory schools.

In addition to extensive playing fields we had three full-size Eton fives courts and an indoor swimming pool. The school and grounds have, of course, long since disappeared from their original site, which has become a heavily built-up area, and I remember some years ago wandering about the maze of roads and lanes which thread between the houses and coming across one with the grandiloquent name of Tabor Avenue. The only memorial I know of to a great headmaster.

One way and another we had a pretty good time there although we had to work very hard. The food, I remember, was first class, a great contrast to what we were given at my previous school. There was very little bullying among the boys, but the conduct of some of the masters would have today produced a flood of summonses for assault by outraged parents. Their methods differed, but I can remember one master only too well not only because I was in his form for some time but because for my sins he came to stay with us for several holidays to coach me for the ordeal which lay ahead. He was a great scholar and no doubt brought me on a lot. But I loathed him and so did the others. He had an ungovernable temper which was always just below the surface and when it rose above it he used to rush at his quarry like an enraged bull, seize him by the short hairs just above his ears and pull upwards until the wretched youth was standing on his toes. In fact there were times when a boy would be lifted right off the floor and suspended in mid air. He was much the same during the holidays he spent with us and made my life a misery.

There was another master who employed a different method. His victims were made to stand on a form and he then proceeded to slap their faces, each cheek in turn, until they almost lost consciousness. On one hot summer afternoon the boy he was dealing with passed out completely and fainted in his arms. There was a bit of a to-do about this and Tabor had to intervene and prohibit this practice in future.

And yet there were hardly any official beatings by Tabor himself, who was intensely proud of the school and a great friend to us all. None the less, and although his bark was far worse than his bite, he was a very irascible man. He used to take the scholarship form in classics and, if things went wrong, this could be quite an ordeal. We used to sit on a long bench in his study facing his writing table and we could always recognise the storm signal when his hand started to stray towards one of the drawers on his right-hand side. This was filled with fives balls, which are not soft. Suddenly the dam would break and with a mighty roar he would wrench out the drawer and hurl them one after another at our bare knees at the range of a few feet until the drawer was empty. Although we got pretty skilled it was difficult to elude them all. It was not really very painful but we used to take away some handsome bruises.

We were not allowed to get away with anything in our exercise books unless it bore his initials. These were not very difficult to copy (I can still) and I am ashamed to say that when the atmosphere was a little sultry or we did not think that our work would stand up to close examination we used to do just that. He never spotted it or, if he did, he gave no sign.

I remember that he did give me a sharp slap on the face one morning when I was showing him my work and sent my glasses flying through the open window. Not content with this he picked up my exercise book and hurled it out as well and I had to retrieve them from a flower bed. Neither had sustained any damage. He was a dear old boy and we were all very fond of him, but like everybody else he had one or two faults.

One of these was that he fancied himself as a medical expert although so far as I know, he had never studied medicine in his life. When we felt ill we had to report to him direct. After describing our symptoms which he listened to very gravely he used to write out some sort of a prescription and command us to deliver it to matron. Generally speaking this consisted of castor oil or senna pods for tummy upsets and ammoniated quinine for colds, but there were other concoctions as well. I was feeling decidedly unwell one morning when I reported to him, and my recollection is that he prescribed Carter's Little Liver Pills though I cannot imagine why. I was also told that I need not do any work and was to spend the day in his private dining room, where there were already one or two other 'patients'. I felt worse and worse as time went on and reported to him again in the afternoon. This time he sent me off to matron to have my temperature taken and I gathered later that it was well over 104. However, I did not remember much about it because I was put to bed where I immediately lost consciousness and the doctor, when he arrived, had very little difficulty in diagnosing pneumonia. Three days later I opened my eyes to find a very pretty nurse bending over me and from then on things began to look up, although it was weeks before I recovered. I often wondered if the Carter's Little Liver Pills had helped me in any way!

Castor Oil Parade, which was taken by matron most evenings, was a ghastly affair. She used to put a little jam in it with the idea of making it more palatable, but it only made it worse, and we used to retreat from the ordeal clutching our stomachs rather like the boys at Dotheboys Hall after Mrs Squeers had served them with brimstone and treacle. All with the exception of one small boy whom the rest of us hated ever afterwards. Having drained his glass to the last dregs with every appearance of satisfaction he licked his lips and announced that it reminded him of strawberries and cream, and he would like to have another glass. Unfortunately she refused, because we would have liked to witness his antics the following morning.

A very odd character arrived at the school one term and I will call him Macdonald, though this was not his real name. He must have been about thirteen years old and could speak French and Italian fluently. In fact he had lived in Italy for several years and the story got around that his father had been killed in a duel, which he had witnessed. Whether there was any truth in this I have no idea, but small boys can be pretty bloody minded at times and someone conceived the idea of reproducing what he described as the 'clash of steel'. This effect can be achieved quite simply by clicking one's fingers in a certain way and, one evening, on the signal being given, about five or six of us (including, I am ashamed to say, myself) surrounded the wretched youth and proceeded to click for all we were worth. The effect was startling because he immediately clapped his hands over his ears and started to scream. This rather frightened us, and somebody yelled at him either to shut up or jump out of the window, which was open at the bottom with a drop of about thirty feet. To our horror he adopted the second alternative and in a second he was out of the window and hanging from the ledge by his hands. Somehow or other we managed to pull him back but it was a dreadful moment and we left him severely alone in the future. I only mention this incident because as will appear I met Macdonald again several years later in circumstances which might have ended more tragically.

In 1910 I made a second bid for a scholarship at Winchester, having failed the previous year. This time I succeeded to the extent of getting on the roll, that is to say being kept back an extra day to undergo an oral examination. But the competition was much too strong and I ended up seventeenth out of more than a hundred candidates, with only nine scholarships to be awarded. However, I obtained a Headmaster's nomination, which was infinitely preferable so far as I was concerned as I was never up to real scholarship standard. The same year Cheam acquired no less than five Eton scholarships, but perhaps it is only fair to mention that there were less than forty candidates and more than twenty scholarships. Tabor seemed very pleased with us all and took us out in turn for a drive in his new Rolls-Royce. This was the first time I had ever been in a car.

3. Winchester

I find it more difficult to write about Winchester, where I arrived for the winter term of 1910. Cheam School has long since moved to another locality and must be very different now. But Winchester remains where it was and I surmise, though I have no personal knowledge, very much as it was in my day. Traditions die hard and so far as this great school is concerned the more they are preserved the better.

My housemaster was George Blore, a splendid character and himself an old Wykehamist, who died a few years ago at the age of ninety. The house was generally known as Chawkers after Charles Hawkins, a previous housemaster.

It was perhaps unfortunate that through lack of vacancies the new entry that term was restricted to four, including myself. The other three are all dead, John Carrick who was killed in the first war, Arthur Wickham who went to New College after the war and became a master at Eton, and R. D. Hog who had an elder brother in college; that is to say he was a scholar. Two more boys arrived the following term, R. T. N. Hickley who was also killed in the first war and M. A. Carthew-Yorstoun who was a regular soldier and became a brigadier in the second war. These were my contemporaries, but probably my closest associate was J. G. McIntyre, now Lord Sorn, who in after years was to become an eminent Scottish judge. We were in the same form and used to work together. He had the misfortune to be seriously wounded in the closing weeks of the first war, during which he had served in the army with considerable distinction, with the result that either a foot or leg had to be amputated. He was a fine athlete and would most certainly have gained his rugger blue at Oxford when he went up to Balliol after the war. Rugger was not one of our games at Winchester but he had played it at his preparatory school.

The head of the house my first year was Max Woosnam, who was one of the greatest athletes or rather games players of his or any other generation. At the end of the year he went to Cambridge where, I think I am right in saying, he got five blues which included soccer, golf, racquets, real tennis and lawn tennis during his first year. He was also a first-class cricketer and played several times for the university. It was always supposed, however, that although he was captain of Lords (the Winchester cricket eleven) he did not care a great deal for the game, and I imagine that with such a wealth of talent he was able to pick and choose. He achieved tremendous fame as a soccer player and, although an amateur, played regularly for, I think, Manchester United or Manchester City. He was also a brilliant lawn tennis player, particularly in doubles which he won with R. Lycett at Wimbledon in 1921, and in which he represented England in the Davis Cup.

Another prefect my first year was Victor Mallet, who entered the Diplomatic Service and ended up as British Ambassador in Rome, and another senior who became a prefect in the following year was Charles Portal (later to become Viscount Portal of Hungerford) who, it is hardly necessary to mention, became a Marshal of the Royal Air Force and Chief of the Air Staff in the second war, having served with great distinction in the first.

Winchester was in my time, and presumably still is, divided into College, where some seventy or eighty scholars were congregated, and ten Houses, each of which contained about forty boys or rather men. There is no such thing as a boy at Winchester and even in your first term you are called a new man. Houses were divided into two groups of five known as 'Commoners' and 'Houses' or 'O.T.H.' Winchester football which could not, of course, be played against any other school took up the winter term (short half) and soccer the spring term (common time). The summer term was called cloister time. During the first part of short half we played fifteen-a-side and the second part six-a-side, and there was great rivalry between teams representing College, Commoners and O.T.H. In September 1914 McIntyre was captain of O.T.H. but a fortnight after term started he left, having been commissioned to the Ayrshire Yeomanry, and I took his place. I remember that we won three out of our four matches, being defeated by Commoners in fifteens. A member of this side was Gilbert Ashton, the eldest of the three famous brothers Gilbert, Hubert and Claud, all of whom in successive years after the war captained Cambridge at cricket and soccer and also got their hockey blues. In fact I believe that Claud was captain of hockey as well. There was an elder brother who was also at Winchester and very good at games, but he was severely wounded in the war and died not very long afterwards.

Winchester football is a grand game, and it is a pity that it should be of such little use after one has left. In 1920, when I was at Oxford, I did go down with a team of old Wykehamists to play against College, but six years had elapsed since my last game and, as I had virtually forgotten most of the rules, I cannot have been very effective. It was all right for the others who had come direct to the university from school.

The great event of cloister time was Eton Match and in 1911, my first summer at Winchester, it virtually coincided with the coronation of King George V and Queen Mary. The match was played at Eton that year and we had three days leave so that we could watch the match and the coronation procession. My family had procured seats for the latter and I can remember what a glorious day it was. In fact it was almost too hot and dozens of servicemen who were lining the route fainted after standing in the sun for several hours with the shade temperature in the high eighties. Our seats were close to the Abbey and we had a splendid view of all the open carriages arriving and disgorging their magnificent occupants. Even now I can recollect the impression made on me, and in fact on everybody, by the arrival of one of His Majesty's Ministers of State, whose name, so I was told, not without a slight frown of disapproval, was Winston Churchill. He cut a tremendous dash which seemed to outshine most of the other distinguished visitors.

I suppose that life at Winchester was fairly tough. We were roused at 6.30 every morning, winter and summer, by the butler flinging open the door with a crash and then proceeding to peal the loudest of hand-bells with a sadistic relish, which I can see and hear now, and which was no doubt sharpened by his having to get up an hour earlier himself.

During the next half-hour we had to have a cold bath, dress, swallow a cup of scalding cocoa and run a quarter of a mile to the school buildings where all the classrooms were. At the first peal of that awful bell the youngest boys had to spring out of bed, seize a towel and rush to the bathroom followed progressively by their elders and betters. Actually these cold baths were our salvation. There were four hip baths under running taps and we had to plunge in and remain a few seconds before making way for the next victim. The shock of that icy water on a bitter winter morning was something which even now makes me shudder, but it certainly woke you up and within a minute or two you were glowing as the blood began to circulate again through your frozen veins, and by the time you were dressed you felt almost ready to face the day. Work proceeded from 7.00 to 7.45 when we all flocked into Chapel before returning to the house for breakfast. After breakfast there was more serious washing and those who had to, shaved. By 9.00 we were back at work, which continued on a normal day until 12.30 and resumed in summer at 2.30 and in winter at 4.30 for nearly two hours, the rest of the afternoon being devoted to games. Finally there was a spell of one and a half hours prep. or toytime as it was called, after the little curtained-off cubicles in which we each worked when at the house and kept all our personal possessions, which were known as toys. So by the end of the day one had done about eight hours work. It is only fair to say that there were three half rems or holidays in the week which meant no work after lunch until toytime, but by and large it must have been a forty-five hour week and even that does not take into account compulsory attendance at Chapel at least twice a day and various roll calls.

Perhaps the oddest of these was the occasion once a year when the whole school had to climb to the top of St. Katharine's Hill, where roll was called. Considering that there were about four hundred and fifty boys this ceremony took a considerable time and, if I ever knew, I have certainly forgotten what it was all about and how the tradition first arose. However, it made quite an enjoyable change. Hills were also memorable for the custom that on a particular Sunday in each term every newcomer had to undergo a series of endurance tests on their ancient flanks. These included running at top speed round the old Roman ditch, negotiating a maze in which you invariably got lost and, worst of all, climbing or descending (I have forgotten which) the face of a very high and steep chalk cliff. This was really frightening particularly if you were inclined to vertigo. In addition you were not dressed for the part, but wearing your Sunday clothes, which consisted for junior boys of an Eton suit and collar, but what on earth you did with your top hat while all this was going on I cannot recollect.

In addition to normal games such as cricket, Winchester football, soccer, racquets, fives, etc., we had a very fine bathing pool known as Gunners Hole, which was really a reach of the river Itchen, converted for the purpose. An incident occurred there one day which nobody who saw it is likely to forget. There was a weighted dummy which was used for life-saving practice, and one of the masters was giving a demonstration. The dummy was thrown in and slowly sank followed a few moments later by the master. Usually he surfaced pretty quickly, but this time there was a long pause and we began to feel rather anxious. However, he came up at last not only unconscious but clutching to his bosom not the dummy but a real corpse. Apparently he had not noticed the difference at first but half-way to the surface he suddenly found himself looking straight into the face of the deceased at a few inches range, and promptly passed out. Though very shocked he soon recovered after he had been dragged out of the pool, and eventually the corpse was removed in a wheelbarrow. It was all rather macabre but the excitement was terrific. Subsequently it turned out to have been a case of suicide. The coincidence of its proximity to the dummy was not so strange as it might seem because the demonstration was taking place in the deepest part of the pool just above the sluice gates which had prevented the body from being washed further down the river.

There was virtually no bullying at Winchester, at any rate so far as my house was concerned. A certain amount of corporal punishment was administered by prefects but it was generally deserved and never excessive. During my first two years, when I was at the receiving end, this relatively happy state of affairs was no doubt due to the high quality of George Blore and the prefects. Beatings, when they occurred, followed a curiously ritualistic pattern. The instrument was a very solid affair, consisting of a wooden fives bat blackened with age and use, about eighteen inches long and more or less evenly divided between blade and handle, and it was always kept on its own special shelf in the prefect's library. I well remember that Max Woosnam was the artist. With his deadly eye and wrists of steel he could and did cause considerably more physical discomfort with three strokes than any of the others with five, one of the reasons being that, when he was operating, each stroke came down on precisely the same spot with a sort of cumulative effect. Beatings were short and sharp but only took place at the end of the day so that if the offence had been committed in the morning you had to wait a very long time before it was expiated and this was not something to which you looked forward with any particular enthusiasm. The drill was that the prefect concerned would invite you to come and see him after prayers. When the time came he invariably considered for a moment, giving the impression that he could not remember why he had required your presence. However, recollection always came and you were told to go and fetch the fives bat, which you presented to him handle first with a little bow, rather as though you were making some sort of a donation.

The proceedings did not take place in the privacy of the library, and anybody who cared to witness them was free to do so. Some time towards the end of my second year, when I would cease to be a 'fag' or 'cad' as it was called, I was beaten by the captain of 'Lords' whose boots I had omitted to clean before an important match. Directly I saw him go into bat I knew there would be trouble but I never guessed that there would be triumph after adversity. At the second blow there was an explosion like the crack of doom, and the fives bat disintegrated into hundreds of fragments which were scattered all over the room, leaving our cricket hero with a fragment of jagged wood in his astonished hand. Portal, who was watching the proceedings, said I had flinched, which was hardly surprising in the circumstances, and wanted the beating to be completed. However this was no longer a practicable proposition and I was released. I went round the room collecting all the larger fragments which I proudly produced for inspection by my friends who were most impressed and seemed to think that I had been singularly honoured by the whole affair. I cannot remember whether a new fives bat was inaugurated but, very shortly after, not only were fives bats proscribed to be replaced by ground ashes but only the senior prefect was allowed to use them. And in any case beatings were becoming far less frequent. During my last two terms, when I was head of the house, I administered not more than a dozen beatings altogether and yet I suppose that when I went to Winchester there were several a week. But let me say again that they were far from being severe, generally well merited and, in my opinion, did a lot more good than harm. I am, of course, talking of my own house, which was one of the best.

I suppose that one of the most illustrious college buildings at Winchester was 'School', which was built in 1687 to replace the original school building which dates back to the fourteenth century and still, I believe, exists as Seventh Chamber beneath 'Hall'.

'School', which has itself only recently been rebuilt, was used for concerts, entertainments, examinations, lectures and so forth and I remember the great pianist, Mark Hambourg, giving a recital there one evening. But what I chiefly recollect is an ancient inscription on the wall which read, 'Aut disce aut disce tertia sors manet caedi', which means something like, 'Either learn or get out or be flogged'. I fear that our founders must have had a rather warped sense of humour.

Head of the School was the Prefect of Hall and the next two senior prefects in College were Prefects of Chapel. One of these in 1912-13 was my brother. During the three years we were at Winchester together I used to see quite a lot of him although, of course, by school standards there was a considerable disparity between our ages.

During the summer term of 1913 somebody got the notion of forming a cricket club to tour a different part of the country each year at the beginning of the summer holidays. The idea caught on and, though I was relatively junior, I was invited with my brother to join the club which was called 'The Trusty Sweaters' after the famous Winchester College emblem of 'The Trusty Servant' and we wore, I remember, white blazers with a splendid coloured replica of the emblem on the breast pocket. We had quite a strong team, including three members of 'Lords', and Wales was chosen for the opening tour, which was a great success. We played matches against Bangor, Pwhelli, Portmadoc and the Shropshire Gentlemen on the Shrewsbury School cricket ground, and wound up with a cricket week a few miles outside Cardiff at a house called Cwrt-y-rala (I hope I have spelt it right) which belonged to the father of J. H. P. (Pat) Brain, who was in my house and a year senior to me. Pat's father had been a great cricketer in his time and Pat himself in later years kept wicket for Glamorganshire in its early days as a first-class county. Cwrt-y-rala was an enormous house with magnificent grounds including a lake and a cricket field, and Pat organised a house party which would be able to provide a series of matches against local teams and winding up with the Trusty Sweaters. The house was so full already that some of us had to sleep elsewhere but I was fortunate enough to share a room with my brother in the house itself, which must have been accommodating at least twenty-five guests as, needless to say, there were several girls in the party as well.

One of the guests was Edward Wyndham Tennant (generally known as Bimbo), the eldest son of Lord Glenconner, who was also in my house at Winchester and became a great friend of mine. He was a charming, witty and brilliant boy but alas, like so many of his generation, he had only two or three more years to live. He joined the Grenadier Guards soon after the outbreak of war and was killed in France in 1916 at the age of nineteen. I was in Egypt at the time and a week after I heard the news I received a letter from him written from the front-line trenches saying he was going over the top at dawn the following morning for the thirteenth time.

This, of course, is only an example of what was happening every day. It is certainly no exaggeration to say that the boys or young men of our generation were being systematically and relentlessly destroyed. I have various photographs of football and cricket teams, house groups, etc. taken at Winchester during the years 1910 to 1915 and, so far as the boys who appear in those groups were concerned, the mortality rate during the 1914 war was at least fifty per cent. There is one football group of fifteen of whom I know that eight were killed and three were wounded. Of the other four only two, so far as I know, survived unharmed, but I have lost trace of the others. Only once since the end of that war have I visited the beautiful cloister which was erected at Winchester as the School War Memorial, to find column after column of names with which I had once been so familiar. Terrible though it was I do not think that the second world war had anything to compare with such a scale of destruction as this.

The Trusty Sweaters had, or rather started, their second and final tour in the summer of 1914 but neither my brother nor I accompanied it. He was at Oxford by then, and in any case we were on the very brink of war, which brought the tour to a swift close.

Instead I went to stay with my friend Carthew-Yorstoun at Sutton Courtney, next door to The Wharf, the country home of the Prime Minister, Mr Asquith, and it was while I was there that war was declared on the 4th August.

I remember meeting at a tennis party Count Metternich (a descendant of the world-famous statesman) who was either the Austrian Ambassador or a senior member of his staff. I have no idea what happened to him.

In September a camp was held at Tidworth Pennings on Salisbury Plain for the University and Public School O.T.C.s which my brother and I attended. As it happened the Oxford University and Winchester lines were next to each other and his tent was only a few yards away from mine. I only saw him once or twice again after that as he went into the army almost immediately and I returned to Winchester for two more terms before following his example.

The O.T.C. began to take up more and more of our time with several parades a week, including long route marches, which we loathed. Some time during short half we had a visit from a friend of mine who had left school at the end of the previous term and obtained a commission with the Berkshire Yeomanry. I was now eighteen and beginning to consider what I should do about the war. He suggested that I should join his regiment but I pointed out that, as I had never been on a horse in my life, this was slightly impracticable. However, I talked it over with my parents who were rather in favour of the idea. With one son already in the gunners and another in the infantry why should not the remaining member of the family join the cavalry? I was going back to Winchester for one more term anyway and my father arranged for me to take riding lessons, which were a welcome change from the ordinary school routine. Unfortunately during that short and my last term I was struck down first with German measles and then by chicken-pox, which I got very badly, so I did not get an awful lot of riding though I remember that on one occasion I was permitted to accompany Herbert Aris, a senior housemaster and commander of the O.T.C., as a kind of supernumerary A.D.C. during a field day. This was a bit of an ordeal but at any rate I did succeed in not falling off my horse in front of the assembled ranks of budding officers. But even when I joined the regiment in the early summer of 1915 I do not suppose that I had ridden more than a dozen times altogether. Fortunately another officer joined at the same time who was almost as bad a rider as I was and for weeks we had to attend a special riding school to get us into some sort of shape. On the other hand I acquired the most beautiful Bedford cord riding breeches and my boots were really something. Unfortunately elegance had been preferred to comfort and at the end of my first day not only was I in agonising pain but I had to endure the humiliation of having both my boots cut off by my batman. Otherwise I should be wearing them still as there was certainly no other way of removing them.

There were, of course, no O.C.T.U.s in those days. One got a commission straight from school and one's military knowledge was made up of service with the school O.T.C. and such information as might be derived from a cursory study of King's Regulations and the manual of infantry or cavalry training as the case might be. To say, therefore, that I had a lot to learn would be a considerable understatement. Still everything has to have a start and at any rate I was in the army.

A short while after I wrote this chapter I was given a copy of Life is a Four Letter Word, written by Nicholas Monsarrat, the first volume of his autobiography, and I was more than taken aback by the account he gives of his time at Winchester in a chapter headed 'A Season in Hell'. No doubt he endeavoured to record his experiences, though in considerably greater detail, as accurately as I have endeavoured to record my own, but the contrast between them is certainly striking. There is no doubt that I was in one of the best houses (personally I think the best) whereas he was obviously in one of the worst, and I suppose that the war may have brought about a lowering of standards. Still, it had been over for several years when Monsarrat went to Winchester and I can only conclude that he was just as unlucky in his, or rather his father's, choice of a house as I was fortunate in mine. I do not pretend that I could honestly have headed my account 'A Season in Heaven' but, by and large, I enjoyed my time at Winchester and I look back with gratitude and affection to those five years now so long ago.

4. The Army – Berkshire Yeomanry

I joined the regiment in May, 1915, at Bearwood, an enormous house near Reading with grounds to match, belonging to the Walters family who owned The Times. A few weeks later the regiment moved to Churn Camp, near Didcot, which was to be our training area throughout the summer. Most of the officers were extremely rich and had several hunters as their private chargers, but I had to make do with whatever horse was available. I was very young, very junior, very ignorant and completely lost, but found it all most exciting. There were six officers in my squadron including a major, a captain and four subalterns, each of whom was in charge of a troop, and throughout the summer we underwent an intensive course of training on those magnificent Berkshire Downs. When we were having squadron or regimental drill (there were four squadrons altogether) we were all of us called on from time to time to take the parade, and it is, or rather was, quite something to find oneself in command of a whole regiment of cavalry comprising anything up to about five hundred men and horses and obliged under the eagle eye of the commanding officer to put them through a series of intricate manoeuvres, which involved giving exactly the right command at exactly the right time, otherwise one was liable to produce a state of indescribable chaos.

The other regiments in the brigade were the Royal Bucks Hussars and the Oxfordshire Yeomanry, and I remember one awful occasion when I was ordered to carry out some troop drill in a vast field in one corner of which a squadron of Bucks were dismounted and our C.O. was having a chat and probably some refreshment with his opposite number. After a bit, I thought it would be fun to have a charge in their direction, just to show them what a fine lot of chaps we were. So I ordered the troop to draw their swords, placed myself in front of them, drew my own sword with a flourish, and we proceeded to advance with increasing tempo in the general direction of the Bucks. By the half-way stage we were at full gallop and at that moment my horse put its foot in a rabbit hole and I went over its head, losing grip of my sword in the process. Neither my horse nor I were hurt but on sitting up I was appalled by the sight of my troop going full blast, despite the valiant efforts of the troop sergeant, and it became obvious, as their reins got longer and longer, that they were completely out of control and a collision was inevitable. The impact was terrific and had it been against an enemy, I am sure it would have been a most successful charge. Still sitting on the ground, a little dazed, I closed my eyes and said a silent prayer. When I opened them I saw a single rider detach himself from one corner of the swirling mass of men and horses and canter slowly but purposefully in my direction. After collecting my horse, which was quietly grazing a few yards away, he came up to me, saluted and said, 'The Colonel wishes to see you, sir', which seemed to me to be quite understandable in the circumstances. I recovered my sword, re-mounted and prepared to meet my doom. I have forgotten what it was but by the grace of God no serious harm had been done, and I am sure my punishment was mild compared with what it might have been.

Both at Bearwood and Churn the officers' mess was on a regimental basis and although, being war-time, we did not wear blues a good deal of ceremony was kept up at dinner. We ate and drank on a pretty expensive, not to say luxurious, scale and when dinner was over a full decanter of port was placed between every two officers. In consequence our mess bills were enormous and no distinction whatever was made between the senior and junior officers, some of whom, like myself, were more or less straight from school. In fact had I not received an allowance from my father I do not know how I would have managed, because my pay and mess bills cancelled out. We also felt a little aggrieved at the fact that those who consumed a good deal more than their share of the more sophisticated and expensive part of both the solid and liquid refreshment provided for the mess were very much better off than we were, but their contribution towards the mess bill was the same as our own.

After summer training was over we moved to King's Lynn. The horse lines were located on a wide expanse of open ground between station and town, the men were billeted in various houses over a wide area and the officers were split up into squadron messes. I shared a house with three other subalterns, and must concede that away from the eagle eye of authority we had a pretty good time during our off duty hours. It was not difficult to get twenty-four hours, or even forty-eight hours leave, which I generally spent in London, catching the last train back around midnight and arriving at King's Lynn about three or four in the morning, which did not leave much time for sleeping before attending early parade. Owing to fairly frequent Zeppelin raids the trains were virtually blacked out after dusk and the journey was a pretty dismal affair.

We formed part of the East Coast defence and one of our duties was to watch out for raiding Zeppelins. It worked like this, and I must admit that it was a most impressive piece of organisation. Every night we provided a series of mounted patrols, each consisting of an officer, a sergeant and about eight men, which set off in time to reach its particular location before dark. Sometimes it was a public house, at others the local post office and occasionally a private house. Double sentries were posted and relieved at regular intervals through the night, while the officer had to remain on duty at the telephone which had been allocated to him. Some of these instruments were antiquated beyond belief, and one would imagine that under normal circumstances it would have taken at least several minutes to put through the simplest local call and yet I cannot remember a single occasion when the response was not instantaneous. Each instrument, and they must have been spread over at least one hundred miles of coast-line, was on a direct line to the War Office in London, and no other call could be put through. Whether or not there were any Zeppelins about we had to report at hourly intervals, and if it was a particularly quiet night, which was not often the case, or conditions were against flying, the War Office would ring at some time in the early hours and give us permission to stand down. Otherwise we were on duty all night. It was an extremely efficient system and ensured that there was no possibility of any enemy aircraft crossing the coast without the War Office being instantly aware of the fact.

Swords, or perhaps I should say sabres, were always a bit of a trial but, of course, we were cavalry in the real sense and not simply mounted infantry, and they were worn by officers and men alike though the latter also carried rifles as well, which were slung in heavy leather buckets attached to the saddles. Later in the war the cavalry, which included most of the yeomanry regiments as well as regular units drawn from Britain and all over the Empire, were to do tremendous execution against the Turks in Palestine under the inspired leadership of Allenby, the greatest of cavalry soldiers. For reasons which I will explain later I never took part in any of these particular encounters, but I cannot imagine anything more thrilling or, for the enemy, more terrifying than a cavalry charge. Incidentally I can say from experience that, whether mounted or on foot, it is not always so easy as it may seem to return a sword to its scabbard. And to pass from the sublime to the ridiculous I remember one awful occasion when John Ressich, a fellow subaltern of mine and afterwards a well-known author, though he died only a few years after the war as a result of wounds he had received in North Africa, had the embarrassing experience of getting his sword jammed in his scabbard the wrong way round when mounting the guard at King's Lynn. This was a ceremony which several of the townspeople used to come and watch every evening and it must have made a happy diversion for them when John, after struggling first of all alone, and then with the help of his sergeant, finally had to abandon the unequal contest and cast his Sam Browne belt, complete with its various accessories, on one side. He was a much older and more sophisticated man than the rest of us and I shall always be grateful to him for his kindness to me when I was a newcomer to the regiment and had very little idea as to what it was all about.

It was while we were at King's Lynn that I was sent on what was called a Pioneer Course at Brightlingsea in Essex. The course lasted three weeks, at the end of which I received a certificate to the effect that I was qualified to build pretty well every sort of bridge which was known at the time and carry out pretty well every sort of demolition that had ever been invented. As I have never been able to make anything with my hands, and have only on the rarest of occasions succeeded in mending a fuse, it will be appreciated that the course was somewhat of a farce. The first two days were taken up in being taught to tie a variety of knots, the only one of which I remember is a dove hitch, and when I got back to the regiment my squadron leader insisted, to my horror, on my giving a lecture to the squadron on this particular form of activity. But what we really enjoyed was the last week of the course when we concentrated on explosives, and I can only shudder when I remember the awful things we did with such lethal objects as detonators, primers and even slabs of gun cotton, and all in the most casual sort of way. Two incidents I remember particularly. The exercise one morning was to blow up a large tree, and we had a splendid time preparing for this by packing into the base of the trunk bags of gunpowder and other explosives to which were attached several yards of red instantaneous fuse and a few inches of black safety fuse. When we were ready we were made to take up our positions under cover about a hundred yards away while the sergeant instructor gallantly lighted the safety fuse with a cigarette. The explosion was timed to take place two minutes later and we watched with bated breath as the seconds ticked by. Nothing happened and after waiting for five minutes the instructor allowed us to get up from where we were crouching and approach the tree to see what had gone wrong. Nothing had gone wrong except the timing, and when we were only a few yards away there was a blinding concussion and very slowly, and very steadily, like a rocket from its launching pad, the entire tree rose into the air where, a few seconds later, it disintegrated into a chaos of flying boughs, pieces of trunk and other fragments which descended on us for the next minute. Even now it seems to me a miracle that no one was hurt.

The other incident occurred on the day we were to carry out a bombing attack from what was supposed to be an exact replica of a front-line trench in France. The novelty of the idea lay in the fact that we were all to manufacture our own bombs, and for this we were provided with a variety of tins, the idea being to fill these with stones and then attach whatever we considered to be suitable in the way of explosives. After an hour all was ready and we crouched on the fire step ready to deliver our respective contributions. Somebody blew a whistle and away went the bombs of all sizes and descriptions, some of which went off in magnificent style and others failed to explode at all. I remember being vaguely aware that the gentleman next to me had been playing about for some time with a biscuit tin which was apparently so heavy, by the time he had finished his preparations, that he was hardly able to tilt it over the parapet let alone hurl it at the supposedly approaching enemy. For a minute or so nothing happened, and then he most unadvisedly poked his nose over the parapet to inspect his handiwork, which immediately blew up in his face with an explosion which put all the others to shame and completely removed his nose in the process. We all felt very subdued as he was carried away on a stretcher.

All this time the first line of the regiment was fighting in Gallipoli and occasionally we were called on to send out drafts of officers and men to replace casualties and so forth, but the prospects of our going abroad as a unit began to fade. Towards the end of 1915 we had to supply a draft of three officers alone and I was very disappointed not to be one of those selected. As it happened, however, one of them got appendicitis and I was ordered to take his place. I remember being given a fortnight's leave, most of which I spent with my family at various places, and I think that this must have been the last occasion (it may have been a month or two before) on which I saw my brother Jack when he was on leave from France. He and I and my father dined together my last night at the newly opened Regent Palace Hotel and I do not remember that when I said goodbye to him before dashing off to catch my train at Liverpool Street I ever considered, though I suppose I must have done, the possibility that I should never see him again. Very soon after this we got our embarkation orders and I came up to London to spend a night with my mother and father at the Euston Hotel before catching the boat train to Liverpool the following morning. I had no idea really where I was going, or even whether I was to join the first line, and in any case the news from Gallipoli was very bad and it looked as though evacuation might be imminent. But I could not really have cared less. All I felt was that I was on the eve of a great adventure, something very different to anything I had experienced before, and so indeed it proved to be.

5. Egypt

It was, I think, on the 16th January 1916, that we sailed from Liverpool on the S.S. Olympic, a slightly older sister ship of the ill-fated Titanic. She was enormous (about 47,000 tons) by the standard of that day and we had on board some eight thousand officers and men in addition to a crew of nine hundred. The troops were accommodated, or rather packed, on eight decks, lying side by side wherever an inch of space could be found and their sufferings, particularly on the lower decks, must have been appalling. There was a gale blowing in the Bay of Biscay and practically everybody was seasick, the men just where they lay. As was usual in the 1914 war the officers were far better off. I shared a first-class stateroom on the top deck with Dick Bartie, one of my two fellow officers from the regiment, who was later killed in Palestine, the other having a cabin to himself. The ship was 'wet' and we could have as many drinks as we wanted and whenever we felt like it, which was quite often. The three of us were fortunate in not having any regimental responsibilities as we were not taking a draft with us, though, of course, we had to take our turn as orderly officers, officers of the watch and so forth.

At night there was an officer of the watch to every two decks who had various duties to perform, including responsibility for the blackout, particularly when we got into the Mediterranean, which was full of enemy submarines which, incidentally, sank the ships in front of and behind us. By that time conditions on the ship were pretty awful, particularly at night, when all the portholes and bulkheads were hermetically sealed. I was in charge one night of 'A' and 'B' decks and I must confess to my shame that I spent most of my tour of duty on 'A', being hardly able to cope with the heat and stench of 'B'. When one realises that below 'B' there were six other decks, each of them hotter and more evil-smelling than the one above, one can only wonder how the men contrived to remain alive. Some of them never moved from where they lay from the time we embarked at Liverpool until we reached our destination seven days later, and I remember seeing dozens of them brought up from somewhere in the bowels of the ship looking like figures of wax, some unable to walk and others unconscious, and being propelled down the gangway to the tenders taking them ashore, where they were borne away on stretchers and disappeared.

Because of our speed we had no escort except for a couple of destroyers which kept us company for about twenty-four hours out of Liverpool, and we pursued a most erratic course, particularly after we passed the Straits of Gibraltar, and I do not suppose the continual changes of course helped to ease the suffering of the wretched men below. We had a four-inch gun fore and aft manned by a naval crew, and I vividly remember one morning when, just as we were repairing to the smoking room for our elevenses, both the guns started to fire and the ship, which was already going at full speed, seemed to go completely mad, swerving and dodging and jigging about in all directions, with fatal results to the contents of the bar. The alarm was sounded and we were ordered to don life-belts and go up on deck, a task which, in the general confusion, was very difficult to perform. The guns were still blazing away merrily and the ship, still at full speed, continuing to take evasive action. However, we were relieved, though considerably annoyed, to find that the gun crews were simply being given some gun practice - the target being an old barrel which had been thrown off the ship. Quite apart from the fact that we had been given no warning, it seemed to us to be a pity to run the risk of attracting the attention of any wandering submarine which might happen to be in the vicinity.

However, there were no more adventures and in due course we found ourselves at Mudros, the harbour of the Greek island of Lemnos, one of the main bases for the operations on Gallipoli, which had now been evacuated. The bay was crowded with troopships and naval craft of all sizes and descriptions, but even if there had been room for the Olympic the water was too shallow, and we had to anchor outside the shelter of the harbour. For some reason, I suppose because of the successful evacuation, there were flags flying in all directions and we had at least two military bands on board, which certainly gave us our money's worth. We stayed on the ship for a day or two and were then split up among a number of smaller ships, some of which were bound for Salonica and others for Egypt, where the first line of my regiment had already been evacuated. And on a wet and rather cold morning towards the end of January the three of us finally disembarked at Alexandria.

On the following day we received orders to report to the commandant of a big staging camp which had been set up on the sea-shore at a place called Sidi Bishr, a few miles outside the city. We were there for several weeks with very little to do and we seemed to spend most of our time savouring the delights of Alexandria. In fact the only thing which I can remember about Sidi Bishr was a truly awful sandstorm. This was nothing like the storms I was to experience later on in the desert, but the camp was on a very sandy beach and the job of holding down the tents was almost impossible. The storm started in the late afternoon and lasted all through the night, by which time hardly a tent was left standing and those which managed to survive were simply held up by the weight of the sand piled up both inside and outside them. Fortunately there were a number of large mess huts where we all took shelter and had a meal of some sort before going back to retrieve our possessions, which were buried feet deep, and get the tents up again. In addition to all this it was bitterly cold and I am afraid that those officers who had neglected to bring anything from England except tropical kit not only suffered considerable discomfort under conditions which would have suited an English November but also, it must be admitted, looked extremely silly and I was very grateful for the fact that I was properly equipped.

While we were at Sidi Bishr we got word that the Berkshire Yeomanry had proceeded to Mersa Matruh and we were expecting to receive orders any day to join them. This little place, which became famous in the second world war, is situated on the coast about 165 miles west of Alexandria, and was a forward base for the operations which had been going on for some time against the Senussi Arabs who were allies of the Turks, and whose function was to attack Egypt from the west at the same time as the Turks moved against the Suez Canal from the east. In fact this joint adventure was to pose quite a serious problem for the British and Commonwealth forces in Egypt until such time as they had been reinforced by some of the troops evacuated from Gallipoli.

In due course I was ordered to report to Mersa Matruh, the other two officers having already gone on in advance. The journey took about twenty-four hours by sea from Alexandria, and the only boat which made the trip was a very ancient P. & O. of about 2000 tons. She was crammed from end to end with troops and stores and an incredible assortment of Egyptians, Arabs, Negroes, etc., some on their own and some with their families, some on business, others for no particular reason which I could discover. I managed to find somewhere on the upper deck to put my sleeping bag and fortunately the weather was fine, but my chief recollection of that night, apart from the smell, is that the ship was infested with rats which not only kept up a continuous squeaking but scurried about all over the place and I was woken up again and again by the weight of their beastly little bodies either running over me or simply standing on my chest and regarding me with a baleful eye.

It was a relief to get to Mersa Matruh and link up with the regiment I had been seeking in vain for so many weeks. But, as so often happens in the army, the regiment had never asked for or been told about this influx from England and, as it was already over strength so far as junior officers were concerned, it soon became clear to me, at any rate, as the most junior of all, that I was not particularly welcome. However, I was posted to one of the squadrons as a kind of supernumerary without any particular job to perform and without a troop to command. Still, I was provided with a horse of sorts and used to get a bit of riding in the evenings which, on one occasion, led to an extremely unpleasant adventure. Some new horses had come in from the remount depot and I thought I would take one of these out. My companion on that evening was that rather odd character, Macdonald, whom I have already mentioned as having been with me at Cheam School, but we had not been together for very long before my horse, which was half Arab and half something else, and which I discovered afterwards was practically unbroken, was frightened by a pack of snarling wild dogs (pi-dogs we called them) which suddenly appeared from behind a hillock, got the bit between his teeth and bolted. There are a series of salt lakes at Mersa Matruh which are for the most part surrounded by sandy beaches, separated by broken rock which extends from the cliffs on either side right into the water, and my horse seemed to be under the impression that this would be a hell of a good place for a gallop. So it was, on the sandy bits, but the rocks were a very different matter and I was scared out of my wits, not so much, I am afraid, on account of the horse's legs, as for my own skin. However, it soon became clear that he was as sure-footed as a cat and, barring accidents, would contrive not to fall and all my concentration was bent on contriving not to fall myself. It was a dreadful ride but eventually, after making a complete circuit of the lakes, we arrived at a wide beach which ran into the sea and my horse decided that this would be a good time to stop. By then, however, I had managed to resume control and I do not know whether he was more astonished or angry when I galloped him into the sea till he was chest high in the water. We then turned round and walked very slowly and very subdued back to camp.

But all this was nothing compared to Macdonald's experience. After my disappearance he resumed the ride which we had planned and proceeded on his way alone, intending to get back to camp about six o'clock. However, by dinner-time there was still no sign of him and we began to get a bit anxious. In accordance with standing orders the only gate into the camp from that side, a massive barbed wire affair, had to be closed at dusk, and it was not until about an hour later that the sound of clattering hooves could be heard coming nearer and nearer. Suddenly there loomed out of the darkness a horse and rider making straight for the gateway and apparently oblivious, until the very last moment, of the fact that it was closed. And then, with a spectacular leap, they were safely over and brought to a standstill. Macdonald staggered into the mess hut and, without pausing a moment except to point to a smoke-blackened bullet hole in the sleeve of his tunic, broke into a torrent of French, and incredibly without a single stutter, although when speaking in English, as I remembered so well from Cheam days, he stammered terribly.

It appeared that after he left me he rode on into the desert, or rather scrub, for a few miles singing away quite happily, when, happening to glance back, he saw an Arab emerge from behind a hillock a few hundred yards away. This did not worry him particularly but a minute or two later he looked back again and there were three Arabs who were followed by two more, one of whom was mounted. It was then, he said, that he began to feel uneasy. After all we were in hostile country and it was unlikely that these gentry had any particularly friendly intentions. Also they were spread out in a line between him and the camp. Suddenly from behind a rock only a few feet away another Arab rose up, put a rifle to his shoulder and fired at Macdonald at point-blank range. No doubt he was saved by his horse swerving away from this unexpected apparition and the bullet went through his tunic without harming him. But he was almost unseated, and for a moment or two it was touch and go whether he could hold on.

However, he regained control and before the Arab could reload and fire again he was galloping hell for leather away from the scene, but also unfortunately still away from the camp. Next minute a bullet whistled past his head, not from the man who had already fired at him, but from the mounted Arab, who seemed to be the leader and was infinitely better armed, and who was now galloping after Macdonald, whose only weapon was a revolver, and firing from the saddle. How long the chase went on he could not remember but gradually he outstripped his pursuer only to be faced with the problem of getting back to camp, now some ten miles away. Things were not made any easier by the fact that it was now beginning to get dark, he was completely lost, he had to circumvent the Arabs and his horse had cast a shoe. However, as already related, he finally made it and, at the end, in spectacular fashion, but it had been a very nasty experience and I felt very grateful to my horse for preventing me from sharing it with him.

It was shortly after this that the advance on Sollum began but, as the regiment was over strength and I was the junior officer, I was left behind to my disappointment.

6. The Senussi War

The Senussi were a powerful sect of religious fanatics somewhat similar to the Touaregs of the Sahara. They were despotically ruled by descendants in direct line of Sidi Mohammed ben Ali es Senussi, who in turn claimed direct descent from the Prophet Mohammed, and had founded the sect in 1835. These Chiefs combined the functions of supreme ruler and religious head of the sect and their followers believed them to be specially selected by the Prophet, with Allah's approval, to be their spiritual and temporal guide.

The headquarters of the sect were originally at Alexandria but Sidi Mohammed's son and successor, Senussi el Mahdi, established himself in the Kufra Oasis in the Libyan Desert. On his death in 1902 his son, Sidi Idris (who has recently been deposed from the throne of Libya) was too young to succeed, and his nephew, Sidi Ahmed, known as the Grand Senussi, became the Chief. Sidi Ahmed had ambitions to establish himself as the ruler of a great Libyan state. He had always maintained good relations with Egypt but, when Turkey came into the war on the side of Germany, an effort was made to induce Sidi Ahmed to proclaim a Jehad or Holy War against the Allies with the object of inflaming religious fanaticism in Egypt and embarrassing those countries which had Mohammedan subjects.

To this end a Turk, Nuri Bey, was sent early in 1915 as an emissary to Sidi Ahmed with instructions to endeavour to embroil him with the British, who had built a motor road westward along the coast from the railhead at Dabaa to Mersa Matruh, Sidi Barrani and Sollum, about 300 miles to the west of Alexandria, where a small frontier post had been established and was protected by a couple of gunboats operating in the Gulf.

At some distance inland there rose the waterless and virtually unexplored escarpment of the great Libyan Plateau, which extends in a wide semi-circle from the vicinity of Matruh to Sollum and stretches as far south as the remote oasis of Siwa, which had by now been established as the forward headquarters of the Senussi. The

British position was, therefore, one of some strength and the Senussi, encamped near Sollum but without artillery, realised that as long as the British maintained command of the sea it was useless for them to attack the posts along the road.

NILE VALLEY
AND
WESTERN DESERT
to illustrate
Operations against the Senussi
1915 - 1917

To digress for a moment, Siwa had been considered a Holy City for centuries and was in ancient times the seat of the Oracle of Jupiter Ammon and later the home and burial place of the greatly venerated Oracle and Saint, Sidi Suliman. Although I was to become very familiar with Mersa Matruh and Sollum, and also the oasis of Baharia further to the south, my company, unlike other units of the Imperial Camel Corps, never reached Siwa which has been described as being unlike any other place in the world. It seems that the town resembles from a distance an ancient castle towering above a forest of waving palms. The original site was on the side of two immense limestone rocks which rise steeply from the level of the plain. As the population increased more and more houses were built on top of the old ones and the town, instead of spreading, began to ascend in the air, house upon house and street over street, until it became more like a beehive than anything else. Fathers built houses for their sons on top of their own until, as can be imagined, their great-grandchildren reached really dizzy heights! In the course of time the inside of the town became a vast warren connected by steep twisting tunnels, narrow and dark, rather like galleries in a coal mine. Although, of course, things are very different today it can be said that prior to the First War very few Christians entered Siwa and came out alive.

However, to return to the British at Sollum, their situation was seriously affected in November, 1915, when an Austrian submarine torpedoed a British armed merchantman, the Tara, from which only three of the ten boats it carried succeeded in getting away. These were taken in tow by the submarine and their occupants handed over as prisoners of the Senussi. They were marched 150 miles into the desert and, as afterwards transpired, received very bad treatment before being rescued in March, 1916, by the Duke of Westminster, who was later awarded the D.S.O., and his squadron of armoured cars which had only just returned from a very successful encounter with a large force of Senussi, which they had almost completely destroyed, including no less than thirty Turkish officers killed or wounded.

After sinking the Tara, the submarine attacked Sollum and managed to convoy to the shore a steamer on which were about 300 Turkish soldiers, some Turkish and German officers and a considerable supply of machine guns and ammunition. They reached the Senussi camp, and a few days later an attack was made on the little British force. The first assault was repulsed but, as the troops at Sollum were at a great distance from the railhead at Dabaa, in a rough country and with communications which could easily be cut by the enemy, it was decided for strategic and political reasons to withdraw them to Mersa Matruh, about 180 miles west of Alexandria.

The country round Matruh was valuable on account of the light sandy soil which produced on the edge of the desert a bountiful supply of barley, which formed the main food supply of the Bedouin in the Western Desert and it was certain, therefore, that if the Senussi seriously intended to undertake any operations against Egypt, they would first of all endeavour to recover the barley fields. To provide against this contingency a strong column was assembled near Dabaa ready to reinforce the troops at Matruh. Aerial reconnaissance showed that the Senussi were gathering in force from the south and moving eastward. There were some patrol encounters with the enemy advance guards, armed with machine guns, which although inconclusive in themselves disclosed that a Senussi army of some 5000 men was gradually collecting in the region of Jebel Medwa near Matruh.

To meet this threat a force was assembled, partly by the railway and road connecting Alexandria and Matruh and partly by sea transport, consisting of a composite infantry brigade, a composite cavalry brigade and a regiment of Sikhs, who were in fact the only fully trained troops. After spending some days in digging trenches, erecting barbcd wire entanglements and generally strengthening the defences, the British commander, Major-General A. Wallace, decided to attack on Christmas Day. Contact was soon made with the Senussi outposts by an infantry column consisting of New Zealanders and the Sikhs and supported by some armoured cars, a mountain battery and, from the sea, the six-inch guns of H.M.S. Clematis. The attack on the Senussi positions was pressed home with great dash and courage, and eventually the ridges which they occupied were stormed and the enemy driven into a deep ravine. Here they made a great stand, assisted by a number of caves which provided excellent natural defences. In consequence it took some time before the ravine was cleared. Unfortunately the encircling movement of the cavalry had been foreseen by Jafar Pasha, a Turkish officer of Arab extraction, who was in command of the Senussi forces, and was delayed by his own mounted troops. In the result, although the whole of their stores as well as flocks of sheep, herds of cattle and a number of camels were captured, the main body of the enemy got away and retreated to Halazin, about twenty miles south of Matruh. It was in the course of this engagement that my friend John Ressich had been very seriously wounded in extremely unpleasant circumstances. I cannot remember whether the whole regiment was involved but

John's squadron was ordered to carry out a charge against the Senussi on an apparently flat expanse of desert. Unfortunately between the opposing sides there was a wadi, that is to say a dried-up water-course, with very steep sides, which was quite invisible until the last moment of the charge when it was too late, and the squadron, or at any rate the leading troop, galloped straight into it with disastrous consequences, and before the remnants could extricate themselves the Senussi counter-attacked and overran the wadi, which was not regained until the following day. I remember talking to one of the survivors of this horrible incident and he told me that the worst part was after dusk when the ghoulish Arab women crept on to the scene with knives and mutilated several of the dead and wounded. There was, however, at least one officer, it may have been John himself though I never saw him again, who got his own back. He saw one of the women emasculate a trooper who was probably already dead and then creep towards him, holding her beastly knife in her teeth. He pretended to be dead but managed somehow to loosen his revolver from its holster and, as she bent over him, he blew her brains out.

During the next few weeks both sides were considerably reinforced and, after another somewhat inconclusive engagement, the Senussi withdrew to the vicinity of Sidi Barrani, where they occupied a strong defensive position on a ridge at Agagia, some fifteen miles to the south. Here they concentrated a force of 8000 men under Nuri Bey. with Jafar Pasha as his second in command. They were well supplied with machine guns under German and Turkish officers, backed by two pieces of artillery. Towards the end of February Major-General W. E. Peyton, who had now taken command of the British forces which had been strengthened by the inclusion of a cavalry brigade, consisting of the Dorset and Bucks Yeomanry regiments, established his advance base at Umgeila, from where it was proposed to make an all out attack on the enemy at Agagia. The battle which followed under the overall command of General Lukin, and which resulted in the complete defeat and rout of the enemy, was distinguished by a charge of the Dorset Yeomanry under Lieutenant-Colonel H. M. Souter in the course of which five officers were shot down and Souter's horse killed under him right in front of Jafar Pasha, who was himself wounded and taken prisoner.

There were several more engagements before Sollum was finally taken, including those in which the Duke of Westminster played such a prominent part with his armoured cars, and the capture of the Madian and Halfaia passes leading up to the top of the escarpment overlooking Sollum Bay, and it is no exaggeration to say that some of the men, particularly the infantry, suffered almost intolerable hardship from the heavy marching, lack of water and tropical heat. Nonetheless the campaign in the north had been virtually completed.

Shortly after the regiment returned to Mersa Matruh from Sollum it was ordered to Cairo and I was sent on with the advance party. It was just then that G.H.Q. decided to form a camel brigade to be known as the Imperial Camel Corps, and in due course we were ordered to supply a detachment of one officer and some thirty N.C.O.s and men to join the new corps. The C.O. asked for volunteers and, as I could see very little future for myself in a regiment which was so overstocked with junior officers, I was one of the first to apply and in due course I got the job. This was something which I have never regretted and which during the next two years was to take me to some very strange places and provide me with some unusual and not unexciting experiences.

7. The Imperial Camel Corps

At the end of 1915 Lieutenant-Colonel Leslie Smith, a splendid and gallant soldier who had already served for twenty years in the Middle East and had won a V.C. in Somaliland some years before, decided, in view of the immense difficulties encountered by the cavalry in maintaining the various outposts and carrying out their constant patrolling which was required throughout thousands of square miles of virtually waterless desert, to approach General Sir John Maxwell, who was at that time G.O.C.-in-C. Egyptian Expeditionary Force, for permission to raise a white man camel corps composed entirely of officers and men recruited from mounted units. This corps was to be a self contained and completely independent fighting force to take over the job of patrolling and maintaining contact with the Senussi in the vast desert areas to the west of the Nile Valley and the north of the Sudan.

At first this proposal was not well received. For one thing he was told that white men could not handle camels and that he would have to recruit native troops, and for another he met with strong opposition from the officers commanding cavalry regiments, who not unreasonably resented the idea of their units being used as reserves for the proposed camel corps. These were nearly all regular or ex-regular officers to whom it was almost an insult to mention camels in the same breath with horses, and even when permission was finally obtained, and the new corps had come into being as the Imperial Camel Corps and already begun to more than justify itself as a fighting force, they persisted in their belief that it was no more than a glorified labour corps. In fact it was often confused with the Egyptian Camel Corps and even more so with the Camel Transport Corps which, although officered by British officers, was in reality a native unit used exclusively for the transport of the vast quantities of water and supplies required for the upkeep of the armies in the field including, I may say, the dozens of cavalry regiments scattered throughout the waterless wastes in which they had to operate.

Incidentally the Camel Transport Corps was afterwards to do a magnificent job and play a vital part in Allenby's campaigns for the conquest of Palestine. I have a vivid recollection of the time after the capture of Beersheba when the forward troops ran out of water and we lay all day under a burning sun without a drop to drink, nor so far as we could see any hope of one, and the arrival late that evening of a large convoy of camels carrying sufficient water for the needs of something like three divisions. I am not exaggerating when I say that it was touch and go whether we should be able to continue.

The first units of the Imperial Camel Corps were derived from the Australian and New Zealand mounted regiments and in due course they made up the 1st, 3rd and 4th Battalions. But my story is concerned with the 2nd Battalion, which was formed in the early months of 1916 and derived almost entirely from British Yeomanry regiments, although later on a company (No. 5) was added from an infantry division. This company was part of a force, under the command of Colonel S. F. Newcombe, who had played a leading part in Lawrence's raiding operations against the Hejaz railway. The force was employed in sabotage work behind the Turkish lines at Beersheba but eventually came to grief when it was surrounded and captured by the enemy, after losing more than half its men killed or wounded.

The other five companies were made up as follows:

No.6 Cheshire, Shropshire, Mongomeryshire and Denbighshire Yeomanries, commanded by Major J. de Knoop and Baron Alan de Rutzen both of whom were killed in action in August, 1916, and later by Captain H. R. Pettit, M.C. and Lieutenant R. Houghton.

No.7 Scottish Horse and Lanarkshire, Fife and Forfar and Ayrshire Yeomanries, commanded by Major F. C.Gregory, M.C., who was killed in action together with his second-in-command Captain C. M. Q. Orchardson, M.C. in December, 1917, and later by Captain E. H. Deas, M.C. and Captain J. J. Bell-Irving. Deas was also awarded a Bar to his M.C.

No.8 Royal Bucks Hussars, 2nd County of London Yeomanry (Westminster Dragoons) and Berkshire and Dorset Yeomanries, commanded by Captain C. W. Mason-MacFarlane, who was killed in action in September, 1916, and later by Captain J. J. Paterson, Major Julian Day, M.C., Captain H. W. Tredinnick, M.C. and myself.

No.9 3rd County of London Yeomanry ('Sharpshooters') and City of London Yeomanry ('Rough Riders'), commanded by Major the Earl Winterton and later by Captain A. E. Newsom, who was killed in action in March, 1918 and Captain Brothers, M.C.

No.10 East Riding of Yorkshire Imperial Yeomanry ('Wenlock's Horse') and Staffordshire and Lincolnshire Yeomanries, commanded by Major T. Bardwell and later by Lieutenant C. H. N. Ashlin, Captain A. G. Wilkinson and Captain J. Lyall, M.C.

The Battalion was commanded by Lieutenant-Colonel Gardner and later by Lieutenant-Colonel R. V. Buxton, D.S.O. and for most of my time with the Camel Corps, the second in command was Lord Winterton.

Each company, which was usually commanded by a Major or Captain and corresponded more or less to a squadron of cavalry, was divided into four sections of about thirty-five men, each commanded by a subaltern. We also had our own medical and supply services and detachments of heavy (Vickers) machine guns, mountain guns from an Indian regiment, sappers and signallers, etc., and at full strength there would be a complement for the five companies of approximately thirty officers and 800 N.C.O.s and men, with the best part of 1000 camels. It was only, however, on the rarest occasions, if at all, that the battalion functioned as a single unit, the idea being that the brigades should be able to operate as completely independent units or, as was more often the case, a series of units at battalion or even company strength. We had tremendous advantages over infantry as we could march thirty or forty miles a day even when the weather was at its hottest, and over cavalry because we were not dependent to anything like the same extent on water. I believe that against all probabilities it was discovered that horses were able to go without water for up to forty-eight hours even in that heat, but we could go for four and, at a pinch, even five days. Every man carried on his camel, in addition to his saddle-bags, a sack of grain for the camel and a tank of water for himself and, though there were occasions when it had to be severely rationed, and washing and shaving were at a discount, we could manage to last out with this for just as long as the camels could go without any water at all. Officers were armed with revolvers (I had to put my precious sword in store in Cairo, where it was stolen) and the men with rifles, and there was also a section of Lewis guns attached to each company. Incidentally these were not very satisfactory under desert conditions owing to continual stoppages from sand, and I remember one occasion when we were training in the desert and sixteen Lewis guns went out of action simultaneously when a slight wind, not by any means a real sandstorm, blew up.

No, there was nothing usual about the Imperial Camel Corps and if one includes the Australian and New Zealand companies, which after all constituted about three-quarters of its entire strength, to say nothing of a splendid Sikh Mounted Battery from the Hong Kong and Singapore R.G.A., which was attached to us, a sprinkling of volunteers from the Rhodesia Mounted Police, a South African mining prospector who had fought against the British in the Boer War, a fruit grower from the Canadian Rockies, a pearl fisherman from Queensland, a noted polo player from the Argentine, and even an American, all of whom for some reason chose to throw in their lot with us, it can be seen at once that, omitting the American, the entire British Empire was well represented in our ranks!

It must have been this which prompted the authorship of the following poem or doggerel, call it what you will, which appeared on the 1st September, 1917, over the name of 'Corporal Cuss' in the second issue of Batrak, the Camel Corps magazine, which was founded and edited by Captain Morgan (probably 'Corporal Cuss' in person) of Brigade Signals. There was only one further issue during the war and it was not until June, 1967, fifty years later, that the fourth issue was published by Laurence Moore, who has since followed it up with nine more. The poem appeared under the heading 'Abassia', which was the barracks outside Cairo where we did our training and which constituted our base.

> From the furthest isles of Orkney
> From the edge of the Sudan
> From the flats of Murrumbidjee,
> Or the purlieus of Japan,
> From amid the waving Pampas,
> Or the banks of Windermere

They have gathered, gathered, gathered
To the Huts of Abassia.

He whose single thought was salmon
Met the rogue who poached for pearls,
And the Billjim made a cobber
Of the darling of the girls:
The Guardsman and the Terrier,
The Plutocrat and Peer –
All are jumbled up together
In the Huts of Abassia.

If you seek for information
On Polo, Maps or Gin,
Beer, Beauty or Ballistics,
You can find it all within:
If you seek the heat of battle
Or you're finding life too drear –
Go and join the 'Curse of Egypt'
In the Huts of Abassia.

Allowing for a little poetic license this seems to me to have been a pretty good and accurate description!

8. About Camels

As a start I would like to explain that there are two completely different species of camel, namely the two humped Asian or Bactrian camel and the one humped Arabian. The Bactrian is larger but has shorter legs and a much thicker coat, which grows longer in winter and enables it to withstand without apparent discomfort the rigours of virtually Siberian conditions. The Arabian is generally spoken of as a dromedary, although the name properly belongs to a special breed of trotting camel like those which were supplied to us from Upper Egypt and the Sudan. Opinions differ as regards loads, distances and speeds but a good dromedary can certainly keep going for twenty-five or even thirty miles a day for weeks on end and at a speed, varying in accordance with conditions and the particular type of camel, from about four to ten miles an hour with a load of 450 lbs or more including the rider. The normal trotting speed, and this is the most comfortable for the rider, is six miles an hour. The speed of a camel can be accurately determined from its tracks.

The hump, which constitutes a reserve of fat, varies in size according to conditions and grows smaller after days of hardship and indifferent food. We were, I remember, under the impression that a camel had four stomachs but this is not correct. The stomach does, however, have a number of separate compartments or pouches each of which carries up to two gallons of a fluid mixture of food and water and this, combined with the ability to subsist on a limited quantity of food, enables the camel to keep going without water for up to five or, if well broken in, six days even under extreme desert conditions, provided that it is not unduly pressed. The swifter breeds can go even faster and further. The sole of the foot, which unites the two toes, is calloused and there are also callosities on the chest and joints, that is to say whatever parts of the body touch the ground and have to carry the weight of the camel when it is couched. A camel also has long sheltering eyelashes, heavy eyelids, slitted nostrils which it can close at will, as for example during a sandstorm, great strength and an acute sense of sight and smell. I have read somewhere that during a particularly bad sandstorm a camel will fall on its knees, stretch its neck along the sand, close its nostrils and remain in that position until the storm has passed, but my own recollection, although this may be at fault, is that they preferred to remain standing with their backs to the wind and their heads lowered towards the ground, and we certainly encountered some pretty severe storms, particularly in the Western Desert.

At the end of a long and arduous patrol, when their reserves of water were exhausted, the sides of the camels would have fallen away showing their ribs, and they would make a concerted rush for the water troughs. Usually each of these accommodated about six camels to start with but, as the minutes went by and gallon after gallon disappeared down their throats, they would visibly swell until at last those on the outside were pushed out of reach and had to be taken to another trough. This is not really surprising when one realises that a thirsty camel can drink from twenty-five to thirty gallons at a time.

During the rutting or syming season, which seemed to occur pretty frequently, a bull camel (and most, if not all, of ours were entires) produces from its mouth a large pouch accompanied by a sort of bubbling roar and a spray of cud which varies in accordance with what it has been eating. If this happens to consist of a particular shrub, probably camel thorn, it is also accompanied by what I can only describe as a condition of extreme halitosis, and it is only the inexperienced who fail to take evasive action in time! However, this was a lesson which we learnt in the very early days.

Curiously enough the dromedary, though of Arabian origin, can be found as far east as India and there was in Palestine, at the same time as ourselves, a company of Bikanir Camel Corps mounted on camels from the Sind. This had been raised and fitted out by the Maharajah of Bikanir himself and was almost a corps d'elite. They were splendid men and I would say that their camels were half as large again as our own. Their saddles were also quite different to ours, and unlike us they rode astride with sometimes two up.

A camel will take a tremendous load but if it considers that it has been too heavily laden it will refuse to rise. Once, however, it has accepted its burden, it will often continue until the last extremity and succumb only to die. We saw plenty of this during our withdrawal from the Jaffa-Jerusalem line after the capture of the latter in November, 1917.

A camel is reputed to be a wild and savage animal by nature and to have no instinct of attachment towards its master. This is something which we who served in the Imperial Camel Corps simply cannot accept although, of course, there were some rogues among those humped angels! Of the four or five which I rode from time to time the one which was certainly outstanding in terms of strength and endurance could be a very tricky customer indeed. My favourite, on the other hand, was the gentlest and most amenable of creatures, and we became very attached to one another, which was just as well since he carried me for well over 2000 miles, or approximately half the total mileage which I covered. Generally speaking, however, the bulls when they are syming can become quite fierce and dangerous and are apt to make savage attacks on their fellows or, for that matter, anybody who happens to be standing around and within reach. We had to learn by experience that in addition to its biting propensities it could deliver a kick like a mule, or perhaps I should say unlike a mule, because a camel kicks sideways instead of backwards which, to begin with, we found very disconcerting indeed. In parts of Turkey camel fighting is a recognised form of sport, in addition to camel racing, and considerable sums of money turn on the results of these grim and savage contests which often end in the death of the vanquished.

Nonetheless, even if beneath the surface some camels may retain a degree of obstinacy and bad temper, domestication although accepted somewhat grudgingly does produce in the main a degree of docility which has been described somewhere, a little unfairly I think, as 'more the result of habitual nonchalance than any outcome of intelligent subservience'!

God only knows what they thought of us, but we certainly thought a lot of them and after all there were occasions when our lives were in their hands or rather in their humps. Incidentally a camel's usefulness has no limits even though it may be dead. Its flesh, provided that, in accordance with good Moslem practice, it has been slaughtered with the knife, is eaten by the Arabs, who seemed to materialise from nowhere whenever one of ours was dying, the milk of the cows, which is good and nutritious, is drunk or made into butter or cheese, its dung is often the only fuel available in parts of the desert, its skin can be tanned into leather and its hair can be woven into various fabrics or used in the manufacture of artists' brushes. So called camel hair brushes are not, however, always derived from this source. Altogether it is indeed a wonderful and unique creature and we came to have a great affection for our comrades in arms.

9. Abassia

At the end of April we assembled for training at Abassia Barracks a few miles out of Cairo and were introduced for the first time to our camels, which obviously liked the look of us even less than we liked the look of them. Most of them, however, were really magnificent animals and we could only hope that they were not quite so supercilious as they looked.

By the time training started in earnest it was getting very hot and, as it turned out, this was the beginning of the hottest summer in Egypt for over forty years, and we were to experience temperatures of anything up to 130 in the shade, and that without any shade except perhaps when we were resting during the hottest part of the day, under cover of a ground sheet supported by four slender poles which were continually blowing down.

Having been accustomed to horses, the men very soon got used to riding camels, though later in the war when No. 5 company was formed from an infantry division they had a lot of difficulty. Probably by then the camels were inferior anyway and a really bad camel can be a very unpleasant customer indeed.

One of the worst I remember was a shaggy bull camel, which was sent to us later in the war with a batch of remounts. He wore a muzzle, which made us suspicious from the start, but we did not realise he was a man-eater! One day, when he was being taken from one part of the lines to another, he suddenly attacked his escort, one of whom was knocked to the ground, whereupon the camel knelt on him and, if it had not been for the muzzle, he would certainly have torn out his throat. Fortunately two of the men were carrying picks and did their utmost to smash the camel's head in. At each blow he roared and flung his head back only to return to the recumbent man on which he was still kneeling. After a few minutes of this he decided to call it a day, got up and wandered off on his own, still roaring his head off. It was decided he should be destroyed and, armed with a shotgun, which apparently had no effect whatsoever, and a rifle, the company commander successfully put an end to his activities for good. After that we had quite a number of the same sort and, by a curious coincidence, they were all found to be dead the morning after their arrival. No enquiry was held though it was tacitly understood that a felony had been committed under extreme provocation. After all the men had quite enough to do fighting a war without having to fight their camels as well.

In any case these bull camels were not only a nuisance but also completely useless. They were constantly rutting and used to spend hours at a time with their hind legs wide apart behaving in a most obscene manner. By the time, after several days of this, that nature was satisfied, they were so weak and worn out that they could hardly stand let alone do any work. And no sooner had they recovered their strength when they started rutting again and the whole process was repeated. I believe I am right in saying that one of the Australian battalions was at one time fitted out with nagas or female camels, but I doubt whether it was a success, and I shudder to think what would have happened if our lot had come along at the wrong, or perhaps I should say, the right moment!

But these were exceptions. In the main they were docile enough, though some of them had a nasty habit of suddenly turning their heads round and trying to bite your knees off. Yet, however much they might complain and grumble, and it must be admitted that they spent a lot of time in this way, their powers of endurance and willingness to go on until they literally dropped were quite remarkable. They may have been ill disposed though I think that appearances were sometimes deceptive, but they were indeed great hearted as I will show later on.

They were also very comfortable to ride, particularly when trotting. There was no up and down movement, just forward and back, and as we packed the wooden saddles with blankets or sheepskins, there was no discomfort at all even after several hours riding. In this way they kept up a steady six miles an hour almost indefinitely. If you pressed them beyond that they would break into a canter or gallop which was quite horrible, and frequently ended in the rider being thrown. There were no stirrups or reins, simply a rope tied on to the camel's nose and leading back on one side. With this and the pressure of your feet on either side of its shoulder you could guide the animal without any difficulty. Occasionally there were pullers which had to be restrained by a small wooden peg fitted into a nostril and attached to the rider by a separate cord. Generally the slightest pull on this did the trick, which is not surprising considering the pain it must have caused, but in very obstinate cases the nostril used to be terribly torn.

I remember that my own camels were called in succession Pharaoh, Mark Antony, Pompey, Tommy, Mick and Mrs. ---- after a favourite great aunt of mine whom he closely resembled! The noise when the camels were mounted was unbelievable. They would be kneeling down and, when the order was given, each man would take hold of his camel by its nose, turn its head towards him, place one foot on its neck and lift himself on to the saddle, and lean well back to counteract the motion of the camel getting up hind legs first. On every single occasion every single camel roared in protest while this was going on and the effect was staggering.

We kept them beautifully clean, at any rate while we were training. It was different later on. There was grooming every morning for at least an hour. The camels were tethered in a hollow square facing inwards, and after the usual washing, combing, scraping and brushing had been completed, accompanied by a continual hissing on the part of the 'groom' which must have astonished the camels, they had to be de-ticked. Camel ticks are unpleasant little beasts, bigger than sheep ticks, and they invariably took up their positions immediately under the camel's tail, where they proceeded to burrow in. I was reminded of a certain tribe of barbarians which, if I remember my Caesar correctly, used to insert their spears when attacked by an enemy mounted on elephants 'in molli parte sub caude', which not unnaturally caused the unfortunate elephants a considerable degree of discomfort. Anyway if the ticks were left undisturbed for a few hours you would find that your camel had what looked, at a distance, like a large bunch of grapes hanging down behind. It was very necessary, therefore, to get the ticks out as soon as possible, and at grooming parade little straw fires were made all round the square into which the ticks were dropped after they had been extracted, and they used to explode like popcorn.

There was one splendid incident. In the course of our training it was decided that we must prepare for the possibility of a gas attack.

Gas masks were extremely primitive in those days and consisted of a hood rather like the Ku-Klux-Klan, made of some evil-smelling material with enormous eye-pieces and nose clips. On the appointed day we had to march on foot through a cloud of chlorine gas, first with our masks on and then with them off. I do not know which was the worse. Somebody then pointed out that it was not much use our surviving a gas attack if the camels did not, and it was decided to make an experiment. There happened to be available at the time a very sick camel, which had not eaten for days and was too weak to stand up. Very suitable for use as a guinea-pig. We all watched as the gas people projected a mass of their noxious compound at the unfortunate animal which disappeared completely for several minutes, at the end of which the cloud began to disperse and the camel was observed, to our great delight, to be standing on its feet for the first time for days and peacefully grazing! The chlorine had obviously met its match.

The barracks at Abassia were old and primitive. The officers were billeted in what were alleged to be the married quarters and we had to contend with a variety of wild life, which included flies by day, mosquitoes by night, bugs at all times and some monstrous black hornets which had taken possession of our hut. They left us alone so long as we did not interfere with them but there was always a chance of some accidental contact and, as we were assured by the local experts that a single sting from one of these creatures was probably fatal and two certainly, it is not surprising that we kept as far away as possible.

After two months our initial training was supposedly complete and my company (No. 8) was ordered to proceed to a camp at a place called Shusha, near Samalut, which was about 150 miles south of Cairo, involving a march of several days, mostly along the west bank of the Nile. It would have been possible to send us by rail but it was felt that a protracted march like this, under reasonably civilised conditions, would be a good experience for us prior to embarking on any desert operations. Shusha was one of the bases from which operations against the Senussi were being conducted in the general direction of the Baharia Oasis, which was one of their principal assembly areas, and a light railway was being built as a line of communication with our forward units.

The opening stages of the march from Abassia were almost unbelievable. To start with we had to ride through the centre of Cairo, and in the second place this was the first occasion on which we had proceeded in full marching order complete with all our stores, provisions, cooking equipment, extra blankets, ammunition, Lewis guns and so forth, all of which had to be packed on spare camels, which had been specially selected to carry what were in fact enormous loads, not only in weight but size. Later on, of course, we got used to packing up all this paraphernalia almost in a matter of minutes and, more important still, packing it correctly so that the load was evenly spread, a vital necessity if saddle sores were to be avoided. But on this first occasion we had no experience of this sort of thing to draw on and it is not surprising that we made a very amateurish job of it, with the result that it was not very long before knots became untied, ropes began to loosen, loads started slipping and various pieces of equipment became detached and fell off.

Furthermore, we had not really learnt to control our camels properly and, what with the difficulty of guiding them through the Cairo traffic and continually having to dismount and pick up odds and ends of equipment which had fallen off the pack camels and struggling to reload them, it was not surprising that before long the column began to split up into little detached groups of camels, spread over a couple of miles or so with hardly any vestige of order or discipline left. On top of all this there were a number of stragglers to be rounded up and guided through the maze of streets which had to be negotiated. No doubt it was a salutary experience but it was also a painfully humiliating one and must have been a source of great amusement to the Egyptian population, who disliked us anyway and were always at pains to show us how much they resented our presence.

Our route to Samalut and Shusha led through a series of quite large towns such as Wasta and Beni Suef and for practically the whole way followed the bank of the river. The heat was terrific and we made a practice of starting off the day's march at about 4 a.m. and continuing for some four hours. We would then rest up during the heat of the day and start off another three-hour trek about 4 p.m.

It was really rather enjoyable, particularly the early morning ride, when it was relatively cool, and all the time we were gaining experience in looking after, managing and packing the camels.

In addition to the towns, we passed through numberless villages surrounded by palm groves and waterholes, which were usually occupied by the enormous water buffaloes used by the fellaheen, as the peasant population is called, for various tasks. These animals could be a bit tricky at times and on one occasion a particularly ferocious-looking specimen chased my batman, who was probably out on a scrounging expedition of some kind, about a quarter of a mile into camp. Everywhere the local population turned out to greet us, though I do not suppose they had the remotest idea who or what we were, and it was rather pleasant to be welcomed with smiling faces in place of the stares and scowls we usually encountered in Cairo. We particularly envied the children who seemed to spend most of their time bathing in the Nile, a refreshment which was denied us on account of that dreadful Egyptian disease bilharziosis. It seems that the waters of the Nile are infected with some sort of parasite or organism which penetrates every orifice of the body, including even the pores of the skin, and then proceeds to eat one's insides away. Not surprisingly, therefore, it was a court-martial offence if one was caught bathing.

At Beni Suef we received an astonishing entertainment. We were greeted by a number of Notables, as they were called, who delivered an invitation to the officers from the Mudir, or Governor of the province, to lunch or rather feast with him at his private residence. This was, of course, an invitation which had to be accepted and in due course we presented ourselves at the gates. It was one of the hottest days of the year and I remember that the thermometer stood at 127. The Mudir was a most peculiar man with a most peculiar sense of humour. Before lunch he conducted us round the garden and about half-way through our tour he suggested we might like to have our boots cleaned. We accepted with some surprise as we had dolled up for the occasion and they were already spotless. He then clapped his hands and there emerged from somewhere a very humble gentleman, clad in very dirty rags, who produced a chair and some brushes and other impedimenta and we all took our turn. The Mudir was delighted and said that he too would have his boots cleaned, but first we must all have some beer. After consuming a bottle he took his seat with another freshly opened one and, directly the boot cleaning ceremony was over, he gave a scream of laughter, poured the whole of the contents over the wretched slave and then literally kicked him into the nearest bushes, where he fell flat on his face surrounded by all his bits and pieces which were strewn in every direction. The Mudir was more convulsed than ever but intimated that the show was over and we must all go into lunch. There were about a dozen people present including the Mudir's A.D.C., some Egyptian officers and various Notables and we all squatted on the floor, something which I have always found very difficult to do, being rather stiff jointed, round a low table where we proceeded to consume the biggest meal with which I have ever been confronted. There were ten courses, but no implements of any kind, and the piece de resistance was a mountain of chicken and rice into which we each in turn plunged our hands and, after finishing what we had succeeded in gathering, licked our fingers, and plunged them in again!

What with the food and beer with which we washed it down and the steadily increasing heat, both from within and without, we were dripping with sweat and almost beginning to lose consciousness when the Mudir announced that it was time for siesta. The fact that there was nothing on which to lie caused him no problem, and he charged out of the room clapping his hands and yelling directions at the top of his voice. We then became aware of a sort of twittering and giggling from the floor above, and caught an occasional glimpse of a dark-robed figure with a white veil which obscured the whole face apart from the eyes peering down on us. This was followed by a procession of servants down the stairs, each of them carrying a mattress which had unmistakably been filched from the Mudir's harem. The mattresses were laid side by side on the floor and we were invited to compose ourselves to rest. Not only was this another invitation which it would have been very impolite and indeed insulting to refuse, but by then we were in such a state of extremity that we would have been quite incapable of refusing anyway. Never shall I forget the overpowering scent of patchouli which accompanied me as I lost consciousness and remained with me throughout my dreams.

An hour or two later it was time to resume our march and, with many protestations of gratitude and goodwill on our part and roars of laughter from our affable host, we proceeded to mount our camels, apart from one of my fellow officers who missed the saddle completely and fell flat on his back on the other side. This incident really completed the Mudir's day for him, and the last thing we heard as we went on our way was that monstrous laughter gradually dying away in the distance.

10. The Desert – Baharia – Fayoum

A day or two later we reached Shusha camp, which was located just on the edge of the desert a mile or two from Samalut. I cannot recollect how many troops it contained or of what they consisted apart from the Royal Bucks Hussars, to which we were attached for rations, etc., and whose commanding officer, Colonel John Grenfell, was, I think, the senior officer in the camp. Their adjutant was 'Tony' Rothschild, and I can remember messing with a squadron whose officers included Major 'Freddie' Cripps, Neil Primrose, Lord Rosebery's son, and Evelyn Rothschild, both of whom were killed in Palestine a year or so later.

The building of the light railway was proceeding apace and now stretched about sixty miles into the desert. Four blockhouses, which were located at intervals of about fifteen miles, had already been built B.1, B.2, B.3, and B.4, and two more were in process of construction.

After we had been at Shusha for two or three weeks it was decided to send a detachment of the Camel Corps to B.4, which was the forward base and Paterson and I, with our respective sections of Westminster Dragoons and Berkshire Yeomanry, were ordered to accompany it, the idea being that Captain Mason MacFarlane should follow later on. It was our first training exercise on any sort of an operational basis and it was quite an exciting prospect.

I should explain here the enormous difficulty of mounting any operations against the Senussi in the Western desert. They were based on various oases far away in the interior including Baharia, Kharga, Farafra and Siwa, but there was no possible means of finding out where they were in strength at any particular time. It was believed that some 2000 tribesmen were gathered at Baharia which was our objective, but nobody seemed to know exactly where Baharia was. Such maps as existed were virtually useless and there were thousands of square miles of desert which appeared on the maps either as a completely blank space or just with the one word 'unexplored'.

There was no doubt that they were 'desert' but the desert varied considerably. Some parts were soft sand, others hard gravel on both of which, particularly the latter, we could make good progress, but it was known that somewhere between us and Baharia there was a vast range of sand dunes more than a hundred miles long, anything up to eight miles wide and in places quite impenetrable. Somehow or other a way through had to be found if we were ever to reach the oasis which was believed to be about fifteen miles on from where the dunes died out.

This was my first experience of the real desert and I found that, despite or perhaps because of its utter silence and loneliness, it had an extraordinary fascination for me. Apart from our little party there was hardly a living creature to be seen. Occasionally one would glimpse the trail of a gazelle or the track of a lizard in the sand, but it was always a mystery to me how they survived, particularly the gazelle. There was no water and hardly any growth except for camel thorn which by some miracle of nature contained an element of moisture. Nor were there any birds to be seen and even insects were rare though occasionally one came across a praying mantis. One night I shared my sleeping bag with a scorpion which was not discovered till the morning. Fortunately we had slept in different compartments. There was also a ferocious species of spider, and at Shusha we used to put on spider fights which invariably ended in the death of one of the combatants and its consumption by the victor. Some of them became champions and I remember that our representative, which was known as 'The Shusha Slosher', had a great reputation throughout the camp, until it succumbed in its turn to a younger and stronger opponent.

It was now midsummer and during the day-time the desert was like a furnace. Violent dust storms blew up from nowhere without any warning and subsided just as quickly perhaps an hour later, by which time one's mouth and ears and nostrils were choked with sand and one's skin, wherever it was exposed, scorched and scarified. But it was not long before our knees and faces, which had started off by assuming a brilliant scarlet colour, became almost black and tough enough to stand up to almost anything in the way of heat which the desert could throw at us. Fortunately the nights were cool and sometimes cold, and we were able to get some sleep which was almost impossible when we were resting during the day. Water, of course, was the great problem, although not so acute at this stage when we were only cut off from fresh supplies for a day or two at a time. Later on when we were on patrol for four or even five consecutive days it was a constant anxiety. All we had for drinking and washing was a goatskin water bottle and a five-gallon tank fixed to the saddle. Owing to the intense evaporation the water in the bottle remained refreshingly cool whatever the conditions, but unfortunately it also diminished the supply and we had to be careful not to run out. I remember this happening on two occasions and it is not a very pleasant experience being without water in the desert even for a few hours especially, as happened once later on, when you are under shell fire.

Our progress to Blockhouse B.4 was relatively uneventful. We trekked during the cooler parts of the day and bedded down at night either in the desert or at one of the intermediate blockhouses. I remember arriving one evening at B.2 and being greeted, to our mutual astonishment, by Geoffrey Byass, who was a captain in the Glamorgan Yeomanry and had been in the same house as myself at Winchester.

A good deal of patrolling was going on in every direction and, apart from the Camel Corps, this was usually carried out by detachments of armoured cars. These were known as the heavy car and light car patrols, and it is curious to realise that although this was fifty years ago the former consisted of Rolls-Royces and the latter of Fords. There were no tracked vehicles in those days, and it was astonishing how these two makes of car were able to cope with virtually any kind of desert, sometimes covering more than one hundred miles in a day. I do not mean they could ride the dunes, this was of course impossible, but they could range far and wide until they found a gap through which to penetrate and, although this generally came to a dead end, they were able to make an occasional break-through and more or less plot the course which would have to be taken by the main body when the time came, months later, for the advance on Baharia.

The dunes were certainly a fearful obstacle but it was not until my second tour of duty when I was stationed at B.6, which had been completed by then and become a railhead, that I came to grips with them for the first time.

Meanwhile there was a lot of patrolling to be done from B.4 but the furthest we could go fell far short of the dunes themselves. After we had been there for a few days I was ordered to take out a patrol with about half a dozen men and penetrate as far as we could into the broken ground which stretched for miles between the blockhouse and the dunes and ascertain whether any sort of Senussi activity was going on. This 'broken ground' was a deadly sort of place. The going was quite good but, owing to the endless number of mounds and hillocks, some of them two or three hundred feet high, it was impossible to see for any distance in any direction or to keep a straight course and, as we found, it was very easy to get lost. There had been a caravan route of some kind but we were never able to discover where it led from and, worse still, where it was going, in addition to which the tracks were constantly diverging and breaking away from each other. There was no indication whether it had been used in recent weeks or months or even years and it was really no use to us at all. Each hillock had a completely flat top, and frequently this was surmounted by a cairn of stones, but we had no idea what they signified.

There was no water, no growth and no sign of life, nothing but sand, gravel, rock and during the day-time a burning shimmering heat which distorted everything into fantastic shapes and images. Things were not made any easier by the fact that we were supposedly in enemy territory and had received orders to be always on the strictest guard and never to show ourselves on any skyline and I must admit that, as our trusty camels bore us further and further into this dreadful wilderness, we began to feel very small and lonely. Our way did not lead straight as we were continually having to circumvent hillocks of various sizes and although, of course, I could with the help of my compass (not one hundred per cent reliable among all those rocks), the sun by day and the stars by night more or less determine the direction in which we were going, I could not forget that B.4 was nothing but a pin point which it would be very easy to miss on the return journey and that our water would not stretch in those conditions beyond four days at the most.

And then I went and got lost, not the patrol just myself, and only for a short time, but it was quite long enough. It was midday and we were resting. I had posted a sentry (not forgetting that he must keep below the skyline) and decided I would have a look round for myself. I should, of course, have singled out some feature of the ground near our little camp and always kept it in sight, but I was new to the game and failed to carry out this very elementary precaution. In consequence when, after wandering about for perhaps half an hour, I decided to return to camp I suddenly realised, with a very unpleasant sensation in the pit of my stomach, that I had not the slightest idea where it was. Everywhere I looked seemed exactly the same, the sun was directly overhead so there were no shadows, there was no breeze, no movement, nothing but absolute stillness and the constant mirage.

I began to panic slightly but had the sense to realise that I must not move from where I was until I had collected my wits, or I might get further and further away from the camp. It was about five minutes later that I saw the figure of a man nearly half a mile away. He was standing quite motionless on the top of a low hillock and seemed to be staring in the opposite direction. Apparently he had not seen me and I thought the best thing I could do was to make a closer inspection. He might be alone or he might have friends, so I proceeded to stalk him, not a very difficult thing to do in all the broken ground which gave such excellent cover. About twenty minutes later I reached a point where I was able to observe the figure without being confused by the mirage, and I can truthfully say that my delight in recognising my own sentry far outweighed my annoyance that he should have so grossly disobeyed orders as to have climbed to the top of the nearest skyline immediately he thought I had been away too long. I, of course, had to admonish him but we both realised that it was not a very convincing exhibition.

It must have been soon after this that we began the return journey. There was, of course, no problem as regards direction. All we had to do was to proceed due east. The difficulty would arise when we emerged into the flat desert when I should have to decide whether we were north or south of B.4, or in a direct line. Otherwise it would be only too easy to miss it, and our water was already running very short. In fact it ran out altogether during the evening of the third day since leaving B.4 which was when we finally broke through with still another fifteen or twenty miles to go before we reached the block house, always assuming that we were in the right direction. I decided to wait until morning before we moved on, and we had the prospect of a very anxious and thirsty night ahead of us. And then, to our intense relief, two tiny specks appeared on the horizon which soon resolved themselves into a couple of Rolls-Royce armoured cars which had been sent out to try and locate us. They had a little water with them, but not quite sufficient for our needs and eventually the water was drained from the radiator of one of the cars which, of course, immobilised it, leaving the other to return to base in the morning and come back with fresh supplies. So it all ended very happily and I was very glad that I had not been called upon to make the final decision.

By this time our company commander Captain Mason MacFarlane, a brilliant regular officer who had come to us from the 7th Hussars, had arrived from Shusha, and after a few days it was decided that I and my section should be relieved and return to Shusha, to be replaced by an officer called Ryan, who commanded the Dorset Yeomanry section of the company. In due course Ryan and his men arrived and we marched out the next day on our trek back to base. I had expected to stay at Shusha for some time but I had only been there a few days when I was ordered to proceed with about thirty men to the Fayoum oasis, which was about sixty miles to the north. The Fayoum is really more than an oasis and covers a wide area of very fertile country separated from the Nile valley by a strip of desert which in places is only about a mile wide. We were to be attached to the Lincolnshire Yeomanry who were camped on the southern fringe of the oasis. More about that later, but first of all I must relate the story of MacFarlane and Ryan.

The former was a brilliant regular officer who not only knew his job inside out but was also a man of intense energy, resource and courage and it was not long before he decided to make a personal reconnaissance of the Baharia itself, provided that a way could be found through the dunes for a patrol mounted on the best and hardiest camels available. At best this was going to be a very hazardous and dangerous mission, but just possible within the limit of five days. It was believed, and so it turned out, that the oasis lay in a deep depression surrounded by a high escarpment and it would, of course, be necessary to remain on the high ground until the patrol could proceed to the lower level under cover of darkness. Eventually, with the help of the armoured cars, a viable route through the dunes was found and a day fixed for the operation to start. On this occasion MacFarlane was accompanied by Paterson and a Sergeant Guppy from the Dorset Yeomanry section. Everything proceeded according to plan, all MacFarlane's calculations turned out to be correct, and on a late afternoon the patrol established itself on top of the cliff from where they could not only see the oasis spread out below them but also observe that a little distance away it could be approached through a gap in the escarpment, which would provide them with a relatively easy access to the lower ground.

Directly it was dark enough they started off and rode down the slope to a point a few hundred yards away from the fringe of the oasis, where they halted and dismounted. MacFarlane then proceeded to carry out a personal reconnaissance on foot which took him right through the oasis to the other side and back, a distance of some nine or ten miles on a moonless night through country which he had never seen and was quite unmapped, and which was infested with a merciless enemy. His orders to Paterson and Guppy were that, if he had not returned by dawn, they were not to wait for him any longer and in fact it was obvious that with the arrival of daylight they would have no chance of survival. The night wore on and the false dawn had already come and gone when they heard the footsteps of a running man and MacFarlane emerged from the darkness which was already lightening.

He was speechless from exhaustion and thirst, but indicated that there was no time to lose, and within seconds they were on their camels and away. At the same time figures could dimly be seen rushing out of the oasis, there was a fusillade of rifle fire but nobody was hit and, before the Arabs could organise any sort of pursuit, the patrol was racing up the slope to the escarpment and going flat out back towards the dunes and safety. Not the least incredible part of this feat of valour and endurance was that on his return MacFarlane was able to reproduce a rough map of the Baharia which turned out to be substantially accurate and this despite the fact that, from the moment he entered the oasis until he left it, he was aware of being shadowed from behind and both sides, and he was never able to understand why his pursuers had not closed in on him until it was just too late.

Some two or three weeks later MacFarlane decided to make another reconnaissance to complete his study of the oasis and to form some idea of the strength in which it was held. It was believed that there were at least 2000 Senussi in the area. On this occasion he was accompanied by Ryan, a Corporal Bolt and two other Dorset men and they made their landfall at the top of the escarpmen sometime in the late afternoon of the second day. It seems that MacFarlane decided that he and Ryan should proceed on foot some way along the top of the cliff to a point where they could get a better view of the oasis. Bolt was ordered to keep all five camels ready saddled for a quick getaway in the event of an emergency, but was told that in any case the two officers would be back within the hour. About an hour later Bolt's little party heard the sound of heavy firing some distance away in the direction in which they had gone. After a minute or two there was silence, but there was no sign of the officers returning and Bolt was faced with the heavy responsibility of deciding what he should do. And then suddenly he became aware that a large party of tribesmen were climbing up the cliff towards him and that, whatever had happened to the officers, he had now got a fight on his own hands.

There ensued a battle which was quite a little epic in its way. From where they lay on the top of the cliff they opened fire on the tribesmen, who were by then some thirty feet below and, besides inflicting several casualties, they were able to pin the remainder of the party down. However, with the approach of darkness it was obvious that, if they stayed there, it would only be a matter of time before they were overwhelmed. Furthermore there was still no sign of MacFarlane and Ryan, and it could only be concluded that they had come to some harm. The only choice seemed to be retreat, but it was very difficult to disengage without being rushed by the enemy, and Bolt decided to put up a bluff. He ordered the other two to take all the camels back a few hundred yards and he would join them as soon as he could. He then took on the enemy single handed, changing his position every few seconds and firing from a different point so as to give the impression that the party was still intact. Fortunately the tribesmen seemed reluctant to come out in the open and rush those last thirty feet. After a final burst of fire Bolt ran literally for his life back to the camels and as the tribesmen appeared over the top of the cliff they were on their way. Two days later the forlorn little party of three exhausted men and five camels arrived back at B.4 and Bolt put in his report.

But, of course, he was in the unhappy position of having returned from a dangerous patrol without his officers and the question arose as to whether his story could be accepted out of hand or whether there should be a court of enquiry or even a court martial. And then, while this was being decided by higher authority, he had a lucky break. A Bedouin was picked up by a patrol and it turned out that he had been a witness of the whole affair. Not only did he corroborate Bolt's account but he was able to tell what had happened to MacFarlane and Ryan. It seems that they had been attacked in the same way as the others but they had not been able to prevent the tribesmen from scaling the cliff. There had been a grim battle at a few yards' range between the two officers, armed only with revolvers, and dozens of tribesmen armed with rifles. Several of the latter were killed but, of course, the outcome was inevitable. The Bedouin believed that one of the revolvers jammed and the other ran out of ammunition, and all that MacFarlane and Ryan could do was to throw first of all their revolvers and then stones at the enemy until after a few seconds they were shot down, and their bodies flung over the cliff, where they were found when the oasis was taken a couple of months later. So instead of a court martial Bolt was recommended for a V.C. as a reward for his outstanding courage and resource but, incomprehensibly, all he received was an Italian decoration, Italy having just come into the war. However, he made up for this later in the war by getting the D.C.M. and Bar. It was widely believed that MacFarlane was also put up for a posthumous V.C., an honour which we all thought he richly deserved.

I heard the news when I was in the Fayoum, where I spent several weeks carrying out various patrol duties. I remember one of these patrols particularly well. For some reason which was a little obscure at the time, and is even more so now, I was ordered to take with me a local Sheikh. Nobody seemed to know whether he was going to disclose to us the whereabouts of a band of Senussi or whether he was going to lead us into a trap or whether he was simply attached as a guide. All I can remember about him is that he was at least six and a half feet tall, and suffered badly from bilharziosis. Neither of us could understand a single word the other said and we took an intense dislike to each other on sight.

It was a very small patrol and my orders were about as vague as they could be apart from the fact that we were to be out in the desert for four days and ascertain whether there was any sign of the elusive Senussi. Late one afternoon we arrived at a range of high dunes and I decided to camp for the night. But we had no sooner dismounted when the Sheikh suddenly took to his heels and bolted through a gap in the nearest dune. I shouted to him to stop but this had no effect and the only thing I could do was to follow him. By then I was convinced that he was going to sell us down the river, not a very apt metaphor in that sandy wilderness, and I thought I might have to shoot him. It was a nightmare chase up and down the dunes, stumbling about in the loose drifting sand, cursing and swearing at each other, sweating like bulls, at least I was, in the blazing heat until finally with a last savage imprecation the old boy squatted down and proceeded to relieve himself. As I have said, he was suffering from bilharziosis and he appeared to be undergoing a particularly acute attack. All the poor man was looking for was a little privacy, and our arrival at the dunes had given him the opportunity. I turned my back and a little later he rose and joined me and we started to walk back to camp. The sun was setting and the dunes were changing moment by moment from dazzling white to yellow then pink and finally blood red, always a magnificent spectacle, when suddenly there appeared on top of one of the dunes a pair of gazelle, first the horns and then the heads pressed close together and frozen into immobility as they caught sight of us below. I think that we were both transfixed for a moment by the sheer beauty of those two little animals in that lovely setting and, although we never spoke a word to each other during our walk back, I felt we had shared an experience which for a moment had helped to bridge our differences. At any rate l do not think that we quarrelled any more.

We had another patrol a few days later which had a tragic instead of a comic sequel. One of the men was a veterinary corporal whose job it was to attend to the various ailments which afflicted our hard worked camels. I suppose that his continual contact with the different kinds of septicaemia from which they suffered had infected him, and I remember that he had a number of bandages on the exposed surfaces of his body such as knees, arms, neck, etc. This did not call for any particular comment as most of us were suffering from septic sores of one kind or another, and indeed this was general throughout the whole of the army in Egypt. The same thing happened, I believe, to the troops in South Africa during the Boer War where they were called 'Veldt' sores. They were due to a variety of causes, such as lack of fresh vegetables, infected water, and bites from various mosquitoes and sand-flies, to say nothing of ordinary flies which pestered us in thousands from morning to night. Even when we went into the desert we always took hundreds of these loathsome little creatures with us on ourselves and our camels, and on long expeditions it was several days before they died out. On shorter ones we simply brought them back with us. I think that everyone was infected in some degree. Even if you simply cut yourself shaving the chances were that it would turn septic and some of the men had sores all over their faces. I had a few myself and they were difficult to cure because of the bristles growing up through the open sores. Anyway, when we were about two days out on patrol the corporal was taken desperately ill. I will not attempt to describe what the unfortunate man had to go through but, mercifully, after a few hours he relapsed into unconsciousness, and we certainly had a problem on our hands. I sent two men back to camp for help and we did our best for the patient until it arrived. After all this time I cannot remember the details but an ambulance of some kind was sent out and he was taken on ahead. After we got back ourselves I was met by the medical officer in charge, who was a very worried man, and he asked me to come with him and see the patient, who had been put into a separate hut. He was still unconscious but while we were with him he went into a terrible convulsion, as though he was suffering from strychnine poisoning, and after a few moments he fell back dead. The M.O. told me that he suspected cholera and was sending in a report to that effect. Supplies of vaccine were rushed into the camp and, pending an autopsy, everybody had to be inoculated. The autopsy took place two days later in the town of Fayoum, but it was not until after several days that we heard that the death had not been caused by cholera, but by some other virus which the medical people had been quite unable to identify. Fortunately it cannot have been contagious or infectious as nobody else succumbed, but they were very anxious days and I cannot say that the detachment from the Camel Corps was exactly popular until the flap eventually died down.

But there were so many diseases about including dysentery, malaria, sand-fly fever, etc., and there was always the danger of typhoid although, of course, we had all been inoculated against this either before we left England or on the ship. There was also an outbreak of plague throughout the Fayoum oasis, where it was probably more or less endemic, and there were several villages which we were not allowed to pass through, even in a car, without taking precautions. We had to stop a few hundred yards short of the village and cover our faces with a sort of gauze mask before driving through hell-for-leather, with orders not to stop under any circumstances whatever, not even if we killed or injured one of the inhabitants. So far as I know there was no accident of this kind but on the one or two occasions when I had to drive, or rather be driven, through one of the villages we always left a trail of dead or injured dogs, chickens, sheep, goats and so forth behind us. I cannot think that this endeared us particularly to the unfortunate villagers, who already had the plague to contend with, but it would have been disastrous if on top of all its other troubles the army had become plague ridden.

Despite these alarms and excursions I thoroughly enjoyed my stay in the Fayoum. The officers of the Lincolnshire Yeomanry were most hospitable although the C.O. who had, I believe, been some years in India, had a liver the size of a football and junior officers like myself were advised in their own interests never to speak to him until midday at the earliest and, if possible, sundown. The regiment had suffered a dreadful experience on the voyage to Egypt. Their ship, which was not in convoy, was attacked by an enemy submarine which surfaced some way astern and although unable to fire its torpedoes was able to keep the ship within range of its gun, which subjected it to a continuous and intense bombardment. The submarine was also able to keep out of range of the ship's only armament which consisted of one or two machine guns! I do not know how many casualties were inflicted but I believe that so far as the men were concerned the roll was not too severe. But the damage caused by shells bursting among the horses below decks was horrible. Dozens of them were killed and no doubt many more were injured so badly that they had to be destroyed. It must have been a terrifying experience.

After about two months I took leave of my hosts and we returned to Shusha, where the final capture of the Baharia was being planned.

Blockhouse B.6 had now been completed and had become a railhead which, of course, enormously eased the problem of supplies. The company had now been taken over by J.J. Paterson, who had originally commanded the detachment from the Westminster Dragoons, and who before the war had been in China with the well-known merchant firm of Jardine Matheson & Company, and returned there when the war was over. In the Second War he was in command of the Hong Kong Home Guard, which put up a terrific resistance against the Japanese until, having run out of food and ammunition, it was forced to surrender after being completely encircled and sustaining heavy casualties.

In point of fact there is little to relate about the operations against the Baharia because the Senussi had seen the writing on the wall and decided to get out while the going was good. The advance took place in November, 1916, and it was interesting to pass once more over the ground which we had patrolled earlier in the year, make our way at last through the range of sand dunes to the open ground beyond and then another fifteen miles to the escarpment surrounding the oasis where MacFarlane and Ryan had died, and down through the gap between the cliffs which they had descended on their earlier patrol to the verge of the oasis itself, which would have looked and seemed peaceful enough had it not been for their bodies, which were found lying at the bottom of the cliff.

My chief recollection of the Baharia is that it was a very beautiful place with a profusion of date palms, groves of oranges and limes and virtually unlimited water and marshland, which abounded with duck of various species, snipe and other waterfowl. A less attractive feature was the fact that most of the Arab children were afflicted with elephantiasis and in many cases their heads were at least twice the normal size, which gave them a grotesque appearance. In the absence of the Senussi fighting men the inhabitants received us peacefully enough and supplied our wants of fresh fruit and vegetables, which were very welcome after months of bully beef and biscuit and other army rations which though quite good of their kind were distinctly monotonous. But the highlight was a truly memorable feast. One of my colleagues borrowed a gun from somewhere and shot several duck and teal which we cooked ourselves over a very slow fire in the largest pot we could lay our hands on and to which we added a magnificent sauce composed of tinned cream, a pound or two of crystallised plums and a whole bottle of port, which we had carried for hundreds of miles waiting for a real occasion to arise. This was the occasion. The sauce was almost black with the consistency of the thickest lentil soup, and we took turns to pour it with loving hands over those marvellous birds. The preparation of the meal took hours and the smell from that fragrant concoction had made us almost demented by the time it was ready to eat. But it was worth waiting for and I have never in my life tasted anything quite so delicious.

We did not stay in the Baharia for more than a few days before returning to B.6 where half the company was to remain for several weeks, including my section of the Berkshire Yeomanry and the section of the Royal Bucks Hussars commanded by a great friend of mine, Merlin Huth. We were attached to the Montgomeryshire Yeomanry who occupied the post and the rest of the company proceeded to Shusha where we rejoined them towards the end of January, 1917.

In preparation for Christmas Day the mess secretary had paid a visit to Cairo and he brought back with him a quantity of delicacies with which to celebrate the occasion. I still have the menu for our dinner which reads as follows:

Sherry	Consomme Julienne
	—
Champagne	Dindon Roti
	Pommes de Terre
	Asperges
	—
	Jambon
	Pois
	—
Brandy	Pouding de Noel
	Mince Pies
	—
Port	Pate de Foie Gras

It was a wonderful repast and we all got distinctly high. It is curious to reflect that the two meals which I have enjoyed most should have taken place under such extraordinary conditions within a month of each other, but I still think that the first of these was the better.

Incidentally, although I cannot believe that this was true, we were told that we were the first Europeans to visit the Baharia. As a matter of fact several of the Egyptian oases including Siwa are supposed to have been visited by Alexander the Great and possibly the Crusaders as well. Certainly in Siwa there was a quantity of chain mail emblazoned with the cross so there may be something in the story.

In the meantime reports had been coming in from Jennings Bramley's Intelligence that the Senussi had withdrawn to the oasis of Farafra, 120 miles further to the south. It was not known whether they intended to make a stand there but this was something which had to be discovered and a force of fifty men was dispatched for this purpose under the command of Jennings Bramley himself, who had been in Egypt for thirty years and held the rank of Bimbashi (Colonel) in the Egyptian army.

It was realised that, if any serious resistance was encountered and they were unable to get into the oasis, they would be faced with the prospect of having to get back without any chance of replenishing their water supplies, a march of 240 miles which would take at least six days to accomplish, and would be a very severe ordeal for men and camels alike. However, in the result, all was well as most of the Senussi had already melted away into the desert and the party returned safely to the Baharia with fifteen prisoners. Mr Mark Ward of Weymouth has given an account of this expedition, in which he took part with a number of other men from No. 8 Company, and he also recalls, something which I do not myself recollect, that some of the patrols which penetrated the great mass of sand dunes which stood between the Baharia and B.6, which was the last of the block houses, were considered to be so dangerous that knock-out pills were issued to be used in the event of capture, as there had been several cases of torture and mutilation on the part of the Senussi. Something of this sort had been witnessed by John Ressich as he lay unable to move at the bottom of the wadi after the disastrous charge which I have already related. On another occasion a Yeomanry officer, whose name I will not divulge, though I knew him well, was so incensed when he came across a party of three or four Senussi horribly mutilating the body of a British soldier that, although normally the gentlest of men, he lined them up in a row and shot them one by one at point blank range with his revolver. The danger of falling into the hands of the

Senussi was well known to everybody, which throws into sharp relief the reply which was given by a very senior officer to a question as to whether there was any news of Mason MacFarlane and Ryan - 'Not so far' he said. 'But they will be all right. The Senussi are gentlemen and will treat them decently'. Well perhaps they would have, but it may have been fortunate for those two brave men that, as it turned out, they were killed on the spot fighting to the last round in their revolvers.

Our stay in this part of the Western desert was now drawing to a close. Huth and I paid one visit to relative civilisation when we had to go to Minia, a town on the Nile, to collect the pay for the men. We travelled by the light railway and had quite an adventure at the outset. B.6 was located in a saucer-like depression and for a mile or so the railway track led up quite a steepish gradient to the higher ground. The engine was pulling a pretty heavy load and having some difficulty in climbing to the top. And then, just as success was in sight, the engine coupling broke. The coaches slowed to a stop and the sensible thing would have been to get out as most of the occupants did, but for some reason we stayed put and gradually the coaches began to go backwards down the incline gathering speed all the time. Before long we were swaying and rocking as the pace increased until it looked rather as though the coaches would become derailed at one of the numerous bends. However, by some miracle they stayed upright and about five minutes after the coupling broke we quietly drew up, much to the astonishment of the station staff, at the platform which we had left so optimistically some twenty minutes earlier, and despite the fact that none of the coaches had any brakes.

Before we left B.6 for good, Huth and I made two other interesting discoveries. Walking along the edge of the dunes one evening we came across a vast area of oyster shells which, although we were anything between 500 and 1000 feet above sea-level, afforded pretty convincing proof that at some remote time in the past the whole of this part of the desert was under the sea. The other discovery was that camels can eat anything. At any rate one of them on which we experimented one day consumed, apparently to its complete satisfaction and without any ill effects whatever, two or three tins of salmon, tins and all, and several boxes of matches. This may sound rather cruel but we had the feeling, based on previous experience, that a camel's digestive processes were capable of absorbing anything he was offered, and how right we were.

On our return to base at Shusha we did not have to wait long before the company was ordered to return to its old quarters at Cairo. The journey was to be made by rail and we made another discovery, which is that camels have a rooted objection to getting into trains. There were ramps leading up to the camel trucks and all the pushing and pulling and swearing in the world would not induce the camels to climb them. However, somebody produced a very bright idea. We wrapped their heads in an assortment of sacks and blankets, turned them round several times so as to get them confused as to direction, manoeuvred their backsides towards the ramps and then pulled for all we were worth in the opposite direction. This was quite sufficient to induce the camels to go backwards up the ramps, and in next to no time we had the whole lot safely entrained and tethered down. Their astonishment and disgust when their head covering was removed were almost pathetic. For once they had been fooled into doing what we wanted and they obviously regarded the whole thing as a very shabby trick.

11. The Southern Oases

If an imaginary line is drawn due south from Sollum on the coast to the Siwa Oasis and from there south east and south to the oases of Baharia, Fararra, Dahkla and Kharga the territory enclosed between that line to the west, the sea to the north and the Nile Valley to the east comprises an area or more than 50,000 square miles, considerable parts of which had to be constantly patrolled after the withdrawal of the main body of the Senussi from the coastal regions into the interior of the Western Desert, and this was precisely the task for which the Imperial Camel Corps had originally been formed.

At about the same time that we had left Abassia for our Baharian adventures the other companies were either sent direct to Sinai to join up with the forces covering the Suez Canal or to various places within the Kharga area to strengthen or replace the cavalry and for that matter infantry units which were already there but, with the approach of summer, were becoming more and more unsuited to the task which lay ahead.

The Kharga expedition included No. 10 Company and to reach the oasis, which lies about 250 miles to the south east of Baharia, they had to proceed by rail from Cairo to the nearest station and from there undertake a march of 100 miles across the intervening desert.

Kharga is a large and well watered oasis with several villages and noted particularly for its fine dates. About 100 miles to the west there is the oasis of Dahkla and, when the Senussi were being driven into the interior from the coastal regions, they were reported to be concentrating at Dahkla as well as Baharia, which was the reason for the decision that Kharga should be occupied so as to keep an eye on their movements. Part of a Scottish Infantry brigade had been sent to this area but the occupation of the outlying posts and the whole of the patrolling in the general direction of Dahkla were made the responsibility of the Camel Corps. Wing Commander Ashlin, who was then a Lieutenant in No. 10 Company, was in charge of the furthermost post which consisted of a stone building surrounded by a wall and was turned into some semblance of a fort. It covered the principal approach to Kharga from the desert and all the long distance patrols operated from this point. Ashlin's command included a platoon of a Highland regiment and he had given orders that no pipes were to play within a quarter of a mile of the camel lines, because the first time the camels heard the pipes there was a stampede and it took several hours to round them up. After this incident the relations between the Scotties and the camels became severely strained and they never succeeded in getting over their mutual distrust and dislike. To the Scotties a camel was always a 'bluidy hump' and it would be interesting to know exactly what the camels thought in return!

Ashlin has given a graphic account of one of the patrols which he led towards the Dahkla Oasis. It was an exceptionally unpleasant one but the story does help to illustrate the dangers and discomforts of operating in those barren and waterless wastes, which were for the most part unmapped and even unexplored. In addition it was now mid-summer and the desert was like a furnace. Kharga Oasis is in a hollow and to get out of it, in the only direction patrols could go towards Dahkla, it was necessary to cover about forty-five miles of flat desert, dotted here and there with a well or waterhole, and then climb an almost perpendicular escarpment between 300 and 400 feet high. There was only one steep path, within a radius of 100 miles in the required direction, leading up to the top of the plateau, and it was particularly hard to find, so much so that, as this was to be their first long patrol, Ashlin took with him as guides two Australians who had been there before with their own company of Imperial Camel Corps and were supposed to know the path well.

I now propose to give the story of what happened in Ashlin's own words which, although I was to have my own fair share of patrolling in the Baharia and other sectors, are far more descriptive and indeed exciting than any I could use at second hand.

This patrol was a particularly long one (seven days). We were supposed to strike some wells reported to be at a certain point on our way. The patrol consisted of eleven all told including the two guides and myself. Fortunately I had picked out my animals carefully and brought four spares.

Nothing untoward happened until we got to the reported wells which we found to be bone dry.

There was a little camel scrub close by which refreshed the animals to some extent and, although we had not been economising particularly with our drinking water, we still had sufficient, with careful rationing, for three days which would just get us back. One of the first lessons taught in the Imperial Camel Corps was to husband one's water supply on such expeditions, and consequently there was no cause for alarm. The going had been heavy, men and animals were tired and a Khamseen (sand storm) was blowing, so we camped for a few hours and tried to get what rest we could with our heads buried in our blankets. The rest refreshed the animals, though it did us little good, and we made good time going back, reaching the edge of the escarpment on the morning of the sixth day without water for the camels. We could see far below us at a distance of thirty miles the dark outline of a small oasis indicating the location of water. All that remained was to find the path down and in five or six hours we would be drinking our fill. Both our guides seemed quite certain that we had struck the edge of the escarpment to the north of the path, so we turned south. The Khamseen, as happens so often in those parts, had completely changed the aspect of the country owing to the shifting sand, so there was some excuse for the guides' mistake. This, however, should not have happened if we had been more experienced.

At the end of three hours' marching there was still no trace of the opening in the escarpment. The camels were showing signs of distress and we began to realise the predicament we were in. The guides were now frankly at a loss, so after a short halt I decided to retrace our steps. It was noon with the heat at its highest but I dared not halt for more than a breather. Naturally our progress was very much slower and it was almost night when we reached the point where we first struck the edge of the escarpment. Darkness was fast falling so there was nothing to do but camp. The animals were suffering acutely and our drinking water was practically all gone. I collected what was left and it did not fill one small water bottle. We spent an anxious night. It was too dark to try and locate the path so we had to wait with what patience we could for the coming of dawn. As soon as it was light enough we started, our progress being now painfully slow as we had to halt frequently and lead the camels over the worst bits of ground.

We had been plodding along for about two hours when one of the weaker animals went mad with thirst. The poor beast was too weak to do any damage and, as it was in agony, we shot it. Shortly after another, fortunately a spare which had gone lame, also went mad and fell over the escarpment. He must have broken his neck because he lay still at the bottom. Towards noon after covering about fifteen miles without finding the path, our worst misfortune overtook us. One of the Australian guides, quite a young boy, began to behave queerly, from thirst, the sun or probably both. He became delirious and so violent that we had to bind him to his saddle. I then decided to give up looking for the path, realising that our only course was to make an attempt to descend the escarpment. This was no task at all for us on foot. The difficulty was to get the camels down, it looked almost impossible without breaking their legs, particularly in their weakened condition. Without camels it was doubtful if we could have traversed those thirty miles of desert to the nearest well. Something had to be done, however and I hoped with luck that two or three animals might reach the bottom uninjured and we could fetch water and help.

We found a place which resembled a very steep chute reaching to about forty feet from the bottom. It zigzagged a little and there was a certain amount of loose sand and stones on the surface. Half the men descended and we rolled the kit and equipment down. Then we tackled the chief problem which was getting the animals to descend, and it was then that they showed their intelligence and good sense. They seemed to know that it was their only chance. We coaxed the first one over the edge and into the chute. As soon as he felt himself going he just sat down on his haunches and slid which was the only possible way of getting down without a broken neck. We got the others down in the same way and in quick succession. The last forty feet was practically a sheer drop but they rolled or scrambled down somehow. They were all, of course, badly cut and scraped by the rocks and some were lamed but actually there were only two serious casualties, both broken legs. These animals had to be shot. Although we only lost four camels some were so weak and lame that they could not be ridden and the less exhausted carried a double burden on this last lap of our journey. It was with very thankful hearts that we made for the well which, owing to this episode, was named the Well of Deliverance and so marked in the survey maps. The camels seemed to sense that water was near for we covered the thirty miles in a little over six hours in spite of their exhausted condition. We subsequently discovered that the Khamseen had obliterated all signs of the path down the escarpment, and a land mark was put up so that there should be no repetition of this unpleasant incident.

I should just like to add that following a survey trek between Kharga and Dahkla this officer had a hill named after him –'Mount Ashlin'.

At the end of July No. 10 Company proceeded to Sinai where it joined up with Nos. 6, 7 and 9 Companies and as part of the Desert Mobile Column became heavily engaged over the next two months in the Battle of Romani and subsequent operations as described in the following chapters. Towards the end of September it returned to Kharga which had been held during its absence in Sinai by a battalion of infantry, who naturally had been unable to maintain the long range desert patrols. Consequently remnants of the Senussi forces had managed to concentrate in the oasis of Dahkla about 100 miles to the west, in the same way as they had been able to occupy the oasis of Baharia 150 miles further to the north, and it was decided that the time had come for both of these places to be captured and the Senussi driven beyond the frontiers of Egypt. Dahkla had always been one of their strongholds although officially administered by the Egyptian Government.

On arrival back in Kharga No. 10 Company immediately resumed its patrolling towards the fringes of Dahkla. These were helped by a water and ration dump which had been established thirty miles to the west of Kharga, apart from which the five-day patrols were over entirely waterless desert. The patrols had now been increased in strength and early in October a small force of about two sections, comprising some sixty rifles and two Lewis guns, encountered a group of Senussi a few miles to the east of the first well in the Dahkla Oasis. The Camel Corps were a good deal more mobile than the Arabs who were soon rounded up. They were mostly on foot although they had with them a few scrawny female camels, each bearing the Senussi brand or wasm which is a tribal brand as distinct from a fendy which denotes a sub-clan. Incidentally each camel of the Imperial Camel Corps had its own regimental number which was branded on its neck. This particular party of Senussi was made up from several sub-clans, but as all their camels bore the regular Senussi wasm, a shortened version of the Arabic word 'Allah', they probably came from the Zawia or Monastery in Dahkla.

There was no other course than to escort all the prisoners back to Kharga, nearly ninety miles away and, as they were on foot, the Camel Corps were unable to ride at the usual short trot of six miles an hour and the whole column had to proceed at a slow walk. At one of the mid-day halts there was a sudden commotion among the Arab women, who had insisted on accompanying their menfolk into captivity, but it was not until it cried out that the Camel Corps realised that one of the women had given birth to a baby. It was explained to the Senussi leader that in two hours time the march would have to be resumed but a spare camel would be provided for the mother and child. This offer was, however, contemptuously refused presumably in order to prove that Senussi women were really tough and sure enough, as the column moved off, the woman was seen to make a sling of her rags, pop the baby in and fling it over her shoulder. And barefoot she made the march which had several more days to go.

Some of the men were clad in tatters of khaki uniform but most wore normal Bedouin clothing. Their arms consisted in the main of German Mausers or Russian rifles, but some of them carried the long Arab Jezel, a smooth bore flintlock about five feet long and usually decorated with mother of pearl inlaid in the butt and the barrel banded with silver. This weapon had a very short range, not more than 200 yards, and fired a home moulded leaden bullet which could tear a nasty hole if it hit its mark. Most of the prisoners claimed to have come from the oasis of Jaghabub or the Jebel Akhdar, both of them hundreds of miles away to the north west in Cyrenaica.

There were several different routes between Kharga and Dahkla all of which had to be constantly patrolled. The desert in this region was exceptionally bare and there was no vegetation for the camels to graze, not even the seemingly dried up camel thorn, which would also have provided fuel for the cooking fires.

In the middle of October, at the same time as No. 8 Company was feeling its way towards the Baharia Oasis, it was decided that No. 10 Company should make an attempt to occupy Dahkla. Major T. Bardwell who had brought it down from Sinai had just taken up an appointment in the Sudan and the Company was commanded by Captain A. G. Wilkinson.

Pending its departure from Kharga it was attached to a Base Camp 'for pay and rations'. Not that pay was of much interest in the desert apart from a little mild gambling, but there was a Y.M.C.A. hut in the Camp, where it was possible to buy a few little luxuries to augment the perpetual bully beef and biscuits. The Camp was a large one and surrounded by barbed wire and piles of sandbags, with sentries perched on towers and protected from the sun by wooden canopies.

The Camp Commandant may have considered that the Camel Corps had its uses but he refused to have the camels within the perimeter of the barbed wire, even though there was plenty of room and, of course, the cameliers stayed with them. After all they had become quite used to sleeping in each others company! Normal rations were issued but no fire-wood, a situation which obviously had to be rectified. Following their last evening in the Camp canteen the cameliers were ordered outside the wire and the gates closed behind them but, unfortunately for the Commandant, he had not allowed for their skill and experience as night raiders. During the night not a single sentry gave the alarm and not a sound was heard except the usual croaking of the bull-frogs, the ticking of crickets and the light tapping of some sort of night bird, accompanied by the howling of jackals and the occasional moaning or bubbling of the camels.

Next morning the Company was saddled up in full 'Marching Order' to move off when the Commandant rode out not to wave farewell but to complain that marauders had almost wrecked his camp. Whole wooden ablution benches and latrine screens (both of which the cameliers regarded with contempt!) had disappeared together with his favourite jackal trap and he wanted to know whether the Camel Corps were responsible. Not surprisingly he got very little change out of that and, although he walked right through the lines of camels peering and prying about in all directions, not a piece of his precious timber was to be seen. It had all been shredded by bayonets into sticks of about eighteen inches and tucked out of sight under the saddle bags and covering furwahs or blankets. I do not think that the cameliers, or buccaneers as I have more than once heard them called, were ever lacking in enterprise!

As it happened Dahkla was eventually taken without a struggle. The Senussi had been given sufficient evidence of the strength and mobility of the Camel Corps during the earlier skirmish and fled as it approached Tenida, the first village, where Headquarters was established while patrols were pushed further into the chain of village oases until finally the most westerly, Qasr el Dahkla, was occupied.

In his account of this expedition Laurence Moore has explained that Dahkla Oasis is rather different from that of Kharga. The villages are closer together and, owing to a much better water supply, it is a good deal more fertile. Dates, various citrus fruits and olives were grown and chickens and eggs could be bought from the villagers. A great escarpment, about 350 feet high, runs east to west, protecting the thirty-mile chain of villages from the prevailing northerly winds. Beyond Qasr el Dahkla the escarpment takes a sudden turn almost at a northern right angle and in this angle the last outpost was established at Bir Sheikh Mohammed, where lovely hot springs ran into deep stone cisterns. Communications were by heliograph so that, in order to get the mirror signals round the bend in the escarpment, three or four men were continually manning a transmitting station up on the highest point at the turn. From Bir Sheikh Mohammed nightly patrols ascended a nearby pass up the cliff and longer ones took trips of several days to the west in track of the Senussi, who were reported to have retreated to the oasis of Kufra, later to be made famous by the woman explorer Rosita Forbes.

Rumours of an impending counter-attack by the Senussi 'Army' were continually being received but it never materialised which was perhaps just as well bearing in mind that the whole of the oasis was more than 100 miles from the nearest base at Kharga (which in any case could not have provided any reinforcements without the use of camels) and held by one company of Imperial Camel Corps and that almost the whole of its population was either of the Senussi Sect or allied to its cause.

No. 10 Company remained in Dahkla until May, 1917, When it was sent to Sollum to relieve No. 8 Company, which had been ordered to proceed to Sinai.

12. Sinai - Romani

Before relating the experiences of the Imperial Camel Corps in Sinai during the latter half of 1916 it might be helpful if I were to go back a bit and give a very brief account of the military situation in July of that year and of the events which led up to it.

In February, 1915, the Turks had made an attempt to invade Egypt across the Sinai Peninsula. The probable reasons for this were (1) to ensure that as many British soldiers as possible were retained to garrison the country and correspondingly reduce the number of troops available for the fighting in France, which would in turn release some of the German troops to strengthen their forces on the Russian front, at that time under considerable pressure and (2) to obtain a Turkish victory, on the only front where this was even remotely possible at the time, so as to counter the unpopularity of the war as a whole in Turkey and the possibility of a revolution.

Unfortunately for the Turks their rather slow and cumbersome movements towards the Suez Canal had been under close observation for several weeks, both by British aerial reconnaissance and patrols of the Egyptian and Bikanir Camel Corps, with the result that by the time the advanced units of the Turkish army which consisted, with its rear echelons, of about 60,000 regular and 10,000 irregular troops under the command of Djemal Pasha with a mixed Turco-German staff reached the Canal, Sir John Maxwell had succeeded in collecting together a force of more than 40,000 men in entrenched positions on its western bank, which had been carefully prepared and strengthened for months previously, with another 30,000 in reserve. These included British, Indian, Australian and New Zealand troops and a considerable part of the native Egyptian army.

The attack when it came at dawn on the 3rd February, was badly conceived and handled and, instead of pushing forward reconnoitring columns to probe the British positions and ascertain how strongly they were held, or alternatively striking with his whole force, the Turkish commander more or less blundered up against the defences with a relatively weak force of not more than two below strength divisions, which were bloodily repulsed, and he never succeeded in getting the main body of his army into action at all. The Turks fought gallantly as usual but to no avail and by nightfall they were in full retreat.

DEFENCE OF SUEZ CANAL 1915-1916

It was estimated that their losses were not less than 4,000 officers and men killed, wounded and taken prisoner, while the British casualties barely totalled sixty. In addition the Turks had lost practically all the pontoons which they had brought up for their intended crossing of the Canal.

No attempt was made to follow the retreating enemy, which was a wise decision in view of the fact that the British troops were not positioned to take the offensive nor were they yet sufficiently trained to take part in a major desert campaign. However, during the following months, a system of military defences was established well to the east of the Canal, pipelines and light railway and motor tracks were laid, and everything possible was done to ensure that, when winter came and conditions had become less rigorous in the wilderness which faced them, the British forces would be so strongly placed that they would not only be able to block any further attack on the Canal but also to take the offensive directly the opportunity arose.

In the meantime the British attack on the Dardanelles and landings in Gallipoli had relieved the pressure by the Turks on other fronts and, although a second attempt on the Canal had been expected and Djemal Pasha had asked for 25,000 German troops to reinforce his battered army, there was very little chance of his request being granted and, in the event, he had to wait some time for reinforcements from any source.

In consequence he refused to make any further move towards the Canal and by the end of 1915 the British were beginning to worry his advanced posts.

In February, 1916, the great German reservoir at Hassana, 100 miles from the Canal, which had taken months to construct, was attacked from the air and virtually destroyed and this was followed by an assault on the oasis of Gifgafa by the Australian Light Horse after a march of 160 miles in three and a half days. The attack was completely successful and the elaborate water works which had been built up by an Austrian engineer, were demolished. These two actions so diminished the enemy's water supplies that he was compelled to draw further back. In addition a small body of British cavalry, which included squadrons from the Warwickshire and Worcestershire Yeomanry and Royal Gloucestershire Hussars, had occupied the important oasis of Katia which lies forty miles to the east of Port Said and fifty miles to the north of Gifgafa from which, however, it is separated by a range of heights, the Jebel Maghara, which were occupied by the enemy in some strength.

In the subsequent weeks there was severe fighting throughout the whole of this area, which included the Duweidar Oasis nearer to the Canal. The Turks were making constant sorties from their positions on the higher ground, and on Easter Sunday they attacked Duweidar at dawn under cover of a dense mist with a force of 2000 men. Defending the oasis was a company of Royal Scots Fusiliers who put up a stout resistance and, although sustaining heavy casualties, succeeded in holding out until they were reinforced by two more companies of the same regiment from a hill a few miles away, and eventually the Turks were routed by a bayonet charge. This action, in which both sides fought with great gallantry, was a vital one because, had Duweidar fallen, the Yeomanry also fighting against heavy odds some fifteen miles away and almost surrounded by a force of 2000 Turks and 1000 Germans and Austrians, would have been completely cut off.

There were several more encounters, which for the most part ended in favour of the British, but early in May, 1916, the Turks increased their strength in Sinai with the arrival of considerable reinforcements, probably from Gallipoli which had been evacuated by the British a few months earlier, and from a few miles away to the east of Katia were keeping a close watch on the movements of the British who were in some strength at Romani. The Turkish base was at El Arish on the coast, nearly 100 miles east of Kantara, the British base on the Canal, and by the end of June an army of about 20,000 men was concentrated there under the command of a German officer, Baron Von Kressenstein. He had by no means abandoned the idea of another direct assault on the Canal and in fact he would certainly by now have assembled a far larger striking force if it had not been for the effect produced by the Arab revolt in the Hejaz headed by Sherif Hussein of Mecca, who declared his independence of the Turks and his intention to sweep them out of Arabia.

On the 18th May, El Arish was subjected to an intense bombardment by the heavy guns of two British monitors which destroyed a fort and caused serious damage to the airfield and other installations. The camp was also set on fire in many places. The monitors were able with their shallow draught to steam very close in shore, and the Turks were so overcome by the fury of the assault that they attempted very little reply and sought shelter in the palms surrounding the camp, where they were shelled by the smaller guns of a sloop which accompanied the monitors and was able to get closer still. The attack was then taken up by several planes of the Royal Flying Corps, which dropped a number of bombs some of which exploded in the middle of a body of 1000 Turkish troops. More important still, several photographs were taken from the air which proved to be of great assistance later on. Kressenstein retaliated by bringing up to El Arish some of his anti-aircraft guns and also by making air raids during June on Kantara, Romani and other places in the vicinity of the Canal.

The assault on El Arish was followed a month later by another air raid, which was also very successful, and Kressenstein's plans were so disrupted by these attacks that he was compelled to delay his advance until late in July. In the meantime Sir Archibald Murray, who had by now succeeded Sir John Maxwell as C.-in-C., was able to complete his preparations. Permanent lines of defence were constructed from Romani to Mahemdia along the coast of the Bay of Tina, where assistance could come from the British naval forces under the command of Vice Admiral Sir Rosslyn Wemyss.

The Turkish army, which consisted of two or three crack infantry divisions and included eight machine gun companies under German officers and partly manned by Germans, was supported by mountain artillery and batteries of four-inch and six-inch howitzers and anti-aircraft guns with Austrian gunners, and indications of the coming offensive were observed by Murray in the middle of July, with the appearance of numerous enemy aircraft over the Romani-Duweidar area. Two days later reports confirmed that the Turks were already moving westward and had reached, in considerable strength, a line stretching for some miles in a south-westerly direction from Bir-el-Abd, about twenty miles due east of Romani, to the oasis of Magheibra.

Four companies of the Imperial Camel Corps - Nos. 6, 7, 9, and 10, which had just returned from Kharga, had now arrived in Sinai, where they were joined by two regiments of Australian Light Horse and one regiment of New Zealand Mounted Rifles to make up a formation, which was known as the Desert Mobile Column, under the overall command of Lieutenant-Colonel (later Brigadier-General) Leslie Smith, V.C. Their orders were to proceed at once to the small oasis of Bir-el-Mahadat and to establish there an advance base of operations. They did not have to wait for very long.

BATTLE OF ROMANI
AUG. 4TH 1916
Situation about 4 p.m.

Turkish main attack →
Turkish holding attack ▪-▪-▸
Principal tracks -----

On the night of the 27th July, Kressenstein made an advance from Magheibra, which was temporarily checked by a New Zealand mounted regiment. In a brief skirmish the Turks lost about fifty men and it was not until the 2nd August that Kressenstein was able to make a reconnaissance in force in the direction of Katia preparatory to launching his main attack across the fifteen miles of desert which lay between his advanced troops and Romani, from where the main British defences stretched towards the coast and straddled the old caravan route, claimed to have been used by Moses in his flight from Egypt to the countries lying to the east of the Sinai Peninsula. This barren strip of desert has countless historical associations having been fought over by Egyptians, Jews, Assyrians, Babylonians, Greeks, Romans, Arabs, French and British and it was here that Napoleon's armies marched in 1799, when he advanced towards El Arish on his way to Acre.

All this time Murray was himself planning an offensive but it was not until the 3rd August that all his formations were in a position to take the field. Indeed for some hours during that day he was in doubt whether he or Kressenstein would strike first, but uncertainly came to an end when at midnight the Turks assaulted in force and drove furiously at the Romani - Mahemdia fortifications. Kressenstein's plan was to press back the British in the south, cut the railway and then attack from the rear, and for some time it seemed as though he had succeeded. The British outposts were driven in and, when part of the line was forced, the situation began to look rather serious. About 3000 Turks made a desperate assault on two enormous sand dunes, held by the Australians and New Zealanders and, although it was repulsed, a second attack for which reinforcements had been brought up met with more success, and by the early hours of the morning both positions had fallen into enemy hands. Meanwhile the whole of the fortifications between Romani and Mahemdia had been under heavy shell fire from the howitzers and other artillery. None the less they did not make any serious impression, nor did further repeated assaults by the Turkish infantry. These attacks were made on the 52nd Division, consisting of territorials from the Lowlands of Scotland, who stood their ground and repelled the enemy at every point. Gradually the tide of battle turned and the time arrived for Murray's counter attack. Reinforcements in the shape of two mounted brigades and two brigades of the East Lancashire Territorials had now arrived on the scene and already the Turks were beginning to fall back. The two great sand dunes were recaptured with a loss of 500 men taken prisoner, a mountain battery and several machine guns, and elsewhere the Turks were beginning to sustain heavy casualties, their confusion being increased by the naval guns which caused havoc in their rear and lines of communication.

Soon they were in full retreat pursued by the cavalry and unable to make any stand until they were back again at Bir-el-Abd which they were, however, forced to evacuate three days later after being nearly surrounded. This defeat, in what came to be called the Battle of Romani, was a major disaster for the Turks, who had suffered severe losses, and it would have been worse had it not been for the intense heat and lack of water which prevented the British from pressing home their advantage, despite the many thousands of transport camels with their loads of water, food, ammunition and other supplies. Although, however, the British advance in the north was, for the time being, halted at Bir-el-Abd it was not long before the Desert Mobile Column reformed after its exertion during the battle and was able to fulfil the principal role which had been assigned to it.

13. After Romani

The task of the mobile column was to make a detour from the south and cut into or get behind the retreating enemy and do as much damage as possible. It was rightly assumed that they could move a great deal faster than the Turks and that this would enable them not only to cut off any stragglers but also, if opportunity arose, to make attacks on the main body and at the same time have the ability to withdraw quickly into the desert should the opposition prove too strong. What actually happened was that, although the enemy lost a number of prisoners during these sorties from their flank, and were forced to abandon quantities of war material, the bulk of their forces were able to carry out a fairly orderly retreat from one prepared position to another, a series of rearguard actions being fought until they reached their strongly fortified base at El Arish.

The chief problem of the Mobile Column was, as usual in those wastes, lack of water. Wells were few and far between and most of these had been fouled or poisoned by the Turks as they retreated. In consequence the brunt of the work had to be borne by the Camel Corps, who had to make sure of the water before the cavalry could advance. Some of the wells had been filled in with sand which took several hours to clear before any water could be obtained. This would have been brackish anyway but its taste was not improved by the occasional dead camel, the pungency of the split trunks of date palms with which the wells were lined, and the chlorine which was added on the instructions of the Medical Officer! The result of all this was a highly flavoured fluid which was only fit to drink with tea. However, the Camel Corps had tremendous assets in their ability, so far as the camels were concerned, to go without water for days at a stretch, their mobility and the fact that they were able to split into self-contained units of any size as the circumstances might require. As a result the enemy were never sure of their numbers and their cavalry were afraid to pursue them in case they got cut off from their retreating main body. But whenever they had prepared positions to cover their retreat, which was naturally very slow and had to follow a fixed route from one well or waterhole to another, they made determined stands. These rearguard actions were almost continuous over a period of nearly two months and they were accompanied by three quite big engagements when the Mobile Column, which had already taken 3000 prisoners, came up with the main body. Casualties were heavy and by this time No. 10 Company alone had been reduced from a strength of five officers, 137 other ranks and 149 camels to two officers, sixty-eight other ranks and seventy-six camels.

SINAI DESERT

Nonetheless contact with the enemy had to be continually maintained and, even when it had taken several hours to dislodge them from their positions, a section or even a company of Camel Corps would be detailed for this purpose.

On one of these occasions, as a detachment of Camel Corps had been making a night march, it was discovered at dawn that one of the camels, which had been proceeding in single file, had lost its rider. There was nothing for it but to go back after him as, alone and dismounted, he would either die of thirst or be murdered by wandering Bedouin. Ashlin, who had by now assumed command of No. 10 Company, relates how he and two of his men with a spare camel went back along their tracks and after riding for about an hour, they noticed vultures circling overhead, a sure sign that something dead or dying was near, and after a close search they discovered the missing man who was lying at the bottom of a small depression dead to the world, fast asleep. When he had fallen from his camel he must either have hit his head on a stone or been kicked by one of the other camels because he remembered nothing when he came to and was so exhausted that, regardless of his predicament, he promptly fell asleep, wisely remaining where he was.

Meanwhile the vultures were all around patiently waiting for him to die. He soon recovered but he was far from popular with the two men who had accompanied Ashlin and naturally did not relish this extra ride after a long march. One of them was so disgusted, Ashlin relates, that he said to the wretched man in the broadest Yorkshire, 'We'd a' left thi to t'bloody vooltures, nobbut we s'ud a' bin sorry for t'poor bods if they'd've etten thee. Thoo'd gi'e owt t'indigestion!'

The Turks employed some of their best troops in these rearguard actions and they were helped by a number of German and Austrian officers, N.C.O.s and gunners who were attached to them. War is usually a pretty nasty affair but sometimes it brings out the best as well as the worst in those who are taking part, as the following incident will illustrate.

Major de Knoop, who was originally in command of No. 6 Company, had been put in charge of all the four Camel Corps companies at Romani and his place as O.C. No. 6 had been taken by Baron Alan de Rutzen, who was hit shortly afterwards while observing the enemy from the top of a high sand dune. He rolled down in full view of the Turks and, fully exposed as he was to intense rifle and machine gun fire, he must have been killed instantly. Attempts to reach him had to be abandoned and it was only after dark that it was possible to search for his body which, however, could not be found. The following morning a Turkish officer, waving a white flag, approached the position held by the Camel Corps, and it was assumed at first that the enemy wished to surrender, but it turned out that this was not the object of his visit. He handed over to Ashlin, who had gone out to meet him, de Rutzen's signet ring, wrist watch and some letters, which had been found in his pockets, and in excellent English said that the night before they had surprised some Bedouin stripping the dead body of a soldier which on investigation proved to be that of a British officer, and they had taken these articles from the Bedouin with the intention of handing them over to the British at the first opportunity, as they thought that the officer's family would be glad to have them. He added, as an afterthought, that they had shot the Bedouin.

Of the three engagements with the main body of the Turks two were of considerable importance and involved the whole of the Mobile Column. The first of these, which was the one in which de Rutzen lost his life, occurred on the 6th and 7th August at Hod-el-Muhamman and Hod-el-Baheir and proved to be a very sticky affair for the Camel Corps, who were ordered to occupy a position which could only be approached over a wide stretch of open ground made up of dry loose sand into which the camels sank up to their knees. In consequence the men had to dismount and lead them floundering across this open space under intense machine gun and shrapnel fire and, although they crossed in small parties, heavy casualties were sustained by men and camels alike. There were numerous acts of conspicuous gallantry. One man faced the inferno four times, in spite of being severely hit himself, and assisted in bringing in three badly wounded men and getting them under cover. Major de Knoop was hit twice, but returned each time to the firing line after having his wounds dressed, to continue directing his men. Unfortunately he did not survive the day. He was hit a third time and died before reaching the improvised first aid post.

Getting the wounded back to the Advanced Casualty Clearing Station was a serious problem for the medical staff who performed wonders. Ashlin has recalled the example set by the Senior Medical Officer, a frail, elderly man, who had been a prominent surgeon in England, and had volunteered from one of the Yeomanry regiments with only the vaguest idea of the sort of conditions with which he would have to cope. His spirit, however, rose above physical handicaps, and those of the Camel Corps, including Ashlin himself, who passed through his hands, would always remember his great capacity for work, his gentleness, patience and unruffled calm. He was labouring under incredible difficulties as the evacuation of the wounded had to be carried out at night on camels, each animal taking two men on a kind of stretcher, called a cacolet, which was strapped on either side of the saddle.

One column of wounded sent back on the second night was put in the charge of a very young and inexperienced officer who had himself been slightly wounded. By now there was such a shortage of officers that no other could be spared. Not surprisingly by morning he had completely lost his way and had it not been for a more experienced officer who, though badly hit in the chest, took charge and a severely wounded signaller who was carried to a high bit of ground and helioed for help, it is doubtful whether anybody would have survived. Fortunately the signals were picked up at Magheibra and, although subjected to several hours of blistering sun, they somehow survived the ordeal and got in safely. Meanwhile the troops in the front line were not only running very short of medical supplies but getting increasingly concerned as to the fate of the column and the message it carried. However, some twelve hours after it had been expected, a party rode in with the supplies and the welcome news of the column's safe arrival. Fortunately the fighting had practically ceased, and the Turks evacuated their positions that night. This gave a few hours of much needed rest before it was time to saddle up once more and follow the retreating enemy.

Two days later an incident occurred which was described in one of the London papers as a mounted charge by the Imperial Camel Corps. What actually happened was this. The Camel Corps scouts suddenly came upon a small enemy ammunition and baggage column consisting of thirty pack mules, a troop of cavalry and about eighty dismounted men, who were crossing an open stretch of ground. The Camel Corps had part of two companies, approximately seventy men in all, a third of whom were ordered to dismount and give covering fire while the remainder, taking advantage of the confusion, charged in extended formation, yelling and firing their rifles from the saddle in the approved Arab style. Needless to say they did not hit anything but, although the Turks put up some slight resistance and managed to get some of their pack animals away, most of them were finally rounded up and surrendered. The result was sixty-eight prisoners taken and fourteen baggage mules. The Camel Corps casualties were two men slightly wounded and seven camels hit. Incidentally it is worth mentioning here that camels show admirable fortitude and patience, even indifference, under fire and unless badly wounded, continue as before, the slightly wounded ones showing no surprise or concern even when their nostrils are pouring blood.

The second major engagement when the Mobile Column came to grips with the Turkish main forces was at Bir-el-Bayud. Two companies of the Camel Corps, No.9 under Lord Winterton and No. 10 under Ashlin, were operating well ahead of the Column when they ran into the southern flank-guard of the enemy. The two companies attacked at once and, after some resistance, the Turks retired on their main body, which was occupying a strong position at Bayud. There had, in fact, been some misconception on both sides. The Camel Corps were under the impression that they were up against the usual rear guard left behind to delay their pursuers and the Turks, as it was afterwards learnt from their prisoners, thought that they were under assault from a much larger body of troops. In consequence the Turks were over-cautious and the Camel Corps over-bold. On reconnoitring they discovered their mistake and that they were confronted by a large body of troops, which outnumbered them about six to one and included several batteries of field and mountain guns.

The enemy had taken up positions on the crest of a range of fairly high sand dunes protecting a small oasis where there were some wells. The Camel Corps were well placed on a slightly higher ridge and, as it was already late in the day and the camels were tired out, and the enemy's artillery fire was doing very little harm, it was decided to remain there for the night and send back a message to Colonel Smith, who was at the advance base at Magheibra with another company of the Camel Corps. He in turn got messages through to the Australian Light Horse and the remaining Camel Corps company, instructing them to proceed at once to Bayud. Colonel Smith arrived just after dawn with the company from Magheibra and decided to engage the enemy with the three companies on the right flank and launch the Australians, who were expected very shortly, in a determined attack from the left where there was more cover. The enemy guns were now opening up but the Camel Corps managed to occupy an advanced position, which they had been able to prepare during the night, and kept up brisk rifle and machine gun fire on the Turkish positions. Meanwhile one of the sergeants, who was a Bisley marksman, had succeeded in establishing himself, well camouflaged, on a small rise overlooking part of the Turkish line from where he did deadly execution against the enemy, killing several of them and wiping out a very troublesome machine gun nest before he was spotted and had to beat a hasty retreat. Sniping played an important part in all these operations and the snipers, who were also trained scouts, did some excellent work.

Unfortunately by noon there was still no sign of the Australians, and the Turks, who had by now got wise to the fact that they were confronted by a very small force, intensified their artillery fire and, under the cover which it provided, pushed forward two battalions with the intention of encircling the Camel Corps who were now coming under severe pressure. However, in order to complete their encircling movement, the Turks had to cross an open space where they came under heavy fire and sustained many casualties. The attack was halted but it was expected that, as soon as they had reformed, it would be resumed. Realising that the situation was becoming rather serious Colonel Smith directed one of the companies, with the spare camels, to show themselves on the summit of a hill some distance away so as to give the impression that reinforcements were approaching and, when they got down into the valley out of sight of the Turks, to double back, go round the hill, and repeat the operation several times making as much noise and raising as much dust as possible.

The ruse succeeded and it was not long before the two attacking battalions retired from such cover as they had been able to obtain and again came under heavy fire during the process. The bluff was kept up until the late afternoon when the Australians at last arrived after their forced march, but it was now too late to try and dislodge the Turks from their prepared positions, particularly as they still greatly outnumbered the combined force of Australians and Camel Corps, and the assault was postponed until the morning when further reinforcements were expected. But by then the bulk of the Turkish troops had got away with their lighter transport and all but two of their heavier guns, leaving behind their dead and a small detachment, to cover their retirement, which put up only a weak resistance and soon surrendered. The position was pretty well untenable anyway on account of the unburied corpses. In that climate the process of decomposition is very rapid. The Camel Corps had lost four officers and thirty-eight other ranks but had inflicted heavy casualties and taken 289 prisoners with a considerable quantity of equipment and the two guns.

It was during this engagement that Ashlin was wounded and he recalls the sufferings to which the badly wounded were exposed during those grim journeys back to the Clearing Station. The distance was fifty miles and part of the travelling had to be done by day under intense heat. The flies were terrible, the water bad and insufficient and, on this occasion, the column was spotted by enemy aircraft and bombed, fortunately without doing any damage apart from adding to the general discomfort and causing further delay. The man who shared his cacolet was badly wounded and died just before the Clearing Station was reached.

It was now late September and the Camel Corps had been marching and fighting continuously for nearly two months. The Turks were in full retreat towards their base at El Arish but it was not until the 23rd December that this was at last occupied by the advancing British forces. During these operations, and the fierce engagements which followed at Maghdaba on the 23rd December and Rafa on the 9th January, units of the Camel Corps, which included, in addition to the Australians and New Zealanders, Nos. 6, 7, and 9 Companies of the 2nd Battalion, played an outstanding part.

Maghdaba lies about twenty-five miles to the south of El Arish and its capture was described in a dispatch from Mr W. T. Massey, one of the British war correspondents, as a brilliant stroke, made under extraordinarily arduous conditions, which resulted in an overwhelming defeat of the Turkish garrison by the mounted troops of the desert column, under the command of lieutenant-general Sir H. Chauvel, and a victory much more far-reaching than the capture of 1300 prisoners would indicate. 'This swift fierce and irresistible attack,' said Mr Massey, 'has produced one of the most important effects of the campaign in Egypt. The sudden rush of mounted troops, twenty-five miles from El Arish, a distance which by all previous experience of desert warfare was considered impossible in a single night, has had an immense moral influence on the Turks whose calculations in Northern Sinai were completely upset - thus the victory at Maghdaba, which added fame to the Anzac Mounted Division and proved the sterling value of the Imperial Camel Corps drawn from British yeomanry and colonial regiments, may be regarded as one of the most important battles of the campaign in Eastern Egypt'.

The Turks were well entrenched in the form of a rough circle 3500 yards in diameter with five large closed works or redoubts. The attack was launched at 8 a.m. The Camel Corps, supported by its own mountain battery and the guns of the Territorial Horse Artillery, began the frontal assault while the Anzac Mounted Division, under the command of Brigadier General E. W. C. Chaytor, moved north of the Turkish positions, under cover of the sand dunes to the east and south east of Maghdaba, to cut off the retreat of the enemy. The battle lasted for eight hours and has been described as being of a desperate character with the Turks offering the most strenuous resistance from the protection of their redoubts.

Shortly after the troops moved off aeroplane messages indicated that some of the enemy were retiring, and the mounted brigades on the east of Maghdaba pushed on quickly so as to complete the envelopment while a reserve brigade was sent forward to assist in the movement. It was soon discovered, however, that only small bodies of the enemy were withdrawing towards their main positions, which were still held in considerable strength. The reserve brigade came under heavy machine gun fire and the other brigades were systematically shelled by the enemy's Krupp mountain guns.

Meanwhile the Camel Corps were also receiving attention from the enemy's guns as they moved across the open plain towards the redoubts, without their line of approach affording the slightest vestige of cover. However, to quote Mr Massey again they continued to advance 'with magnificent steadiness'.

The reserve brigade, unable to go forward without further serious losses among its horses, swung to its flank to assist in the frontal assault which was beginning to slow down in places. One of the redoubts was blown to pieces but the others succeeded in maintaining their fire, the British gunners being hampered by mirage and the flat nature of the ground which prevented the establishment of forward observation posts. However, in the early afternoon the advance was resumed all along the line, and during the next two hours the fighting reached its greatest intensity. Aircraft attacked the redoubts, the guns increased their fire and the troopers, dismounting, joined with the Camel Corps in making repeated assaults.

A further danger appeared when it was reported that no water could be found so that, unless the position could be taken before the end of the day, the thirsty troops and their thirstier mounts would be forced to withdraw to El Arish. So the order was given to push the attack with all possible speed and from then onward the pressure was increased at all points. A detachment of Australian Light Horse on the enemy's left captured a small redoubt to the west of the enemy's position taking 100 prisoners. A little later two regiments of Light Horse were within 200 yards on the North east and in touch with the Camel Corps coming in from the north west. The New Zealand Mounted Rifles were also within reach of their objective. Half an hour later the second line of defence had come under attack from the combined forces and one of the main redoubts was carried after a dashing charge, all its occupants including the Turkish commandant being taken prisoner. Immediately afterwards another detachment of Light Horse charged, mounted, with the bayonet and soon after 4 p.m. what were left of the gallant Turkish defenders had surrendered.

But it was not long before the desert column was to be called on for further exertions. On the 27th December reports were received from the air reconnaissance that the Turks were preparing a strongly entrenched position at Magruntein covering the little town of Rafa, thirty miles east of El Arish and on the Sinai and Palestine border. Although the position was of no particular strategic value it was felt that it would be bad policy to allow its fortification to be completed, and on the night of the 8th January Lieutenant-General Sir Philip Chetwode commanding the desert column, which again consisted of a mounted division of Australians and New Zealanders, the Imperial Camel Corps, the Territorial Horse Artillery and some British Yeomanry set out from El Arish and, covering the distance in only twelve hours, launched the attack at dawn on the 9th January, the Turks being once more completely taken by surprise by the swiftness of the British advance coming so soon after the capture of Maghdaba.

For its size the Turkish position was formidable. Three series of works, facing south-east, south-west and west, were connected by trenches dominated by a redoubt 2000 yards west of Rafa. In addition on all sides the ground was so level as almost to constitute a glacis and without cover of any kind for the advancing troops. However, the guns soon began to register hits and, after a heavy bombardment, the New Zealand Mounted Rifles attacked the eastern defences, with the Australian Light Horse on their left and the Camel Corps coming in from the south. By 11 a.m. these defences had been taken with a loss to the enemy of 160 prisoners in addition to killed and wounded, and Rafa itself was in British occupation.

But there still remained the strong south-western and western defences and the main redoubt itself. Soon after mid-day the attacking troops had been redeployed and while the New Zealanders and Australians mounted a fresh assault from the south-west the Camel Corps and Yeomanry attacked from the west. Very soon the entire position was encircled apart from a small gap to the north-west but the Horse Artillery dashed forward to support the attack at close quarters and by 2 p.m. the gap had been closed.

At 3.30 p.m. a message was received from the air force that a large column of relieving Turkish troops was approaching from the east and General Chetwode ordered a general attack to be made on the redoubt by all the available forces and pressed home to the utmost, leaving the relief column to the attentions of the aircraft. Spurred on by the need for speed the storming parties, splendidly supported by the gunners, burst into the redoubt and by 5.30 p.m., just ten hours after the action had started, the Turks at last conceded defeat and surrendered. A small force was detailed to assist the aircraft in dealing with the relief column which was soon dispersed.

In the whole of this operation the British had sustained 487 casualties of which seventy-one were killed while the Turks, in addition to about 600 killed and wounded, had lost thirty-five officers and 1600 men taken prisoner. They had also lost several guns and a quantity of other equipment.

The engagements at Maghdaba and Rafa were followed in March and April by two attempts to assault and capture the town of Gaza, but the Turks, who occupied strongly fortified positions, put up a very stout resistance, and on both occasions the British forces, which included the 52nd, 53rd and 54th infantry divisions in addition to the Desert Column, were beaten back and, after sustaining heavy casualties, compelled to withdraw from the ground they had gained during the early stages of the fighting.

14. The Desert - Sollum

It is now time to return to No. 8 Company which at the end of January, 1917, was on its way back to Abassia after the completion of the Baharia operations.

The few weeks we spent at Abassia were relatively uneventful. We had hoped that at the end of this period of training we would be sent to the Palestine front but as it turned out we had not yet finished with the Western desert, where the Senussi war was now in its closing stages.

Our destination this time was Sollum, about 150 miles beyond Mersa Matruh, and within a few miles of the Libyan border. Unfortunately there was one officer who was not able to accompany us, though he joined us later on at Matruh. I happened to be sharing a hut with him at the time and was woken up one night to find him sitting on his bed groaning with pain, swearing like a trooper and jigging about like a marionette. It turned out that he was suffering from a total stricture and, as he had imbibed quite a fair amount of refreshment that evening, he was in a pretty bad way, and it was obvious that unless he could be relieved fairly quickly the consequences might be disastrous. After some delay we managed to get hold of the camp doctor who did what was necessary, though the process lasted more than two hours, and next day the victim was sent off to hospital, where he underwent a minor operation. Before he departed he related to me the story which had led up to this unhappy and extremely painful climax. He had been in London not long after the war broke out and just after he had received his commission. One evening he was crossing Waterloo Bridge when he saw a girl who was walking a few yards ahead of him suddenly leap on to the parapet with the obvious intention of jumping into the river. However, he just managed to reach her as she took off and succeeded after a bit of a struggle in dragging her back to safety. Not surprisingly she was in a pretty hysterical condition and he had quite a job calming her down and escorting her off the bridge. Even then he dared not leave her and decided the only thing to do was to take her home by which time she had recovered a bit and asked him in for a cup of tea of all things. He continued to comfort her, but unfortunately in more ways than one, with what turned out to be exceedingly painful and unpleasant results for himself. He recovered quickly enough but the complaint had left him with a tendency to stricture, although he had never had it anything like so badly as on this occasion. There is a moral somewhere in this story but I am not quite sure what it is, apart from the obvious one that we live in an ungrateful world.

A day or two after this we started off on our long trek to Sollum by way of Alamein, Daba, Mersa Matruh, Sidi Barrani and other places which were to become famous in another war. It was a season of sudden sandstorms and alternations of heat and cold which at times became almost intolerable. We rested for several days at Mersa Matruh where among other activities, such as quail shooting, we used to bathe in the salt lakes, taking care to protect our eyes, and popping up to the surface like corks when we dived in. No doubt it was, or would have been, a pleasant existence but I can only recollect it, and for two reasons, as a time of pain and deep personal sorrow. The first and far the least important was that one day I was thrown by one of my camels and although not seriously injured I hurt my back rather badly. The camel was a lively creature at the best of times, but on this occasion I found him almost uncontrollable. The camel lines were located just outside the barbed-wire perimeter and the camel had been brought in through the gate to the officers' quarters which were just inside. The moment I mounted and made for the gate the camel took charge and galloped straight at the barbed wire which was about fifteen feet wide. I suppose I loosened my grip with the intention of dismounting if I got the chance but, whatever the reason, I was flung up in the air and landed flat on my back. I can just remember the animal floundering about in the middle of the wire before I more or less lost consciousness and was carried off to my tent on a stretcher. Afterwards the stretcher party told me that I had, for a few moments, managed to lift myself up on one elbow and let out a stream of obscenities which impressed them far more than anything I had ever done or said before. In fact, for some time after I was treated with the greatest respect. But I was pretty roughly shaken up and a little concussed as well, and it was weeks before I completely recovered.

A day or two after this incident, I had a cable from my father to say that my brother Jack had been killed in France. I had not seen him since we had almost casually said goodbye to each other at the Regent Palace Hotel some eighteen months earlier, but all our lives we had been very close to each other and his death came as a great shock to me when I was already feeling in pretty poor shape. I became depressed and almost unapproachable, but I shall never forget the kindness and sympathy which I had from everybody during that rather grim period in my existence.

In due course we arrived at Sollum which had been captured from the Senussi the previous year. There was still a certain amount of activity going on, but the operations were in their final stages and the Senussi were in no condition to take any further offensive. In fact the Arab population, at any rate throughout the coastal district of the Western desert, were by now in a state of starvation, and refugee camps had been set up to relieve their distress, and as time went on more and more of the women and children and older men were being rounded up and brought in. Most of them were in a shocking condition, particularly the children, and I can well remember how they used to follow behind the camels and pick out and eat the undigested grains of corn from their droppings.

Despite the fact, however, that the grand design under which Egypt was to be squeezed by the Turks invading from the east and the Senussi from the west had collapsed in ruins there was no official peace. Detachments from the Turkish army did in fact reach the Suez Canal but were easily repelled, and at one time the Senussi threat had been a very real one, but Egypt was no longer in any danger and although, of course, the war against the Turks was to continue for another eighteen months, the Senussi were now fading completely out of the picture.

But patrolling was still going on, and the last in which I took part turned out to be quite an exciting one. I only had five or six men with me and my orders were to make a five-day reconnaissance, first of all due west to the Libyan frontier, then south as far as we could go in the time, then east and north so as to reach the sea on the evening of the fourth day and then back to Sollum along the coast. The coastal district is bounded by an escarpment several hundred feet high which converges on the sea as you travel west, and Sollum lies at the point where it reaches the sea. First of all, therefore, we had to climb the escarpment by a rough track which led up from the camp, and after that we would be remaining on the high ground until we hit the escarpment again several miles to the east and couple of miles or so from the sea. Unfortunately during the whole of the time the sky was covered by heavy cloud, and it was impossible to take any bearings from the sun or the stars. I, therefore, had to rely on my compass, which I distrusted anyway because it always seemed to differ from my own ideas! In fact when the time came to make our first change of direction to the south I was almost convinced that the compass was wrong, and for the remainder of the patrol I was in a state of considerable anxiety that we might be heading in the wrong direction, with what could only be a disastrous result. Whether it was due to the humidity in the atmosphere or to some other reason there was a constant succession of mirages which made everything seem very unreal. Once or twice we came across a solitary Arab who passed us without a word and with hardly a glance. Otherwise the desert was or seemed to be nothing but an empty wilderness of rock and sand.

Sometime during the third day, however, when we must have been at our furthest point we rounded a range of hillocks which had for some time obscured our view on that side and saw to our consternation an enormous Bedouin encampment about half a mile away. There was no chance of taking cover as they had already seen us and we could see and hear a lot of rushing about, with dogs barking and men shouting and, what was more alarming, running for their camels. Equally disconcerting was the realisation that the encampment was exactly in the direction in which we were heading. This was obviously an occasion for discretion rather than valour, and for testing the speed of our camels. They responded nobly, probably because they were almost as scared as we were by all the sudden commotion, and we soon began to draw away from our pursuers, who eventually dropped out of sight. By then we were badly off our course in addition to which we were continually changing direction in case the Bedouin had not given up the chase, and by the time we camped for the night about twenty miles further on I for one had not the remotest idea where we were. However, the immediate objective was not to get caught and, although I do not know whether the Bedouin were Senussi or their friends, all the Arabs in that region were hostile and none of us cared very much for the idea of falling into their hands.

There was no incident during the night and the following morning I decided that, wherever we were, the time had come to turn north in the general direction of the Mediterranean. We started early and kept going all day. By midday we were all, including the camels, pretty tired and thirsty and there was still no sign of a break. But in the late afternoon for no apparent reason the camels suddenly started to perk up a bit and lengthen their stride, although it was not until some time later that we were able to detect a freshness in the air which could only mean the sea.

This was a great relief in more ways than one, especially to myself. I hope and think, however, that I had succeeded in disguising from my men the fact that I really had not had a clue as to our position for at any rate the last two days. Eventually we reached the edge of the escarpment and looked down on the sea a few miles away. We could see no way down and I decided to camp for the night. The camels were unloaded and unsaddled, the blankets were spread, our cook began to prepare a meal and we all prepared to settle down for a good night's rest when suddenly we were attacked not by Arabs but by ticks!

There were thousands of them coming at us from all directions. In a moment they were climbing up our legs on to our bare knees and then up the length of our bodies. We were all yelling and swearing, the camels were bellowing, and if there was an Arab within ten miles he must have heard us. We seemed to be at the hub of a wheel of which the spokes were long black lines of these revolting little crab like creatures, much bigger than an ordinary sheep tick. I had often heard of what an army of ants can do in some parts of the world, but an invasion of ticks was something quite new. Our bodies were crawling with them and within minutes they had exercises in loading up and making a quick getaway from, so to speak, a standing start, but I am willing to bet that on this occasion all records were comfortably beaten when we cleared out of that horrible place. I have earlier described how after a meal of blood the ticks used to hang from the camels like obscene bunches of grapes, and we were in no mood to test what would be the effect on the human body. So we carried on along the escarpment for another mile or two and were fortunate enough to find a gap which was not too steep for us to take the camels down to sea-level, where we thankfully set up our camp once more without a tick in sight. I quite enjoyed my dinner of porridge which was all we had left of our rations. The next day we proceeded by easy stages along the few miles back to Sollum, where we were thankful to have our first wash, shave and change of clothes for five days.

The track up the escarpment from Sollum was a pretty rough sort of affair and we had to take out working parties to try and improve it. I have often wondered whether this was the site of Halfaya Pass which became so well known to the Eighth Army during the Second World War. Probably not, but in those days it was the only track which existed.

We had a rather humorous incident at Sollum. An Italian cruiser had anchored in the bay (the Italians were, of course, our allies in the first war) and they sent out two boats with an enormous net like a seine to see whether they could get any fish. When the boats landed and they started to pull in the net it was soon apparent that their efforts were going to be successful. The sea was literally boiling with fish which turned out to be a shoal of barracuda, and as they were brought nearer to land the Italian sailors became so excited that they seemed to have some difficulty in collecting the catch. In this, how ever, they were helped by the British and from every unit in the camp there could be observed a mess corporal sauntering towards the beach with a large sack over his shoulder. Undaunted by screams of rage and shaking of fists by the Italians the corporals walked into the seething mass of fish and filled up their sacks, and then calmly retraced their steps to their respective kitchens. There was really no reason why our allies should have been so angry, because their boats were already so full of fish that they nearly sank on their way back to the cruiser, but angry they certainly were and their gestures were quite unmistakable. And in any case the corporals were only putting into practice one of the basic precepts of their training, namely to show initiative and enterprise on every possible occasion, and I doubt very much whether they regarded the possibility of their actions leading to an international incident as being in any way their concern.

That is the last thing I can remember of Sollum because a week or two later the news for which we had been waiting and hoping for so long came at last. We were to leave the Western desert and join the army which was facing the Turks in Palestine.

Before leaving the Senussi campaign, however, there is one more story I should like to relate in a rather lighter vein, for which I am indebted to certain characters in No. 10 Company, which had come up from the Kharga and Dahkla oases to relieve us at Sollum.

On the eastern tip of the Gulf of Sollum there is a place called Bag-Bag. It is, or was, almost nothing at all, a pile of glaring white sand-dunes with a very brackish well. A mile away there was a Bedouin encampment whose Sheikh, a one-eyed old gentleman, about eighty years of age, was known as Sidi Barrani and who was paid a retainer in return for tipping off the British whenever a supply column was attempting to get through to the Senussi in Cyrenaica. The Bedouin were particularly attracted to the Medical Service and Sidi Barrani asked for something to relieve the constipation from which he habitually suffered. He was given a handful of 'Number Nines', well known to every British soldier in the First War, and he subsequently reported that they were indeed 'most powerful medicine'!

Whether or not it was in gratitude for this deliverance he afterwards, as a great honour, invited some of the cameliers to witness the circumcision of his son, aged six. (If he was indeed eighty years old he must have been a remarkable old man!) There was a great feast and the members of the tribe, including both sexes and all ages, danced round the fires singing and shouting and banging gongs. Suddenly 'before our very eyes' the Sheikh ed Din (or the Ulema) performed the operation 'neat' with a well whetted old French table knife! The cameliers were asked to testify that those outside the tent heard no cry from the very brave boy, which they were able to do quite truthfully because the din drowned his screams! Then the Ulema took some darkish powder from a bag and flung it over the wound. Later that night the mother of the boy sent over and asked for the 'Doctor' and some of the men went over with the R.A.M.C. corporal, who had provided the old man with his 'most powerful medicine' and he cleaned and dressed the poor little chap properly. It transpired that the darkish powder, which had been hoped would congeal the blood, was finely ground coffee!

Sidi Barrani once related that, during the Senussi occupation, a German officer in gorgeous white uniform and a 'gold' helmet visited him and prayed with the Faithful. He understood that the Germans were an Islamic nation and that they were being called upon to respond to a Jehad (Holy War). It was explained to him that in fact the Reformed Christian religion had begun in Germany where there were no Moslems. In the British Empire, on the other hand, there were millions of good Moslems and many of them were fighting the Turks side by side with the Christians. Let us hope that Sidi Barrani was duly impressed!

(1) The author on 'Mick' after inspection by General Allenby.

(2) Lt Merlin Huth, Abassia, January 1917

(3) Lt Inchbald, Abassia, January 1917

(4) Captain C.W. Mason-Macfarlane. (O.C. No. 8 Company). Killed at the Bahria Oasis in September 1916

(5) Captain J.J. Peterson

(6) Camels being exercised

(7) No. 10 Company on the march

(8) Bikanir Camel Corps

(9) No. 8 Company section

(10) Trekking

(11) Lt. Huth, No. 8 Company, Western Desert, 1916

(12) Lt Alan F.J. Baron de Rutzen
(O.C. No. 6 Company).
Killed at Romani in August 1916

(13) Major F.C. Gregory, M.C.
(O.C. No. 7 Company).
Killed near Jaffa in November 1917

(14) Captain A.F. Newsom.
(O.C. No. 8 Company).
Killed at Amman in March 1918

(15) Captain J.A. Lyall, M.C.
(O.C. No. 10 Company, 1918)

(16) Lieutentant Geoffrey Inchbald of No. 8 Company feeding his camel in the Western Desert, 1916

(17) "Signalling by heliograph on the summit of Gobel Libni", Sinai, summer 1917. Patrol commanded by Lieutentant Inchbald (seated right)

(18) Men of No. 18 Company, somewhere in Sinai, 1917

(19) 'Mick, Mark, Tommy'

(20) Huth's camel 'Cheops' up to his shoulders in salt marsh

(21) Near El Arish

(22) Mid-day halt by the Nile

(23) Turkish machine gun being used against its previous owners at Mudowra

(24) The Imperial nature of the Camel Corps

(25) Part of the Hejaz Assault Column in the Wadi Rumm

(26) The Assault Column trekking along the Hejaz Railway

(27) Pumping installation at Mudowra with redoubts in background

(28) Pumping installation at Mudowra being destroyed

(29) Typical rough country at the Wadi Ithm Hejaz Assault Column

(30) Passing through cactus hedges, Palestine

(31) Imperial Camel Corps in the line, Amman 29th March 1918

(32) Presentation of decorations at Ferry Post after return from Hejaz to the Suex Canal in August 1918

15. El Arish - Sinai

In Palestine our immediate destination was El Arish, which was a very pleasant little seaside resort about forty miles west of Beersheba and thirty miles south of Gaza. This involved a pretty long journey. First of all we had to trek all the way back to Alexandria which took several days, then we had to proceed by rail to Kantara, which was the principal base on the Suez Canal for the military operations in Palestine, and finally, also by rail, to El Arish. There were three lines of communication through Sinai from Kantara to the front, consisting of the railway, a meshed wire track to facilitate marching over the sand and, last but not least, the water pipeline on which the army's existence virtually depended, and which was continually subject to raids by Turkish cavalry patrols for the purpose of cutting out sections of the line.

We reached El Arish in mid-June, 1917, just before the arrival in Egypt of General Sir Edmund Allenby, who had been sent out to take over the command of the army from Sir Archibald Murray. Allenby's arrival in Egypt was like a breath of fresh air, which was soon to take on the dimensions of a gale. His predecessor had not proved to be a very inspiring leader and the morale of the Egyptian Expeditionary Force, as it was called, was at a rather low ebb. For some reason Murray had retained his H.Q. at the Savoy Hotel in Cairo, instead of somewhere a good deal nearer the front line which was about 200 miles away and stretched from Gaza to Beersheba. On two occasions an attempt had been made to capture Gaza, where the Turks were entrenched in very strong positions, but both of these had failed and there was a general feeling of listlessness and depression.

The first section of the army to feel the effect of the gale which I have mentioned was G.H.Q. itself, and I hope that Mr Brian Gardner will forgive me for quoting the following extract from his excellent book *Allenby*, published by Cassell in 1965.

'A number of staff officers who had been spending much time propping up the bar at Shepheard's Hotel soon found themselves on a boat home, as did a few elderly regimental colonels and one divisional commander.'

Except for the divisional commander I can confirm this from my own personal experience because, as it happens, I paid a visit to Shepheard's a few months before Allenby's arrival and again a short time afterwards, and the difference was truly amazing. I have never seen or thought it possible to see such an array of brass gathered together as I found in the bars and dining rooms on the first occasion, nor so few as on my second visit. The removal of all this dead wood made a tremendous impression on the army's morale and incidentally it was the first time I ever heard the expression 'being given the order of the bowler hat'.

One of the first things that Allenby did was to carry out his expressed intention of visiting as many of the front-line troops as it was humanly possible to do, and the day came when, although we were still in reserve, it was announced that he was going to inspect us. This turned out to be quite a memorable encounter. We were drawn up in line mounted on our camels when we saw a cloud of dust which heralded the approach of half a dozen horsemen proceeding at full gallop towards a point about a quarter of a mile to our front. Leading the posse was a gigantic man mounted on a gigantic horse, who could not possibly have been mistaken for anybody but our new commander-in-chief. On arrival at the point he swung round his horse and galloped straight at the centre of our line and did not pull up until he was about fifty yards away. And there he sat and we looked at each other. What he thought of us I cannot say but certainly we had none of us ever seen anybody or anything quite so impressive. Camels and horses have a natural antipathy and they are always very uneasy in each other's company. Certainly our camels had shown unmistakable signs of their nervousness and distrust at the approach of this giant equestrian figure out of the blue and the noise of their complaining filled the air. Fortunately, however, they were all equally affected so that although they backed several yards they maintained a straight line. After the inspection Allenby insisted on speaking personally to each of the officers and we all dismounted and went up to him in turn. He leant down, shook us by the hand, said a few words of encouragement and departed, as he had come, in a cloud of dust followed by his staff. The next time I saw him was a year later when I was in hospital in Alexandria.

Our life in El Arish was rather pleasant. There was a lot of refitting and re-equipping to be done before we could be ready to take part in the campaign which Allenby was planning for the autumn, and our duties were confined to patrolling the surrounding areas. Some of these were carried out at company strength and lasted for several days, but the one which I recollect most clearly was quite a small patrol, which I had to take out to a place called Gebel Libni in the Sinai desert in order to determine whether this would be a suitable location for the establishment of a heliograph station.

Gebel Libni was about two days' march away. It was a curious and vaguely sinister rock formation more than 1000 feet high. It had no particular peak but there were dozens of pinnacles pointing like fingers to the sky and there were several caves and crevices leading right into the centre of the formation, which stood out against the flatness of the surrounding desert like a black and monstrous growth. There seemed to be something evil about the place which was in no way decreased by the fact that it was the home of hordes of vultures. As we approached it in the late evening we disturbed a desert hare which jumped out of a bush of some kind, probably camel thorn, and ran off into the desert. Immediately a vulture detached itself from one of the pinnacles and a few moments later it swooped down on the running hare and started to climb again very slowly with the wretched animal in its talons. Somebody fired a rifle at it and it dropped the hare and flew back to its pinnacle squawking with rage. When we picked it up the hare was quite dead, not only from the fall, but the fearful wounds inflicted by the talons. We had it for dinner and it was delicious. The whole time while it was being skinned, cleaned, cooked and eaten we were watched by the vulture and his friends who occupied every point of vantage on the rocks. After dinner I thought I would try and shoot one with a rifle. It was a long shot, about two hundred yards, and when I saw a puff of feathers and dust where the bullet struck the rock just behind it I thought I had succeeded. However, it flew away apparently unharmed. Later on I walked up to the rocks and into one of the crevices, but it was a horrible place and I was glad to get back to my companions.

Next day we climbed up to a sort of plateau quite near the top which seemed to be about the only place where we could set up the heliograph apparatus. To one side of this there was a vulture's eyrie, which was very little more than a circular depression about

142

eight feet in diameter. It was covered with droppings, blood and bits of skin and bones, the relics no doubt of many a delightful meal, and it stank to high heaven. We did not want to stay there longer than we had to, especially with all those filthy creatures watching us from the surrounding rocks, and I for one was very relieved when our signallers succeeded in establishing helio contact with the next observation post, which I estimated to be at least thirty miles away. I was afterwards told that it was nearer sixty.

For weeks after this little expedition I was invariably addressed in the mess and introduced to visitors as Gebel Libni. I took a photograph of the place which I still have and whether through some fault in the film or the exposure, or for some other reason, it seems to be overshadowed by a vast and brooding figure. Perhaps it was there all the time. I can well believe it!

Our recreations at El Arish included bathing and cricket. In June in the Eastern Mediterranean the water is beginning to get very warm and, in fact, we found it almost too warm and in consequence rather enervating. However, it was pleasant and we usually took the camels into the sea with us and gave them a good scrubbing, the last they were to have for many a long day. Cricket in the cool of the evening, played on a coconut matting pitch, was delightful and we had several matches against a West Indian regiment, which happened to be encamped nearby. I had already played a bit in Cairo when we were training during the previous summer, generally at the Gezira Club. I remember one match when the temperature was 108 in the shade and cold drinks were brought out after each over! It so happened on that occasion that I went in first and batted for over two hours, at the end of which time I was bowled all over the place by Mike Falcon of Norfolk fame, and retired to the pavilion where I more or less passed out for the rest of the day. I remember that Cotter, the Australian fast bowler, was also going to play for the opposing side, but fortunately for us he did not do so.

El Arish had a large population of chameleons and we had several of these fascinating little creatures for pets. They certainly lived up to their reputation for changing colour and merging into the background. They also helped enormously to keep down the flies, which they collected at the end of their darting tongues in vast quantities. Tortoises too were always wandering about the camp, and

I was woken one morning by a little jerboa sitting on my chest and gazing at me intently with its saucer-like eyes. Very foolishly I put out my hand to touch it and it promptly bit one of my fingers to the bone.

One other thing which I remember at this time was that the name of Colonel Lawrence was coming into prominence, and we were officially warned against shooting at any strangers without making due enquiry first, as it was believed that Lawrence was somewhere in the vicinity on one of his mysterious missions and, of course, wearing Arab dress!

Whether this report was true I cannot say but I certainly never met up with him myself. In fact, so far as I am aware, the first member of the Camel Corps to encounter Lawrence was Laurence Moore, whose No. 10 Company returned in August from Sollum, where it had been relieved by No. 6 Company, and rejoined the Imperial Camel Brigade.

At some time during the operations which are described in the next chapter two of the New Zealand companies were sent on a reconnaissance mission into the Negev, the desert area running from Beersheba down to the Gulf of Akaba, and Moore had orders to fix up a line of heliograph stations to cover them.

This is his account of what happened.

I was visiting one of these stations one day when the look-out reported a group of about half a dozen Arabs approaching from the south east, the approximate direction of Akaba. We signalled them to come in and I was sent forward, as interpreter, to interrogate them. I called out in my very sketchy Arabic 'Who are you - where are you from - where are you going?' but realised that this was unnecessary when I saw that their leader was obviously a European, who had made no attempt at disguise beyond the fact that he wore Arab clothing. A fair, smallish built man with rather a large head, clothed in a brown Arab aba covering an immaculately white undergarment: on his head he wore a cream coloured kffeyeh, the usual Arab headcloth held down by a double twisted agal or headrope (which the Arab takes off at night and uses to hobble his camel's legs, whereas each of our camels carried a rope round

144

his neck which we used for the same purpose). The agal of this obvious European was made of black wool and the stiffening pieces were bound in gold wire. We had vaguely heard of a British officer doing marvellous things with a force of Arab guerrillas somewhere away to our right and we had been warned of the possibility of his appearance in our vicinity, and sure enough this was the man. He introduced himself as (I think) Captain Lawrence and asked to be taken to Descorps, the H.Q. of Desert Mounted Corps. I could not go all the way back with him but I did ride with him the greater part of the day as far as the H.Q. of the Imperial Camel Brigade, commanded by Brigadier-General Leslie Smith, V.C.

During the course of the march I listened in very intently and was able to follow most of the conversation. Lawrence was obviously treating most of his companions as equals and I discovered later that they were minor sheriffs, representing the King of the Hejaz, and on their way to be presented to G.H.Q. They had one or two servants with them and I chatted with them quite freely, mostly about the problems of the immediate march, and all the time I was most anxious to ask Lawrence how one could get into his outfit. I did not realise it at the time but in point of fact we were in his outfit from that day on. He had come across to see Allenby about the possibility of a link between the British right and the Arab army away to the east. As things turned out later on it was we, the Camel Corps, who were to help provide the link.

16. Palestine – Advance On Jerusalem

We stayed at El Arish until September when we began moving forward to take up our positions for the attack on the Gaza Beersheba line which was planned for the end of October and in which virtually the whole of the Camel Brigade was to become involved as part of the newly formed Desert Mounted Corps, which also included four cavalry divisions, under the command of an Australian, Lieutenant-General Sir H. Chauvel.

The remainder of the army had also been reorganised, since the arrival from England of substantial reinforcements, into 20th Corps, consisting of four infantry divisions and four brigades of heavy artillery, under the command of Lieutenant-General Sir P. W. Chetwode, and 21st Corps, consisting of three infantry divisions and three brigades of heavy artillery, under the command of Lieutenant-General E. S. Bulfin. For the forthcoming operations, therefore General Allenby had at his disposal a force of nearly 100,000 men with an effective fighting strength of about 75,000. Against this the Turks had only 35,000 men in the line but the enormous superiority of the British was largely counter-balanced by the strength of the Turkish positions and the general nature of the country which lent itself easily to defence.

On the 15th October I celebrated my twenty-first birthday but I cannot remember exactly where we were. My fellow officers, including those from No. 7 company commanded by Major Gregory, did their best for me and somebody had managed to arrange for a case of beer to be sent up from somewhere in the rear. We sat down to a splendid repast and the first bottle was opened. Directly the stopper was removed there was a minor explosion and a stream of foam shot up to the top of the tent, and ran down the sides. Nor did it stop until the bottle was empty. Without a word being spoken each of the remaining bottles was opened in turn and behaved in exactly the same way, not one of them yielding a single drop to drink!

Gregory was a splendid man. Although I think he was British

by birth he had spent most of his life abroad in search of adventure and when war broke out he was pearl fishing somewhere near the Great Barrier Reef off the coast of Queensland. I had first met him when I was on the pioneer course in England, which I have already described, and we were billeted together in the same house. I had formed a great admiration for him and he had already made his mark as a soldier and natural leader with a tremendous driving force. It was a great loss to the Camel Corps when he was killed a few weeks later.

Very soon after my birthday we moved up to a place called Khalasa, which was on the extreme right flank of the line and about fifteen miles south of Beersheba. Moore has made the point that the reason why the Camel Corps was deployed on the right - as had also been the case at Romani - was apparently due to the simple but erroneous belief on the part of G.H.Q. that, because the camels could go for several days without water, their riders could do the same! In consequence of this delusion they suffered badly from thirst in comparison with the infantry, who as a general rule occupied the coastal regions where water, though brackish, was plentiful, and the cavalry in the central section where there were also a few wells, the Camel Corps being left to enjoy the amenities of a burning desert where there were hardly any wells at all. However, it must be admitted that this was precisely the sort of country for which it had been trained.

Despite the lateness of the year there was a heatwave which lasted several days with temperatures of up to 110. This was nearly my undoing. I had been on outpost duty since dawn under a pitiless sun and spent most of the day staring through binoculars in the general direction of the enemy lines, and catching an occasional glimpse of a Turkish cavalry patrol. I can only describe the desert on that occasion as a shimmering white-hot furnace and as the day wore on I began to feel pretty awful, with a blinding headache which got worse and worse until it was time to withdraw and report back to battalion H.Q. I used to suffer badly from migraine, and this sort of thing had happened to me once or twice before, but never so severely as this. For some reason I was temporarily in command of the company and I remember Lord Winterton coming out of his tent to instruct me on the dispositions we were to make for the night. I was feeling so ill by then that I did not hear, or at any rate, take in a word he said and it was fortunate that I had my company sergeant major, Guppy, with me at the time.

A few moments after Lord Winterton walked away I collapsed and spent the next quarter of an hour lying on the ground and being violently sick. They got me away eventually and for the next three days I lay under a ground sheet with a sharp attack of sunstroke, and with the knowledge imparted to me by the M.O. that unless I recovered by the time we were to move forward to our final position I would have to be evacuated to hospital. Fortunately I just made it. Our orders came through on the third evening, and although I was still pretty shaky I was allowed to rejoin the company in time for its departure on the following morning.

A day or two later we took up our final position to the west of Beersheba, and at the end of October the attack which was to result a few weeks later in the capture of Jerusalem was launched on the Turkish positions. It seems that the Turkish, or rather German High Command, under General von Falkenhayn, was in two minds as to whether the main attack would be delivered at Gaza or Beersheba. Gaza seemed to be the more likely, and it had already been subjected to an intense artillery bombardment, supported by guns from Allied warships. But in fact Allenby had decided that the main, or at any rate, the initial offensive should be directed at Beersheba. If successful this would mean that the whole of the Turkish line could be turned from its eastern and unprotected flank and Gaza itself would become virtually untenable. This is precisely what happened. The attack on Beersheba was made by 20th Corps, under Lieutenant-General Sir Philip Chetwode, and Desert Mounted Corps, and one of its main features was the charge of a brigade of Australian Light Horse, which overran the Turkish defences and ended in the capture of the vitally important wells before they could be demolished. Prior to this the town had been subjected to a heavy bombardment by our guns which preceded an attack by the infantry from the west and south.

My company was in reserve at this stage and we were interested observers of the bombardment as the guns were stretched out on either side of us, and we could see the Turkish positions a mile or so away erupting in a solid mass of exploding shells. For some reason which I cannot explain, but probably with the idea of calming our excitement over our first contact with real war, Lord Winterton took the opportunity during a brief pause to deliver a lecture to some of the junior officers, including myself, on the subject of parliamentary procedure!

BATTLE OF BEERSHEBA

Later that day we entered Beersheba and reached the railway station which was apparently deserted. There were a number of railway wagons in a siding and several of the men rushed forward to see what they could find. Fortunately we stopped them just in time. The wagons turned out to be a vast booby trap. They were packed with explosives which were wired to the doors. Had any of these been opened the whole contraption would have gone up in an explosion which would not only have destroyed us all, but most of what was left of Beersheba as well. This was an extremely lucky escape as I do not think that we would have thought of booby traps at all if it had not been for an incident which occurred a few minutes earlier when one of the men picked up a bottle of beer, which was lying a few yards away, with fatal results to himself. It turned out afterwards that practically every object of interest in that particular area was a booby trap. Somebody had certainly been very busy.

It would be convenient at this point to mention that on the 30th October, the day before the attack on Beersheba, Colonel S. F. Newcombe's party which consisted of seventy men from No. 5 Company Imperial Camel Corps, a detachment of sixteen men from the 21st London Regiment of the 60th Division and some Arab scouts, moved into the desert east of the town with the object of raising the local Bedouin in revolt against the Turks at the moment of Allenby's offensive, and blocking the road north to Hebron and Jerusalem after Beersheba had fallen. The party was exceptionally strong in fire-power for its size, being armed with ten heavy machine guns in addition to a number of Lewis guns and explosives.

In his book *T. E. Lawrence - In Arabia and After*, which was first published by Jonathan Cape in 1934, the late Sir Basil Liddell Hart described the effect on the Turkish High Command when, on the evening of the 31st October, Newcombe and his men moved down to the Beersheba-Hebron road and cut the telegraph line to Jerusalem. In fact it spread such alarm behind the Turkish lines that, in the enemy's imagination, the bulk of the British Army could only be advancing north of the Hebron road and straight for Jerusalem. In consequence they not only dispatched their one division in general reserve towards Hebron but also drew off reserves from the Sheria sector to meet the supposed threat to their left flank.

Newcombe's hopes of a rising by the Bedouin were, however, disappointed as they preferred to wait on events before committing themselves. Furthermore there was no sign of the hoped for advance by British cavalry to his relief and, as the hours slipped away, his chances of extricating his little party were becoming more and more remote.

On the 1st November an attack by about 100 Turks was repulsed with loss but Liddell Hart describes how, on the next morning, converging forces of the enemy from Hebron and Dhariyeh succeeded in clearing away the obstructions, which for forty hours had disrupted all communications with Jerusalem, and, after twenty of his men had been killed, many others wounded and most of his machine guns disabled during the ensuing battle, Newcombe was forced to surrender when the Turks, who were under German command, had reached positions from which they would have been able to shoot down all the survivors. It could be argued that he had been unwise not to withdraw a few hours earlier while the way was still open. Be that as it may, however, the entire operation had shown a magnificent example of initiative, courage and determination and perhaps it would be true to say that even the loss of those brave men was outweighed by the almost panic effect on the morale of the Turks and the consequent interference with the dispositions they had made in the face of Allenby's general offensive following the capture of Beersheba. This is shown by the fact that, on the evening of Newcombe's surrender, no less than two Turkish divisions and two cavalry regiments were deployed in the hills near the Hebron road with a third division on the way. And there they remained to take part in a series of ineffective actions on the British Army's flank until on the 6th November Chetwode's divisions crashed into and through the Sheria defences where only two Turkish regiments had been left to hold six miles of front.

I cannot help feeling that in the story of the Imperial Camel Corps this episode must surely rank as one of its finer achievements.

I must now pick up the threads of my main narrative. After the fall of Beersheba the Turks had to some extent reorganised and begun to take up positions to the north and north-west and a day or two later the 53rd Division and part of Desert Mounted Corps, including ourselves, were faced with the Turkish 19th Division at a place called Tel Khuweilfe. Although it was now November the heat was unbearable with the temperature officially 107 in the shade, but there was no shade. The day before Khuweilfe was taken my company lay out under the blazing sun from early morning to dusk without any water at all. There was virtually no cover and any movement attracted the attention of a Turkish battery posted on higher ground. As the day wore on things began to look rather serious. Our throats and lips were parched and our tongues became swollen and blackened, and some of the men were in really bad shape. We opened tins of peas and marmalade and drank, if you can call it drinking, the hot grease and vegetable matter, which did not really help very much. I had a flask of brandy with me and although it would, of course, have been fatal to drink any I found some relief from moistening my lips and then sucking them. A rumour had gone round that the wells at Beersheba had not been captured intact after all and that in any case the water had been poisoned. I do not think that there was any truth in this, but certainly the delay in bringing up a supply of water did nothing to discourage it.

However, that evening a convoy of camel transport with water tanks did succeed in making its way to the front-line area, but it was only just in time. Had it arrived a few hours later there could have been a real disaster and, as it was, the convoy was rushed by members

MEDITERRANEAN

Sh. Redwan

Sheikh Hasan

Dunes

Sand

Sheikh Ajlin

GAZA

BRITISH

Cactus

Ali el Muntar

Hedges

Samsons Ridge

Sand Dunes

Area

GREEN HILL

THE LABYRINTH

UMBRELLA HILL

FRONT

OUTPOST HILL

LINE

ATTACK ON GAZA
November 1st/2nd

Turkish Trenches ~
British Front Line ---

0   1000   2000
Yards

of an infantry unit who had been without water for the best part of two days, and were driven almost mad with thirst. This only resulted in a lot of the precious liquid being wasted, but eventually the water reached its various destinations and the situation was restored. But if there had been further delay, or had the Turks been able to counter-attack and destroy the convoy, something like two and perhaps three divisions would have been put out of action. This was a truly horrible day.

The next day we passed through Khuweilfe which was littered with Turkish corpses already in an advanced state of decomposition. By this time Gaza itself had been captured and the whole of the Turkish forces were in retreat, although far from being demoralised. In fact, considering what they had been called upon to endure (the bombardment of Gaza alone from land and sea had lasted for four days) they were still fighting with tremendous courage and tenacity and there was no semblance of a rout. In defence the Turks are as good fighters as any in the world (as they showed in the Korean war) and I think that everyone was full of admiration for the stubbornness with which they conducted their retreat, although exposed to a series of dazzling cavalry charges by the Yeomanry and Australian Light Horse.

After Khuweilfe, Desert Mounted Corps and the 60th Division executed a turning movement to the north-west in the general direction of Huj and Askalon, which is on the sea. The days seemed to pass very rapidly and after all this time my recollections are somewhat blurred, but I can vividly remember a day, or rather night, when I was marooned with four companions in the most appalling thunderstorm I have ever experienced. As second in command of the company it was my job to bring up the rear and make sure that there were no stragglers. Sometime towards dusk one of the men was taken ill with a severe attack of dysentery and for a time was quite unable to proceed. I had a corporal and my batman with me and we managed to get hold of the M.O. who was somewhere in the front. While he was attending to the casualty the rest of the column moved forward and in the pitch darkness we completely lost touch. It was then that the thunderstorm caught us. It lasted for several hours, in fact for the whole of the night. The flashes of lightning coming from a dozen places at once and running along the ground all round us in vivid blue streaks accompanied by a continuous roll of thunder and a solid wall of rain, which turned the place into a quagmire, were really quite frightening. There was no question of our dismounting under those conditions and we crouched on our camels protecting our saddle bags as best we could. Somehow the casualty survived the ordeal, although he was so weak that he seemed to be in danger of falling off every minute. The camels were in an abject state of misery and remained standing the whole time in a tight little circle with their heads facing inwards and moaning their discomfort to each other. The skies cleared sometime after dawn and we were able to proceed, though we did not catch up with the rest of the column for several hours.

Meanwhile the cavalry were in full pursuit of the retreating Turks and it was the role of the Camel Corps to act as a screen between them and the infantry. At night we would relieve the cavalry, when we could catch up with them, and give them some much-needed rest and the opportunity to water their horses, always assuming that there was any water available.

One night I had to take my section to relieve a Unit of my old friends in Fayoum, the Lincolnshire Yeomanry. After they had drawn back we moved forward in search of a better position for the night and rounding a corner we came in sight of a solitary Turkish field gun, guarding a cleft between two small hills. It was only about a hundred yards away and in the vivid light of a full moon we could clearly see the gun crew, one of whom was in the act of putting a shell into the breech, but there was no sound whatever except for the mournful sighs of a dying camel, which had come from God knows where (it was not one of ours). We took such cover as was available and waited to see what would happen next. Nothing happened at all and we gradually became aware of the immobility of the men behind the gun. After a few minutes we began to make our way cautiously forward, but there was still no sound or movement and as we got closer it became apparent that all of them were dead. They had been killed just where they stood, serving their gun to the last. Yet another instance of the courage of the ordinary Turkish soldier and his refusal to accept defeat. With one exception all of them were still standing at the gun and they gave the impression not so much of having been killed as having suddenly ceased to live. Their faces were unmarked and showed no trace of fear or even excitement. There was a field telephone close by and we traced the wire to the edge of a small prominence not more than fifty yards away, where we came across the body of a German officer, who had presumably been in command of this forlorn hope. I am afraid that there was nothing we could do except relieve him of his revolver and binoculars, which would be of no use to him any more.

YEOMANRY CHARGE AT HUJ
Nov 8th 1917

5.9 Battery
DISORGANISED TURKISH INF.
2 TROOPS WAR. YEO.
Mountain Batty
TURKISH INF.
1 SQDN. WOR. YEO.
M.GUNS
Austrian By
4 TPS. WOR.YEO.
1½ SQDNS. WOR. YEO.
1½ SQDNS. WAR. YEO.
TURKISH INF.
1 SQDN. WAR. YEO.
1 SQDNS. WORCESTER YEO.
1½ SQDNS. WARWICK YEO.
Advance of 60th Div.

0   500   1000
Yards

8TH MOUNTED B.DE
El Kubeibe
Zernukah
W. Shellal el Ghor
Yebnah
BERKS YEO.
DORSET YEO.
BUCKS YEO.
MACHINE GUN SQDN
El Mughar
Akir
BERKS BATT. R.H.A
Wadi Jamus
Beshshit
155TH B.DE (52ND DIV.)
Katrah
¼ F.A. B.DE (52ND DIV.)

YEOMANRY CHARGE AT EL MUGHAR
Turkish position shown ▄▄▄

0   1000   2000   3000
Yards

There is no doubt that the impact of the cavalry played a tremendous part in the campaign and the one which finally broke the Turkish armies in the following year. I do not know how many cavalry regiments there were in Palestine, but I know that we used to talk in terms of 100,000 horses, which surely must have been an exaggeration. Nonetheless it was one of the greatest, although certainly the last, of the cavalry wars and I think that when their doom was finally sealed by the advent of modern weapons, with their terrific fire power, the last remaining romance went out of war for ever.

Not that the weapons which they had to face in Palestine could be accurately described as anything but modern. It was more that the Turks simply did not have enough guns and particularly machine guns, to make the work of the cavalry virtually impossible. Nonetheless some of the charges were carried out against almost impossible odds. Outstanding was that of the Warwickshire and Worcestershire Yeomanry against twelve guns which they captured, though at the expense of severe casualties. In the final stages the shells were bursting almost at the muzzles of the guns. Nearly all the Austrian gunners were killed at their posts and the Yeomanry swept on to attack the Turkish infantry who were in support, many of whom were killed or captured, while losing several machine guns into the bargain. Other charges, in addition to those of the Australians and New Zealanders, were carried out by my own regiment the Berkshire Yeomanry and also the Dorsetshire Yeomanry and Royal Bucks Hussars. It was on one of these occasions that Evelyn Rothschild and Neil Primrose were killed.

We passed through the battlefield a few hours later. There were many corpses lying around, and by an incredible and unhappy coincidence our company sergeant major, who was a Dorset Yeoman, stumbled over one of the bodies only to discover it was that of his own brother.

Day after day the advance continued without a break on the heels of the retreating Turks, who although they put up tremendous resistance in countless engagements large and small, were becoming dispirited though never demoralised, under the tremendous pressure which was being exerted on them. We always seemed to be just in or out of the line and I have the confused recollection of being constantly on the march for hours and even days on end, from which a few isolated instances stand out.

There was the capture of Yebna at dawn by our forward troops and tremendous excitement following a rumour that the redoubtable General von Falkenhayn himself had only escaped with minutes to spare.

There was also an occasion when we were held up by having to cross a steep wadi, where a Turkish mule train had been caught and destroyed. The place was littered with dead men and mules and overturned wagons through which the crossing had to be negotiated in almost total darkness. My batman, Neville, was riding in the rear of the column on my spare camel and he was sent up with a message for me. Unfortunately it was never delivered. In the general noise and confusion the camel bolted and went clean over the edge of the wadi, a drop of about fifteen feet, carrying my batman with him. That was the end of the camel, and for a time my batman as well. He rejoined the company a few months later and was there when I left, but I fear he was either killed or died during or soon after the Jordan valley operations in the following year.

A few days later there was the capture or rather liberation of a Jewish settlement called Richon le Zion. I do not recollect that there was any fighting, nor that we were received by the 'liberated' Jews with any particular enthusiasm, although they seemed to be quite friendly. We had pretty well run out of food by then and the nearest supply column was miles in the rear. In fact we were pretty desperate and, as there was no question of requisitioning anything, we had to negotiate with our newly acquired friends for the purchase of sufficient food to keep us going. I seem to remember that they charged us a pretty stiff price and that for about two days we lived on a diet of semolina. This was just about enough to keep us from starvation until our rations arrived one evening and we were able to consume vast quantities of bully beef and biscuit as we rode along into the night.

We took no part in the capture of Jerusalem itself and I shall not attempt to describe that feat of arms. We were assigned to a force consisting of one mounted and one infantry division, whose task was to secure the coastal region far to the north-west, while the bulk of the army was engaged in the Jerusalem sector. This deployment of his forces was afterwards referred to, at any rate by us, as Allenby's bluff. Admittedly we were very thin on the ground and as far as I know there were no reserves behind us at all, so that if the Turks had counter-attacked in strength they must have broken through. But they seem to have been completely in the dark as to Allenby's real intentions and it may well be that they did regard the build up in the Jerusalem area as a screen for delivery of the main assault on the extreme right of their line as they faced towards the south and west.

On the 16th November Jaffa (or Joppa as it used to be called), the seaport of Jerusalem, was taken and a line was established in the vicinity of the river Auja. That was the furthest point which we reached and there as it happened we were to stay for several days. By this time our camels were in a pretty deplorable condition. Most of them had not been unsaddled for days and were suffering from severe sores, and even the most elementary grooming had been impossible since the attack on Beersheba nearly a month earlier. Even now very little could be done for them as we were constantly on the alert to move off at a moment's notice.

Our own front line consisted of three or four strong points on slightly higher ground than the surrounding plain with lateral and communicating trenches. Each of these was manned day and night in about half-company strength and I cannot say that they were particularly comfortable. The Turkish positions were not far away and although, despite many false alarms particularly at night, they did not launch an attack we were under intermittent shell fire the whole time and the trenches were continually being blown in and having to be restored. One of the casualties was Major Gregory, who was killed when a 5.9 shell fell on the strong point he was commanding. This was a sad loss to the battalion as he was one of our best officers.

How long we remained in this sector of the line I cannot remember, but I do not think that it was until after the surrender of Jerusalem on the 9th December, that we were taken into reserve to rest and refit after a campaign which had lasted for exactly six weeks, for the greater part of which we had been constantly on the move. By now the condition of the camels, which had been bad enough before, was almost desperate. Some of them were almost too weak to stand up and most of them were past hope of curing. In many cases they had cavities on each side of their humps so deep that you could have buried a cricket ball in them. These cavities were, of course septic and the raw flesh was alive with maggots. God only knows what these once splendid animals must have suffered but they complained no more than usual, and stuck it out until they collapsed from exhaustion. Cruel though it may sound we had to saddle and load up the worst cases in order to preserve, if we could, those animals which had relatively minor sores by retaining them as spares. But in the event very few of them recovered. There was one pathetic march which I can vividly remember. Again I had to bring up the rear of the column, but this time with the veterinary instead of the medical officer. Camels were collapsing one after another and as there was no hope of ever getting them to their feet again their riders or loads, as the case might be, were being transferred to spares, many of which were to collapse in their turn before very long. As the column moved slowly forward we caught up with the fallen camels and put them out of their misery. How many were shot I cannot say, but looking back along the route we had passed we could see an endless line of corpses fading into the distance. They had served us faithfully, poor devils, and we had become very attached to them, or at least to most of them.

In addition to sores and general weakness most of the camels had also developed a peculiarly virulent form of mange, but unfortunately they did not keep it to themselves. No doubt we were not in particularly good shape. Most of us were already suffering from septic sores particularly behind the knees and on our faces, which made shaving hell. However, we had done very little of this lately. Whether it was due to our poor condition or whether it would have happened anyway I have no idea but, anyway, we were quite suddenly infected with the mange ourselves. Hardly anyone escaped. It was not too bad by day, but directly our bodies warmed up in our blankets at night (the weather had now become very cold and wet) the irritation became unbearable. It was impossible to sleep and the worst sufferers spent the whole night walking about. I doubt whether I have ever heard, before or since, such a variety of language. Our parlous condition was reported to the higher medical authorities and a special decontamination centre was established for our benefit. In the meantime we were put out of bounds, no other unit being allowed to approach us.

I cannot remember how long it was before we were passed as 'clean' again, but it must have been several days. During that time many of the remaining camels had to be destroyed or evacuated and towards the end of December we were ordered back to Rafa near the coast, a few miles north of El Arish, to recuperate and to receive a fresh supply of camels from the remount depot in the rear. There was no further outbreak of mange, but curiously enough I became infected again when I was in hospital in London in August of the following year.

OPERATIONS ROUND **JERUSALEM** November 18th-December 9th 1917

Towards the end of December the Turks launched a heavy counter-attack with the object of retaking Jerusalem, but it failed to accomplish very much and they were finally driven back about fifteen miles to the north of the city. This brought an end to the winter campaign, which had lasted two months, during the first six weeks of which alone 25,000 casualties had been inflicted on the Turks in addition to the 12,000 captured. Volume 4 of 'A Popular History of The Great War' edited by Sir J. A. Hammerton, records the following laconic sentence in Allenby's order of the day issued on the 15th December: 'In forty days many strong positions have been captured and the Force has advanced sixty miles on a thirty mile front'.

It was widely believed that Allenby was held in the greatest admiration and respect by the ordinary Turkish soldier who thought that some supernatural and almost godlike figure had descended on them with the name of Allah Bey.

They also had a saying, which was alleged to have come down through the centuries, that Jerusalem would fall when the waters of Egypt flowed into the city. It may well be, therefore, that the famous pipeline from Kantara had a significance for them which went far beyond the mere supply of water.

17. Rafa - Cairo

The end of the year saw us back at Rafa, which had become a large military base. How we got there I have no idea whatever, although I suppose we must have marched with the few remaining camels at our disposal.

We camped among the dunes not far from the sea and my first recollection is of dining on New Year's Eve with the officers of another company which had been recruited from a number of Scottish Yeomanry regiments. I cannot remember them very distinctly, but I have some recollection that the C.O. was a Captain Dees and that there was another officer called Bell-Irving, who had been in China before the war and, like Paterson, was associated with the firm of Jardine, Matheson & Co. It is, of course, quite an experience to dine with Scotsmen on that night and particularly when one is able to relax for the first time for several weeks, if not months. Unfortunately I am unable to supply any details beyond the fact that immediately on arrival at the marquee, where they had their mess, I was presented with a tumbler of neat whisky which was followed after a short interval by another. I was told afterwards that it was about half an hour later that I passed out completely and had to be carried by a stretcher party over the dunes to my own quarters a few hundred yards away. My batman was very solicitous on my arrival there, by which time I was beginning to come round a bit, and suggested a prairie oyster of all things. This had an immediate and violent effect although not the one which was intended, and my health began to improve. In fact I was perfectly all right next morning and paid a courtesy call on my hosts to make my apologies. Unfortunately there was nobody to whom I could deliver them as they were all, shall I say, fast asleep and in fact I heard afterwards that one of them had slept for thirty-six hours. I am not particularly proud of this story but I feel that there may have been extenuating circumstances!

Talking of whisky I remember an occasion in the Fayoum oasis when some officers rode over from a neighbouring unit for lunch. It was a blazing hot day. Their senior officer was an exceptionally good-looking man, a brilliant conversationalist and altogether a most attractive personality. With the others he accepted the offer of a drink and by the time they left some three hours later he had consumed precisely thirteen whiskies, and they were not small ones. They apparently had no effect whatever. A few nights later we rode over to have dinner with them and were welcomed by his second in command, who apologised for the fact that the C.O. had not greeted us himself, but he was feeling out of sorts. We discovered him sitting in the mess by himself, but he gave no sign of recognition or even awareness that there were any guests at all, and during the entire evening he did not speak one single word to anyone. It seems that his potations when he visited us were a more or less daily occurrence and, of course, you cannot make a habit of consuming a whole bottle of whisky in the middle of the day during a summer like that without it catching up with you sooner or later. In his case it was sooner because we heard a few months later that he had shot himself. It seemed a terrible waste.

Not long after our arrival at Rafa we were all given in turn a few days leave, and in due course Merlin Huth and I proceeded to Cairo where we put up at Shepheard's which succeeded in maintaining the highest possible standard of living throughout the entire war, and it would be an understatement to say that we made the most of it, helped by the fact that our pay had been piling up for months and we had plenty of funds at our disposal. There were at least three bars, one of which was presided over by a gentleman called Hannibal, and was alleged to be the second largest in the world, the first being somewhere in Shanghai. There were also two enormous dining rooms and the food was absolutely superb in its own right, and not simply by contrast with what we had been consuming during the last few months. We used to lunch every day in one or other of these, but if the weather was warm enough, which in early February was not always the case, we dined on the terrace overlooking the street. During the day we made various expeditions to places like Heluan, Heliopolis, near our old quarters at Abassia, the beautiful Barrage Gardens, and, of course, Mena, where we inspected the Sphinx and climbed to the top of the Cheops Pyramid, only to be confronted by a very talkative character selling soft drinks at probably very exorbitant prices. It was not so bad going up, but when we started to descend it was quite a different matter and I seem to remember that, when we finally overcame our giddiness, we proceeded backwards lowering ourselves very gingerly from block to block. There was a story, though I cannot vouch for it, that just about that time three Australian soldiers, who had also been enjoying their leave, had a wager as to which of them could get to the bottom first, with fatal results as they were all killed. Certainly if you did have the misfortune to slip there was nothing to stop you until you reached the bottom.

Night life in Cairo during the first war was a pretty hectic and disreputable affair and I think the less I say about it the better. The trouble was that the more conventional forms of entertainment were denied to us. I cannot remember that anything very much was done to keep the troops amused and we were left very much to our own devices. There were one or two theatres and music halls, including the Kursaal, but we found the performances very dull and conducted in pretty well every language except English.

I had quite an unusual experience at the Kursaal one night. We had booked seats imagining it would be the usual music-hall show, but when we got inside we found they were putting on some kind of traditional Arab play and that the whole gallery had been reserved for Egyptian ladies. There was a white lace curtain running along the top, and below we could see a line of faces all adorned with a white yashmak. This so intrigued me that instead of looking where we were going to our seats in the front row of the stalls I kept my eyes fixed on the yashmaks. A moment later I tripped and fell, there was a tremendous bang and I found myself in the orchestra pit, sitting on the big drum which was still vibrating with the shock. Somewhat crestfallen and a little pained I climbed out with the assistance of Merlin Huth. However, the audience seemed to be highly amused, particularly the yashmaks, to whom I bowed with as much dignity as I could muster before sinking with relief into my seat.

It was during this leave that I again came across Macdonald, who always seemed to be involved in scenes of violence. One evening he was out on the tiles with another officer and they eventually found themselves in a particularly low dive, somewhere in the native quarter of Waza, as I seem to remember it was called. There was a small stage with some sort of cabaret going on and the audience sat around drinking at little tables. They ordered a bottle of something or other and settled down to enjoy the show. The lights were lowered and after a while Macdonald turned round to say something to his companion and discovered that, although only a few moments had elapsed since the bottle had been brought, he was apparently only half conscious and slowly slipping to the floor. Macdonald's own glass was untouched but the other one half empty. In the half light he noticed that the waiter was watching them intently and, pretending to take a swig at his 'wine' he beckoned him over. The waiter shuffled along and Macdonald pointed to something on the table and, as the waiter bent down to look, grasped the bottle and smashed it down on to the back of his head. As he said afterwards he could feel the skull cave in, and he was pretty certain that he had killed him. The lights were still low and, half carrying and half dragging his companion, he made for the exit. He had just reached it when the lights came on and pandemonium broke out behind him. Somebody threw a bottle which smashed against the wall, but somehow or other he managed to struggle down a narrow passage into the street, which was only a few yards wide, still supporting the dead weight of his companion. That, of course, would have been the end (many members of H.M. forces disappeared in Cairo without trace) had it not been for the miraculous arrival at that moment of an empty gharry. Somehow he managed to climb in with his heavy burden and as the crowd erupted out of the building the driver, who acted with considerable promptitude, whipped up his horse into a gallop and within seconds they were, so to speak, out of range. A very narrow escape. It turned out, as Macdonald had immediately suspected, that his companion had been heavily drugged.

I never saw Macdonald again, but heard later on that he had returned to England, joined the R.F.C. and been shot down while piloting a dirigible across the Channel. I was never able to verify whether this was true or not.

At the end of our leave we returned to Rafa where there was not a great deal to do except to prepare for the next operation whatever it might be and have an occasional jackal hunt. There were dozens of these creatures in the vicinity of the camp, and their howling at night almost drove us round the bend.

But there was one day which does stand out in my mind. It was decided to take advantage of the fact that practically the whole of the Camel Brigade was assembled at Rafa to hold a sort of gymkhana. I believe that there had been one or two of these before, but at a time when our company had been detached from the main body. It turned out to be rather a splendid affair. There were trotting races, galloping races, wrestling on camel-back, musical chairs, tug of wars (or should it be tugs of war?), sack races (not on camels), stunt riding, which included trotting and even galloping with the rider standing up behind the camel's hump, and prizes for such things as the best turned out section. So far as the latter is concerned, it is surprising what a little spit and polish can do even under desert conditions.

It was somewhere about this time that I received a letter from home saying that my surviving brother was going to be married shortly and suggesting that, as I had now been overseas for more than two years, it might be a good idea if I were to apply for a spell of home leave and attend the wedding. I thought that this was a good idea too. Unfortunately these things take a long time to arrange. My application was approved in succession by my commanding officer, the brigadier and the divisional commander. There remained apparently one more hurdle to surmount but it was not until several weeks later, when I had almost forgotten about it, that my application was returned with a note from the corps commander to the effect that, as he had just read an account of my brother's wedding in a paper which had come out from England, it was too late and he would have to deny himself the privilege of falling in with my suggestion!

18. The Raid on Amman

The resumption of hostilities after the winter lull, particularly in the Jordan Valley, led to the capture of Jericho on the 21st February, 1918, and by the end of the month the west bank of the Jordan had been completely cleared of the enemy from Jericho to the Dead Sea. In consequence the opportunity had now arisen to erect a crossing of the river and put into operation the plan which had been concocted between Allenby and Lawrence for a raid in force on the Hejaz railway by the British from the west acting in conjunction with the Arabs to the east. Although we knew nothing about it at the time the Camel Corps had been selected to play a leading part in this operation, and on the 10th March we were ordered to proceed to the Jordan Valley. I cannot remember very much about the first part of this journey, which was by easy stages, but in due course we found ourselves at King Solomon's Pools, a few miles south of the city and quite close to Bethlehem.

We stayed there for several days and naturally most of us took advantage of this to spend a day in Bethlehem, where we visited the Church of the Nativity and I purchased a small crucifix alleged, of course, if not guaranteed, to have been made from the wood of the True Cross. I surmise that if all the wood which has been sold over the ages as part of the True Cross was added together it would make a good sized forest. Nonetheless my little crucifix did at least originate from the spot where Christ was born and I sent it home to my mother to her great delight.

By the 18th March we were on the move again, and in the early hours of the morning we topped a rise and saw Jerusalem spread before us. There was, I remember, a full moon and the city seemed to be bathed in silver. A beautiful sight which I shall never forget. Nor shall I forget the incredible silence as we passed through from one end to the other. There was not a soul to be seen, and the only sound came from our camels as they padded their way stealthily through the streets. Later on we passed the Mount of Olives and began our descent through the Judaean Hills towards the Jordan Valley and the Dead Sea. About half-way down we turned north from the road and camped for the night on the edge of a steep wadi. Next morning we were informed that a crossing of the Jordan had been effected and that we were to take part in a large-scale raid on Amman in Transjordania, with the object of blowing up sections of the Hejaz railway, which ran through the town on its way from Damascus to Medina, and which was the chief line of communication for the Turks in the defence of Syria from Lawrence and his Arabs. The information that we should be starting on the following day, however, was incorrect as I had hardly wrapped myself in my blankets with the idea of getting a good night's sleep while we had the chance, when the order came through that we were to march at midnight.

By dawn we were within sight of Jericho and reaching the floor of the Jordan Valley, the lowest place on earth (1300 feet below sea-level) and one of the hottest. During the summer months it is quite intolerable and, even though it was only March, the contrast between the conditions we encountered there and the cold and wet we had recently experienced on the higher ground was startling. All the morning was spent in traversing the wide expanse between the foothills and the river, but the ground was hard and level and we made such good time that by midday we had reached the Dead Sea, where we halted for a meal.

The day was overcast and the water grey and uninviting with a ring of what looked like dirty soap-suds round the edge. I had bathed several times in the salt lakes at Mersa Matruh but they were clean and sparkling, whereas this vast expanse of water seemed to be just dirty and in fact as well as in name - dead. We crossed the river by a pontoon bridge which had been hastily erected by the sappers. The far side was pitted with shell craters and it was evident that the original crossing had been no easy task. The country now seemed to change, and for some reason we were diverted off the track and had to make our way for hours across a horrible swamp which meant very heavy going for the camels and considerably delayed our progress. There was an almost tropical variety of birds, some of which I had never come across before, including hundreds of storks which flew all round us with their pink legs trailing behind. And then it began to rain, a pitiless downpour, which was to last for forty-eight hours and turn the track through the Moabite hills or rather mountains, which we were now approaching, into a morass. We had now been marching for some eighteen hours, except for the midday break by the Dead Sea, but this was only the beginning and after a two hour halt to snatch a meal and a few minutes' sleep we were on our way again. It was a grim night but at least we kept on the move and, so far, the track was on comparatively level ground.

However in the early hours of the morning we began the ascent and when dawn broke we must have reached an altitude of about 1000 feet and it was now that our troubles really began. As the track climbed up through the hills the sides grew steeper and steeper with sheer cliffs on one side and a precipice on the other. The camels struggled gamely but they were neither accustomed to such appalling conditions nor designed by nature to overcome them. The rain continued without a break, the track became worse and worse as the mud was churned up by the troops in front, and the camels at last began to falter as they struggled to keep their footing. Many of them did the splits with their legs splaying out in either direction, others slipped and went over the side of the ravine, and even if they were not fatally injured by the fall there was no chance of getting them back again so that we had to climb down, remove their loads and shoot them where they lay. I think they must have welcomed being put out of their misery.

What with the rain and various traffic jams on the narrow track we did not seem to make much progress that day or the following night and it was pretty obvious that we were getting further and further behind schedule and the chances of surprising the Turks becoming more and more remote. Somewhere away on our left was the 60th (London) Division. A considerable part of Desert Mounted Corps, including various units of Australian Light Horse and New Zealand Mounted Rifles and most of the Camel Brigade, was also involved. Heavy fighting took place to the north and west in the region of Es Salt which was eventually occupied on the 25th March, and the Turkish or rather German High Command must by now have been alerted to the fact that the Hejaz railway and possibly Amman itself were in danger.

The weather got worse and worse and with the prospect of yet another night without rest, the third in succession, the situation was far from encouraging. With darkness progress became slower and slower and was not helped by the fact that on at least one occasion we had to cross a small stream which could only be negotiated in single file. This created such interminable delay that it became difficult to avoid dropping off to sleep. I know that I dozed off myself for a few moments only to wake up and find the whole of my section, which was at that point riding four abreast, fast asleep, both camels and men, and that we could neither see nor hear anything in front of us. In the pitch darkness it was even impossible to see the track, such as it was, and the only thing to do was to leave it to the instinct of the camels to find their way. Some time later to my great relief we caught up with the column just as its rear files were crossing the stream. By dawn the rain had eased off a little but we were still several miles short of our immediate objective, which was a line of low hills to be used as a springboard for the impending attack on the Turkish positions. We still had to traverse some narrow defiles and it became necessary to dismount and lead the camels through as best we could. This is the only time I have seen men fall asleep as they walked, even in mid stride, and there were so many delays that we did not reach our positions until midday, some seventy-six hours after we had started out so hopefully. I remember that the junior officers tossed up as to who should be duty officer. I was one of the lucky ones and slept for seventeen hours without a break.

In the early morning we stood to arms and were briefed by the intelligence officer as regards the situation generally and the task which we were supposed to perform. The only thing I can remember was his insistence that the Turks had been completely taken by surprise (we found this rather difficult to believe), that they had no guns and that, if the attack was pressed home, they would not have time to bring up any artillery before our final objective had been reached. Considering that they were sitting astride the railway which was their principal line of communication, it seemed to us that this was highly improbable, and it very soon became apparent that it was also wholly inaccurate because the moment we left the cover of the hills (leaving our camels in the rear) the first salvoes arrived, and as we were already within range of rifle and machine gun fire from the Turkish trenches less than half a mile away on a completely open plain we began to sustain quite heavy casualties and by the time we had got within 500 yards of the enemy we became completely bogged down and unable to advance any further. The same situation was developing on our left and right and things began to look a little serious. We dug in for the night, which was relatively uneventful.

On the following morning our camels were brought up from the rear and placed in a small wadi just behind our position. Our company commander at the time was a man called Tredinnick, who had taken over a few weeks earlier from Julian Day who had in turn succeeded Paterson but was now at battalion H.Q. Tredinnick was, I imagine, of Cornish extraction but was residing in South Africa at the outbreak of war. He was a splendid soldier and had already been awarded the M.C. Tredinnick was worried about the camels and decided to move them further back which was very fortunate for all concerned because shortly after their departure, the wadi was heavily shelled and undoubtedly most of the camels would have been destroyed.

The Turks had now got the range of our positions all along the line and it was impossible to make a move without attracting a heavy burst of shell fire. In consequence we spent a most frustrating day and were not cheered up by the knowledge that the Turks were being continually reinforced, whereas there was nothing behind us at all. After dusk, however, we were able to make some progress on our right and eventually established ourselves in a trench of sorts about a hundred yards from the Turkish forward positions. The next morning was decidedly uncomfortable because in addition to shell fire we were being sniped at continually from the rear. It must be remembered that we were in hostile country and it would be true to say that at least half the Arab population in the villages were pro-Turkish and many of them in Turkish pay. I have no doubt that the position would have been very different if the raid had looked like being a success, and in fact in the earlier stages the villagers had turned out to welcome us. But they had now discovered that far from being a general advance by Allenby's army, which they had thought to be the case, this was a relatively small operation and one which was already beginning to founder. Inevitably, therefore, the Turks would be reoccupying all the country through which had passed and it was not unnatural that enthusiasm for the Turkish cause, whether real or feigned, was from now on to be the order of the day.

On the rocky hillside to our right flank and behind us there were a number of small caves large enough to hold perhaps a couple of men, and as the sniping continued all that afternoon we were able to pinpoint the little puffs of smoke which issued from the mouth of each cave. Next morning came retribution. A couple of patrols were sent out and after climbing to the top of the hill some distance to the rear they were able to come down on the caves from above where they could not be seen and nonchalantly toss a Mills bomb inside. There was no more sniping. The following day the Turkish trenches were stormed by No. 9 Company, commanded by Pat Newsom, but at very heavy cost, Newsom himself and two of the other three officers being killed. Newsom had led the attack and was shot through the back at close range either by a German or an Austrian soldier, who had a moment before put his hands up and surrendered. Fighting was heavy and continuous and casualties began to grow alarmingly. These included Julian Day, who had come up to the front line, and who was severely wounded in the arm and shoulder.

Meanwhile, other forward units of the Camel Brigade and Light Horse had succeeded in reaching and blowing up several sections of the railway line, but not the station at Amman, which was stoutly defended by the enemy, now in considerable force. That was virtually the end of the raid which had, I am afraid, accomplished very little. This was mainly due to the truly appalling weather in the early stages and the consequent delay and lack of surprise. I have seen it reported somewhere that during one of those awful nights on that mountain track the column had taken some twelve hours to cover two hundred yards.

Sometime during that uneasy night the orders came to disengage, not quite so easy as it sounds with the enemy only a few yards away. We filed very quietly out of our positions and, as part of the rear guard, lay for hours at ten-yard intervals under cover of darkness while the wounded were being evacuated and the remainder of the column was reorganised for the retreat back to the Jordan Valley. It seems that the Turks were completely unaware of what was going on. Otherwise they would surely have counter-attacked before we could reach the cover of the hills and, even so, it was surprising that no attempt was made to molest the column as it snaked its way through those narrow defiles.

It was rough going and the wounded must have suffered pretty badly but there was no rain and we made steady progress. What I chiefly remember was the expression on the faces of the villagers, who spat in the dust as we passed and made signs indicative of their keen desire to cut our throats given the chance. In due course we reached the river at the bridge of Ghoraniyeh (the troops called it by another name which sounded very similar but meant something quite different!) and crossed over to Jericho and the plain beyond. Here we had our final adventure as we were caught in the open by a squadron of German planes which proceeded to bomb us somewhat casually. The attack was not pressed home, but we were extremely frightened on account of the fact that several of the camels were still laden with explosives which had been intended for the demolition of the railway, and a direct hit on one of these would have had highly unpleasant consequences for us all.

That was the end of this operation which is described in Sir J. A. Hammerton's History as follows. His reference to Arabs is, of course, to those fighting under Lawrence's command.

It appeared as though Allenby were beginning a new offensive along the whole of his line. But this was not the fact. His main purpose was a raid in some force on the Hejaz railway in conjunction with the Arabs on the east. Allenby's operations had been designed to clear his front in order that such a raid could be carried out. They had succeeded, and he began to make his preparations. His objective was Amman (Rabboth Amon), lying in a direct line some thirty miles east of Jericho, or about twenty-five miles beyond the Jordan, in the Bible land of Gilead.

Early in March the success of the Arabs in raiding the railway and wiping out isolated Turkish posts had so irritated the German command that a strong force had been dispatched south towards Maan both to curb Arab activities and to protect that vital depot. At Shobek the Arabs had been severely handled, but this reverse had not quenched their ardour or seriously limited their attacks on the railway. The Turkish force had therefore to remain at Maan. Allenby, by striking at Amman, was hoping to achieve one or more of three possible results. If the Turks remained at Maan his advance to Amman would be by so much the less resisted. He should, therefore, be able to seize the station and cut off the Turks in the south. If, however, they retired in order to resist his attack on Amman, then the Arabs should be able to occupy Maan. In any event, by careful co-operation, it might be possible for the two forces to make contact, and for the first time link up Allenby's main force with Allenby's right wing, as the Arab army eventually was named.

None of these expectations was wholly realised. The raid into Transjordania was begun on March 21st by sections of the 20th corps assisted by part of the desert mounted corps. But the Turks made surprisingly strong resistance, and a whole day was spent in forcing the passage of the river. This delay was to prove serious eventually, but for the moment the troops pushed on. Difficult country and terrible weather further delayed the advance, and it was not until the evening of March 25th that Es Salt, to the north and west of Amman, was occupied. Everywhere the advance had been slow and painful, the Turks defending themselves with great courage. The railway north and south of Amman was finally reached by several patrols, and a number of culverts and several lengths of track were destroyed. But Amman itself proved invulnerable. In spite of heavy artillery bombardment and exemplary bravery among the British attacks, the Turks beat off attack after attack. By April 1st it was clear the raid had failed. Enemy reinforcements were pouring in from the north, seriously threatening the communications of the raiding force. Retreat was imperative, so Major General Shea, in command of the operations, ordered the withdrawal. By April 2nd the British troops were back in the Jordan Valley.

The disappointment was felt keenly by the British, and the Turks were correspondingly elated. In particular it was a happy augury for von Sanders. But the repulse at Amman was not a serious reverse, and although the raid had achieved little, the

Turks had no cause for jubilation. Weather, difficult country, and the twenty-four hours' delay in crossing the Jordan had been the main factors in the failure. But great credit must be given to a German battalion of the Asia Corps, which fought with admirable determination. By its steadiness, bravery and discipline it did much to hold up the British advance, and provided a strong backbone on which the heterogeneous Turkish forces rallied.

In other words we got a bloody nose!

19. The Jordan Valley – Musellabeh

Shortly after our return to the valley Tredinnick was appointed adjutant to the battalion, and I was given command of the company which I retained until my departure from the scene a month later. I do not know whether it was exceptional or not but by mid-April the place was becoming like a furnace. It was not only that on most days the temperature rose to nearly 100, but at that low altitude the air such as it was seemed to be stagnant and unwholesome. Conditions were not improved by the fact that when at dawn the mosquitoes desisted from their attacks the flies took over, and if there were thousands of mosquitoes there were millions of flies. At meal-times their attentions became unbearable and it was impossible to raise a mug to one's lips without having to force one's way through the black mass clustered on the brim. I tried an experiment one evening and instead of drinking I banged my mug hard on the table so that the flies all fell into the tea and were drowned. I counted more than two hundred corpses. It said a lot for the many injections we had received that we did not have an epidemic of typhoid. Some of the mosquitoes were of a particularly unpleasant kind, and for those men unfortunate enough to become infected produced a malignant form of malaria. Curiously enough I did not develop the disease until two months after I left the valley, and even then in a form which is euphemistically described as benign.

A few miles to the north of Jericho there is a hill called Musellabeh. It is on the Judaean side of the valley, and rising sharply from the plain it is quite a feature of the landscape. I do not know when it was first occupied by our troops, which were extended from the hills on the west to the Jordan river on the east, but there was no doubt as to its being the strongest point in the line, and with the prospect of a counter-attack by the Turks it was vital that we should retain it. Although I have referred to the Judaean hills, and the Moabite hills on the other side, it must be remembered that some of these rose to as much as 3000 feet above sea-level, and therefore nearly 4500 feet above the level of the valley. This gave the impression that we were surrounded on both sides by mountains rather than hills, and they certainly created a formidable rampart.

Despite its importance, and the fact that so long as it remained in our hands the Turks would be unable to take full advantage of any gains they might make on the lower ground, Musellabeh could not be held in more than company strength owing to the restricted area on the top of the hill. I remember it well because early in April I was ordered with my company to take over command of the hill from an infantry unit which had been occupying the place for some time. It was certainly an odd sort of place. Company H.Q. was set up in a small cave formed by an overhang of rock some forty or fifty yards to the rear of the trenches which lipped the northern edge of the hill but were so shallow because the hill itself was not much more than a solid mass of rock, that they gave very little cover anyway. From these there was a splendid field of vision in some directions, but it did not include the ground immediately below the hill which, owing to its steep sides, was completely hidden from the defenders. Moreover, the enemy had several batteries, mostly German, hidden in the hills to the west, and although we could not see them we knew very well that they could see us. There were also various shallow wadis leading from the hills which would give the enemy infantry an easy avenue of approach under cover of darkness to the broken ground below the hill, where they would be out of sight from above. Finally there was another hill in front of Musellabeh, which effectively screened any preparations for an attack which might be going on behind. It will be seen, therefore, that although in one sense Musellabeh was undoubtedly a very strong point in defence, in another it was highly vulnerable.

We remained in Musellabeh for several days doing what we could to strengthen the defences, and although it was perfectly obvious that an attack was imminent we had a relatively peaceful time, apart from sporadic bursts of shell fire which were mostly on the lower ground and did little damage.

In due course we were relieved by one of the Australian companies and I handed over to its commanding officer, Captain Mills, who had already been awarded the M.C. and was to get another very well deserved one a few days later. It was either on that or the next night that I was woken up from our position in the rear by the noise of a furious bombardment, and to see the whole of Musellabeh literally exploding into flame under a hurricane of shells. It did not seem possible that anybody could still be alive on that rocky exposed little plateau. As it happened, however, the Australians did not sustain many casualties on that occasion and, although the bombardment was followed up by an infantry attack, this was broken up by our artillery before it could be pressed home and the enemy retired in some confusion. The main attack came two days later and is vividly described by Oliver Hogue in his book The Cameliers, which was published in London by Andrew Melrose Ltd. in 1919. Hogue was an Australian who served with the Imperial Camel Corps, and his book contains an account of the deeds (and, as he put it, the misdeeds) of the Australian and New Zealand contingents which formed the greater part of that most unusual and short-lived institution.

The attack, as he described it, was again preceded by a violent bombardment under cover of which, accompanied by heavy fire from German machine gunners posted on the hill to which I have referred, the enemy were able to make their way into the 'dead' ground below Musellabeh where they were out of sight and from where they launched a concerted frontal attack up the steep side of the hill on the Australian positions. But if the enemy was outside the vision of the Australians, although only a few yards separated them, the reverse was also the case and the battle developed into a bombing duel with the Turks hurling up their grenades from below and the Australians 'lobbing theirs gently on the brow of the hill in such a way that the momentum caused them to roll nicely on to the Turks before exploding'.

Still it was touch and go and in places the Australians ran out of bombs and were reduced to heaving large boulders over the brow of the hill on to the hidden enemy. Eventually, however, the attacks which had been coming from the sides as well as from the front, began to fade away and the Australians remained 'the undisputed masters of Musellabeh'. Not, however, before they had sustained heavy casualties, including all the officers on the hill, one of whom was killed and the rest wounded. That was the last attempt by the enemy to capture Musellabeh, and although for several more days the Australian defenders were subjected to heavy shell fire the fighting was virtually over. It was indeed a triumph and Allenby came in person to congratulate them on their performance. Many decorations were awarded, including Military Crosses to Mills and two of his officers, and Allenby in an order of the day proclaimed that, to commemorate the defence, Musellabeh would in future be known as 'The Camel's Hump'.

20. The Bridge

The rest of April passed peacefully enough apart from the heat, flies and mosquitoes and an occasional exchange of shell fire between the opposing batteries.

There was quite a variety of game in the valley and I remember borrowing a gun from somewhere one evening and having a little expedition on my own during which I shot three different species of partridge, which made a welcome addition to the larder.

However, just before midnight on 30th April, I was woken by the intelligence officer (the same gentleman who had told us just before the attack on Amman that the Turks had no guns) who informed me that our troops on the other side of the river were attacking the Turkish positions at dawn and that my company had been ordered to go forward on the west bank and destroy a bridge which was a vital link in the Turkish lateral line of communication. The unit which held our front line in this sector was to stay put and we were to pass through it on our way to the bridge. Two guides from the unit in question would be reporting to me at 4 a.m. and would conduct us to the place from which we were to make the attack at dawn so as to coincide with the advance on the other side. A battery of guns was also moving into position so as to give us covering fire.

It did not seem to me that I was being given a great deal of time to mount this operation, and in fact the chance of making a preliminary reconnaissance of the ground would have been negligible anyway, and what chance there was disappeared entirely when the guides, who reported punctually enough, proceeded to lose their way, with the result that we arrived at the front line an hour late. I hurriedly reported to the colonel in charge of the sector, who did not seem to know much more about the terrain than I did myself. He handed over to me several boxes of Mills bombs, which I afterwards discovered had not been primed and were quite useless, and told me that the Turks were in considerable strength and that for the last week his men had been having a very bad time. Nobody seemed to know exactly where the bridge was and what with this, the lateness of the hour (dawn was already breaking) and the fact that I only had about seventy men under my command, I began to be a little depressed and was not made any happier by the news that our supporting guns had not arrived. It seems that their guides had also lost their way!

I went forward to make some sort of a reconnaissance leaving Merlin Huth to bring up the company. Unfortunately there was little to see except that for the first few hundred yards we should be in broken ground where we should be invisible from the enemy, after which on our main front we would have to emerge on a flat plain about 600 yards short of the Turkish trenches. On our right flank bordering the river the broken ground continued and I ordered Huth to take a section and probe this as far as he could. It was now broad daylight and as the supporting barrage, which we had been promised, failed to materialise our situation could hardly be described as reassuring.

It would be convenient here to refer to Hammerton's description of the operations which had been proceeding on the other side of the Jordan, and I fear that these too had been a flop. The idea had been to destroy the enemy force at Shunet Nimri, a few miles east of the bridge of Ghoraniyeh, and reoccupy Es Salt pending relief by Lawrence and his Arabs. The 60th Division was again involved, with the assistance of a mounted division. All went well at first and the 60th succeeded in occupying the outskirts of Shunet Nimri, but found themselves unable to proceed any further in the face of stubborn opposition. The mounted troops moved northwards round the right of the Shunet Nimri position and succeeded in capturing Es Salt, leaving an Australian brigade to protect their left flank, but in the early morning of the 1st May this brigade was heavily attacked by a Turkish cavalry division supported by infantry, which had crossed during the night from the west bank of the Jordan over a bridge, which I fear may have been the one I had been supposed to destroy. The Australians and in turn the troops at Es Salt and Shunet Nimri were forced to withdraw and in fact only got away with the utmost difficulty, several of their guns and part of their transport having to be abandoned in the process. Thus, although by the 4th May they managed to re-cross the Jordan with very little loss, there can be no disputing the fact that the raid, if you can call it that, was as much a reverse as the earlier one on Amman.

Directly we emerged on to the plain we came under heavy rifle and machine gun fire and began to sustain casualties, which we could not afford if we were going to do anything about that wretched bridge which we had not seen yet, and in fact never did see. I do not know how long we continued to make any progress but as the Turkish fire increased, not only from the front but the flanks as well, supported by shrapnel from their guns, it became obvious that we could not go on much longer. I sent a runner to Huth on my right to tell him to hold his ground as long as he could, and from his position in the broken ground help to cover our withdrawal in the centre, and another runner to my two Lewis gun teams on our left with instructions to do the same. The first runner was killed before he could deliver his message and in the event Huth and his remaining men only got away by the skin of their teeth. The Lewis gunners put up a great performance and continued firing up to the last possible moment. By now we were in a pretty bad way in the centre, and all the men in my leading section had been killed or wounded. I managed to work out some sort of orders for our general withdrawal by stages which, were splendidly carried out. Unfortunately it was at this critical moment that I was knocked head over heels like a rabbit by a bullet which passed through my left forearm fracturing both the bones. It made a bit of a mess but I was helped by two of my men who converged on me from different directions and refused to leave my side until they had brought me safely back to cover. The interesting thing about this is that they were the black sheep of the company, constantly getting into trouble and being punished for one offence or another. I had cursed them many times before but on this occasion they had my fervent blessing. Meanwhile the Turks were scrambling from their trenches in the hope, I suppose, of delivering the coup de grace, but our guns had arrived at last and although they had not been able to help us in our advance they put down a very effective barrage to cover our retreat. So ended an operation which I do not think could ever have succeeded, even if we had managed to get within bombing distance of the Turks, bearing in mind that the bombs we were carrying were nothing more than useless lumps of metal. It was a sad day. A third of the company had been killed or wounded and to make matters worse several of the latter had been taken prisoner.

I had supposed that our failure to carry out our task would not go down very well with my superiors and was more than relieved when I received in hospital a few days later a very kind and encouraging letter from Major Robin Buxton, now commanding the battalion, which showed that my fears on this score were quite unfounded.

After getting back to the front line about two hours after leaving it we rested for some time, but as the day wore on it was decided that the walking wounded should make their way to the nearest dressing station which was some distance to the rear, and leaving Huth in command of the company, I accompanied them. It was a slow and painful journey, but eventually we arrived at a cluster of bell tents, which were occupied by an Australian medical unit which treated us with the utmost kindness and efficiency. In those days it was usual for the anti-tetanus injection to be made in the stomach, and I remember the M.O. standing over the bed on which I was lying and struggling to reach me with his needle through a horde of buzzing flies, which, as I have already described, presented an almost insoluble problem in the Jordan Valley, even under conditions which were made as hygienic as possible. Quite rightly no attempt was made to dress our wounds and in fact it was not until three days later that I had my bandages removed for the first time. The next stage in my journey was by cacolet and I remember that I occupied one of the stretchers and my sergeant major the other. At the next dressing station we became separated and my last link with the men with whom I had been serving for the last two years was severed, apart from those who were able to come and see me in hospital in Alexandria when they were on leave.

From there I proceeded on a led horse and some time in the evening arrived at the main casualty clearing station where I remained for some time before joining up with a convoy of motor ambulances which took us to a hospital in Jerusalem where we arrived about midnight. My particular ambulance had no lights and the driver had only the tail-lights of the one in front and the head-lights of the one behind to guide him on that precipitous and winding road so that it was a rather hair-raising experience.

I only spent one night in Jerusalem and on the following day was conveyed to the railway station, from where several of us accomplished the next part of the journey in a closed wagon, the floor of which was covered in straw. Incidentally it is curious to reflect that, although during the last six weeks I had passed twice through Jerusalem and spent one night there, I had scarcely seen the place at all or, so far as I can remember, any of its inhabitants.

21. Alexandria

The second and third nights we spent at successive field hospitals and it was on the latter occasion that my bandages were removed for the first time and my wound dressed. By then I was beginning to feel decidedly the worse for wear as I had lost a quantity of blood and was still doing so. However, we were now to experience the comparative comfort of a hospital train and we spent the fourth night in another field hospital at Kantara on the canal. On the following morning we crossed the canal and travelled on another hospital train to Alexandria, which we reached late that night, and were finally accommodated in a large base hospital after a journey which had lasted five days since I and my companions, all of whom came from different units, had become casualties. I must confess that after the wonderful treatment we had received all the way down the line we found the base hospital a somewhat impersonal and comfortless place. We were told that as it was so late our wounds would not be examined until the morning. As, however, mine had obviously turned septic I insisted on having immediate attention, and after removing the bandages the nurse hurriedly fetched a doctor who did whatever was necessary.

I remained in that hospital for three months and I can truthfully say that never throughout the whole of my service with the army had we been so badly fed. In fact we were half starved and it was quite obvious that we were not even getting the rations to which we were entitled. Any of us who were able to get out for the day used to come back laden with various forms of cooked meats from the shops in Alexandria, which were eaten with relish but, of course, in the early days very few of us were able to get out. When you got to know them the nursing and medical staff turned out to be very decent people, but obsessed by regulations which always seem to become more and more disregarded the nearer you get to the front line. And I suppose that anyway it was a bit of a bore for them being stuck at a base hospital although it had its advantages. But I shall always remember one ward sister with gratitude and affection. It is rare, indeed, when one is having a rather painful dressing to look up and see that the sister in charge is silently crying. I have long since forgotten her name, but I think she loved us all and we certainly loved her.

During the whole of that time I and my little party of travelling companions from Jordan remained together in the same ward - with one exception. He was an infantry officer who had been wounded, though not too badly in the foot. But for some reason the wound went wrong from the start, and not long after we reached Alexandria his foot had to be amputated. But the operation was too late and it soon became necessary for him to undergo a second operation, when his leg was amputated above the knee. But once again the poison had spread too fast and after another short interval his leg was removed at the hip. Three major operations in two months! He was in a room by himself across the corridor and his sufferings were almost unendurable. We were on the same hospital ship a month after his last operation and I remember that he had lost four stone and looked like a skeleton. I never discovered whether he survived or not but he was supposed to be on the way to recovery.

Those three months seemed to be very long ones. There was nothing to do and I do not remember that we were ever provided with any sort of entertainment. Some time during the first month we were enlivened by a visit from Allenby on one of his tours of inspection. He spent a long time in the ward and insisted on talking to us all and enquiring how we came to be there, what units we came from and in what particular section of the line we had been serving. He gave the appearance, and I am sure it was perfectly genuine, of really being interested in our various experiences. He was a great soldier and a great man, and I think that we were all of us proud to have served under his command.

As soon as we were able to get about we were given leave to spend the days in Alexandria, and even when this began to pall it at any rate gave us the opportunity of having a decent meal. We were made honorary members of nearly all the clubs and the standard of food was as high as ever. But there was no doubt as to our unpopularity with the Egyptians as a whole. My arm was, of course, in a sling and I was frequently jostled quite deliberately and got into the habit of taking evasive action whenever a pedestrian approached.

Unfortunately my arm refused to heal and after I had been in hospital a month it was opened up and some bone splinters which were the cause of the trouble were removed. When I was recovering from the operation an officer, who was being discharged from hospital, came up to me and throwing a couple of books on my bed said he felt sure that I could do with some literature and promptly departed. Literature! I picked them up and found that they were just about the last word in pornography. God knows where he had got them but it was notorious that there was a highly organised civilian racket going on at the time in the printing and distribution among the troops of books of this sort. In fact it had become such a scandal that an army order had just been published to the effect that any officer or man found in possession of any pornographic material would be court martialled. I decided that there were two things I had to do, first read them, and secondly get rid of them as quickly and effectively as possible! The first part of the programme was relatively easy but the second was not. The only suitable receptacle in more ways than one was the loo. There were four of these together, at the end of the corridor which led to the business end of the floor, where during the day-time there were always a number of doctors and nurses going about their lawful business, in addition to which the loos, none of which worked properly, were generally occupied. It would have been relatively simple if only one journey had been necessary but this was far from being the case and for several nights running I crept furtively along the corridor and disposed of as many pages as I could, but not as many as I would have liked on account of the poor flushing and consequent tendency of the drains to become blocked. Even so my nocturnal peregrinations were observed and I was forced to explain them by saying that I was suffering from a mild attack of dysentery from which I rapidly recovered after the last page had disappeared!

One look at my arm a few days after the operation was sufficient to convince the medical board that I should return to England on the next available hospital ship, which was due to call on its way from the Persian Gulf a few days later, and it was then that I was struck down by a cruel stroke of fate. I suddenly began to feel dreadfully ill and developed a high fever. The obvious explanation was malaria but blood tests proved to be negative and it was decided that I was probably suffering from a severe attack of infective jaundice (I had never heard of such a thing) and would have to be isolated. I certainly looked incredibly yellow! A final decision was to be made next day by which time, however, my temperature had dropped to normal and as I steadily continued to improve I was allowed to stay in the ward under observation for the next week. I recovered completely but on the day before I was finally cleared the hospital ship sailed and I was told that the next one was not due for another month. It was two and a half years since I had sailed from England and I was almost in despair. And as became evident later it had been malaria all the time.

The weeks dragged by but in due course the next ship arrived and twelve of us were to go on board next morning. On our arrival, however, we found that the ship was almost full with sick and wounded from the Mesopotamian campaign, and were told that only eleven of us could be squeezed in. How the matter was decided I am not quite sure but I believe we drew lots. Anyway one poor devil had to go ashore again and, while feeling desperately sorry for him, I could only thank God that I had been spared a second and even worse disappointment.

22. The Hejaz Assault Column

Here I would like to return for a moment to my companions whom I had left in the Jordan Valley three months earlier, and who were to take part in one of the more romantic and exciting episodes in the whole of the short-lived history of the Imperial Camel Corps.

Some time after the raid on Amman and the conclusion of the operations in the Jordan Valley which I have already described, Allenby came to the decision that the main body of the Camel Corps should be disbanded. Camels were hardly suitable for the sort of country over which any future advance would have to be made and in any case he was in need of the additional cavalry which the Camel Corps could supply. Although, however, most of them were to go to stiffen the newly arrived Indian cavalry brigades Allenby acceded to Lawrence's request that a detachment of 300 men and 400 camels should be loaned to him for operations against and beyond the Hejaz railway. This was placed under the command of Major Buxton, who was later promoted to Lieutenant-Colonel and awarded the D.S.O. Laurence Moore went in charge of signals and I propose to give an account of the operations which followed in his own words.

We rode back through Jericho and Jerusalem, over the Judaean hills, through Beersheba and across the Sinai desert to our base at Ismailia on the Suez Canal, where we were to refit and change our camels. The remaining 3000 camels were to be presented to Lawrence and we thought we might as well select the best for ourselves before we followed them.

We picked up extra ammunition and large supplies of explosives to take with us and trekked over the south eastern lobe of the Sinai Peninsula through Nakhl to Akaba. Lawrence came out to meet us and rode the last day in our company during which he warned us of the kind of greeting we might expect on our arrival. In spite of his warning, however, we were not quite prepared for what actually happened. There were thousands of Arabs milling around on foot, on horse, on camel, all of them blazing away with their rifles into the air in what Lawrence called a feu de joie, but which we thought a shocking waste of small arms ammunition brought across the Mediterranean at considerable risk by the Royal and Merchant Navies. Several bullets came uncomfortably close and, when we eventually halted, some of the men found bullet holes clean through their solar topees. This probably was one of the reasons why some of the British troops in that sector subsequently discarded them in favour of a khaki Arab headcloth which presented no target above the skull. Later on we went to swim in the sea, the Gulf of Akaba, while the Arabs sat on the shore taking pot shots in our direction with the bullets pinging and splashing all round our heads. When we mildly remonstrated they said that they were protecting us by driving off the sharks!

Lawrence gave us another talk after our arrival and explained that the Arabs of Arabia were quite different – more independent and tougher – from those in Egypt or the Western Desert and he begged us, whatever happened and however provocative or aggressive they might appear to be, not to show any signs of annoyance or fear but rather to 'turn the other cheek'. He asked us this, he said, not only because of our western understanding but because they were so many and we were so few. That night, as usual, we 'formed square' a useful formation, with the camels on the outside, saddlery on the inside and men inside that. The camels kept off the cold wind of the desert and would help protect us against a sudden sandstorm or the odd stray bullet. There were no enemy within 100 miles so we lighted up our fires, and there were many because the Camel Corps always messed in groups of four. Meanwhile the bullets continued to whistle over our heads as the Arabs capered around and cracked away with their rifles. If anybody interferes with the tea-making process of the British soldier there is usually a pretty violent re-action and, when eventually one or two of the tea billies were punctured by the flying bullets, a couple of our men picked up some Mills bombs and were on the point of sailing into the Arabs when Lawrence arrived on the scene and restrained them. He stood in the middle of the square, flung back his aba, showing his white undergarment and, illumined by the countless fires, raised his hand. Immediately the firing ceased, the hubbub died down and we had a peaceful night.

It was either that night or the next that Lawrence asked Major Buxton for permission to address the men and explain why he had sent for us, a most unusual experience during World War One, when it was only on very rare occasions for a commander to take the troops into his confidence. The Arabs, he said, would sit on the hilltops taking pot shots at the enemy but they would not tackle strongly fortified positions. Also they would never attack in the dark and, unless we assaulted some of the Turkish positions during the hours of darkness, we would have no chance of surprising them. He had told the Arabs that we were the bravest soldiers in the world and he begged us to live up to the reputation he had built up for us because, he went on to say, if we did fail in any of our attacks the Arabs might well interfere with our retreat. They would certainly snipe at us from the hilltops and deny us the use of their wells.

He also begged us, as soon as we captured a Turkish position, to clear out and leave it to the Arabs whose principal interest in war was loot. We rather chuckled at this because some of the Camel Corps lads were pretty quick and handy with loot themselves, particularly if there was any liquor around, which only occurred if there had been some German officers in the position. We were also on the look out for certain articles of equipment such as Zeiss or Goertz binoculars and prismatic compasses, Luger automatic pistols, Mauser telescopic sights and a rather natty line in bivouac sheets, which were very popular with the Turkish officers. The Arabs on the other hand looked for, in descending order, horses - preferably mares - camels, sheep or goats and, failing any of these, women. I do not remember that we were ever able to provide them with any of the latter!

The following day we went out to do our first job for Lawrence, which was to capture and destroy the Turkish fortress at Mudowra, roughly half way along the railway line between Damascus and Medina, and a watering point for the locomotives. If we could destroy the pumping station we could put the line out of action for a very long time. We marched out of Akaba with Lawrence at the head of the column and his bodyguard, forty hand picked Arabs from different tribes, whom we naturally called 'The Forty Thieves'. They were most handsomely caparisoned with fancy waistcoats, stripes and polka dots, their hair perfumed, greased and ringleted, quite desperate characters really but faithful in their service to Lawrence.

I rode with them most of the way until we reached the watering place at Rumm. The spring was in reality nothing more than a trickle of water percolating through a layer of porous or fissured rock on a shelf about 300 feet up an almost vertical cliff, and all the water had to be collected up there and lowered to the ground in canvas buckets. It took us more than thirty hours to water our 400 camels. Meanwhile Lawrence went off for two days with Buxton and some of the other officers including my company commander, Captain Joe Lyall, all dressed up as Arabs but with rifles under their cloaks, to reconnoitre the position of Mudowra and, while they were away, some trouble arose at the spring. Some of our men called down and asked me to come up and help with some Arabs who were chivvying them off the shelf with the risk of a horrible fall. I clambered up and asked the Arabs what it was all about and announced that I was in the service of the Sherif Feisal. They took one look at me and said 'Min Int?' (Who are you?). In perfect truth I replied 'Ismi Hurrence,' (My name is Laurence) and when I saw their look of incredulity I quickly added 'Ahu Hurrence' (the brother of Lawrence). At least, I thought, I am his brother in arms! None of them apparently had ever seen Lawrence but eventually they found a little chap at the back who claimed that he had, and they dragged him forward and confronted him with me. He took one look and announced 'Yea, the same mad blue eyes, the same red face. Verily this is the brother of Lawrence'. There was immediate peace, and it was amazing to us that the very mention of Lawrence's name to a crowd of Arabs, who had never seen him but only heard of his reputation, could produce such a moving effect. It transpired later that they were a sub-clan of the Amran/Howeitat, the local tribe to whose Sheikh we had paid 100 golden sovereigns for permission to water from the 'spring'.

Lawrence warned us to drink deeply of the waters of Rumm because, if we failed at Mudowra, the Howeitat would forbid us the use of their water on the way back. So it was up to us to succeed as this was the only hope of our next drink. Fortunately the tactical plan, which had been drawn up by Buxton, worked perfectly and the operation was a complete success. We approached the strongly fortified positions from the rear in complete darkness during the early hours of the morning and, when daylight came, we had captured nearly the whole position except for one redoubt, a natural hill surmounted by stone sangars. Protected as it was by one or two field guns and several heavy machine guns it was a bit too tough for our small raiding party, which had been sent out to make a diversion from the front, to take by assault. However, Lawrence provided for this. When the light was good a couple of planes of the Hejaz flight came over and I had the job of controlling what must have been one of the first ever ground to-air-controlled bombardments. We had no radio so the planes spoke to me in Morse by Klaxon horn, and I was able to tell them where I was by smoke bomb and put out letter signals by prearranged code. After the planes had each dropped, from almost ground level, a couple of sixty pound bombs on to the stony Northern Redoubt, the Turks came streaming out, waving any dirty rag that could serve as a white flag, and I gave the planes the signal 'Cease Fire'.

Our prisoners outnumbered ourselves and, as we obviously could not spare anyone to escort them, they had to be taken back to Akaba by the Arabs. Lawrence knew perfectly well that, if he paid the Bedouin in advance, they would march the prisoners behind the nearest hill and shoot the lot, so they were paid at the rate of one pound in gold for each prisoner who arrived at Akaba alive, which they all did. The Turkish officers strongly objected to this arrangement, but they had to put up with it.

The nearest Field Ambulance was back in Akaba, and our wounded had a most gruelling journey. Captain Lyall, who was badly hit by what was almost the last shot in the action as he was conducting his prisoners from the Southern Redoubt over the 300 yards or so of open ground to the station buildings, told me later that, after some three days of painful progress in the blistering heat, they were all in a bad way, but a plane came over and dropped a note telling them to camp where they were until R.A.F. trucks arrived to pick them up and take them on to a rough landing ground, where they arrived about midnight. Next day they were carried to Akaba, but some of them did not survive. One of those who died just as he reached the hospital was my friend Corporal Jack Freeman, who was posthumously awarded the D.C.M.

Meanwhile, after handing over the captured rifles and S.A.A. to the Arabs, we threw the field guns with their ammunition into the well and blew up the whole lot, together with the pumps and other machinery, generally making a complete wreck of the place. One of our demolition experts was Bimbashi Peake of the Egyptian Army, later to become famous as Peake Pasha*, founder of the Jordanian Arab Legion. Afterwards we rode up the railway line for several miles, blowing up every bridge and culvert on the way. (In point of fact, although the well at Mudowra, which later became a fort of the Arab Legion under Glubb Pasha, must have been reconstructed, and parts of the line further to the north have certainly been repaired, I do not believe that a single train has passed through Mudowra since that day, and even the Arab historians agree that the line was not completely severed until by the Imperial Camel Corps in August, 1918.) And then at last, as the dusk came, we turned towards the east and melted into the desert night and I must confess that it was quite a thrill, as our camels daintily picked their way over the metals, to realise that we were indeed a British force at large behind the enemy lines.

We rode about 100 miles east, then about the same distance to the north, and finally we turned west towards the railway again. To avoid the Turkish or rather German planes we moved only during the hours of darkness. In the daylight and moonlight we lay up in the cracks and crannies of the various wadis. We could move only at the walk, about three miles per hour, because of the enormous loads of ammunition and explosives, which we had to carry with us, so it all took a long, long time.

During one the midday halts Arthur Collins (who was responsible for keeping track of the gold we paid to the Arabs for water, guides or other services) and I were seeking what shelter we could find from the glaring sun under an army blanket strung across some of my signal flags, when we suddenly observed that an Arab, armed with a rifle, was apparently stalking Lawrence, who was himself sheltering under a similar contraption a few yards away and reading as usual. As we caught sight of him the Arab flattened out to take aim and I grabbed for a gun but he beat me to it and fired. The bullet sent up a flurry of sand and feathers about a yard from where Lawrence lay and the Arab calmly walked forward and picked up the shattered remnants of a small sand grouse, which he had blown to bits, and carried them away. Lawrence merely raised his head for a moment and then resumed his reading. We agreed that it was a most fortunate occurrence that the Arab, who turned out to be one of Lawrence's bodyguard, had beaten me to the draw. Otherwise there might have been severe repercussions leading to an international, or rather inter allied crisis!

One night we were halted and told we were just east of the railway at Kissela, five miles south of Amman, where lay our second objective, the very same viaduct and tunnel complex against which we had failed, from the other or western side, the previous March. Lawrence had persuaded Allenby that, where a whole division and more had a few months earlier failed in a frontal attack, a handful of determined men properly equipped, each one an expert in his own job, might succeed if they could attack by the back door. And here we were, within three miles of our former position on the other side of the railway line, although we had ridden rather more than 1000 miles to get there.

In the result, however, we were to be disappointed. By now,

owing to casualties and other reasons, our effective strength had been reduced to less than 200 and reconnaissance established the fact that a Turkish cavalry regiment was actually stabling its horses in the very viaduct we were to blow up, so that although we were confident that we could overcome them Lawrence and Buxton decided that we would be unable to do so in sufficient time before heavy reinforcements arrived from Amman, and with deep regret the whole affair was called off. So once again Amman defeated us.

Lawrence then announced that he had orders from Allenby that, in the event of our being unable to demolish the viaduct, we were to make the Turks aware of our presence and give them the impression that we were a much larger force than in fact we were. This we did in many ways. First of all every man opened three or four tins of bully beef, which was the only food that ever arrived with the caravans, and destroyed or burnt the contents leaving the tins lying about. This was no particular sacrifice because we found it impossible to eat it in that savage heat and the Arabs never ate it anyway. We lighted fires, making a great deal of noise in the process, the light cars were ordered to criss-cross the desert in every direction to make a lot of tracks, and we dropped the camel dung, which we carried for our fires, to add to our camels' normal droppings and give the impression that we had with us three or four times the number of camels which would be required by a relatively small raiding party such as in fact we were. My own contribution was to scribble some meaningless rubbish on army signal forms and leave them scattered around. And then once more we melted away into the eastern desert, with the Turkish cavalry probing cautiously behind us. It is worth mentioning here that the Arabs very rarely fed their camels on hard corn so that their droppings were easily distinguished from those of our own camels, which contained grains of dhurra, a kind of millet. Since the whole object was to deceive the enemy into thinking that the Camel Corps was present in considerable strength we had to confine ourselves to the latter.

Some days later, after dividing into small groups scattered over a wide front, so that any aerial reconnaissance by the enemy would find it difficult to calculate our numbers, we arrived at the oasis and fort of Azrak, where we bathed in the springs, and there occurred the sort of unfortunate incident which had always seemed just around the corner, so to speak, but had never actually happened until now. While we were watering, Lieutenant Rowan, of our No. 7 Company, momentarily forgot the advice given by Lawrence to 'turn the other cheek'. The Arabs as usual were chivvying our fellows off the watering point. I was close to Rowan★ at the time and saw and heard him raise his sjambok and curse them in what we used to call Cairo Arabic. The Arabs muttered and slunk away and a little later there was a shot from the rim of the crowd which killed him instantly. Lawrence referred to this incident in Seven Pillars of Wisdom and said that it was an accident caused by an Arab, who had dropped his rifle, while shooting fish in the fort pool, but I cannot help the feeling, which is shared by my comrades who were there at the time, that it would have been virtually impossible for a bullet from a dropped rifle to have killed a man standing on a plinth with his head above the rest of the crowd some fifty feet away, and that the incident may have had a more sinister explanation, which might have been omitted for reasons of political expediency!

In due course we returned to the railway and engaged in various diversions and demolitions in the vicinity of Maan, which has held by a full division of Turkish troops, until at last we arrived at the Headquarters of the Sherif Feisal (later King of Iraq) at Abu el Lissan, where he reviewed us with his G.O.C. Jafar Pasha, who had been captured by the Dorset Yeomanry

AUTHOR'S NOTE: Rowan was the intelligence officer at Battalion H. Q. who had told us the previous March, mistakenly as it turned out, that the Turks had no artillery at Amman, and had a few weeks later woken me in the early hours of the morning with orders from H. Q. to take my company down to the Jordan and destroy the bridge which formed part of the Turkish lateral lines of communication. Some time after I had returned to England I heard, though I have forgotten from what source, that Rowan had been killed by an Arab. Nothing was said about an accident.

during a charge against the Senussi, and had subsequently been released after the Arab revolt to take command of their 'regular' army. We understood that we were to receive a Hejaz medal, but it never materialised!

After we left Abu el Lissan we made an expedition, again and for the last time led by Lawrence, to the famous gorge at Petra and returned from there to one of our bases at Beersheba, where our camels had a long awaited graze and rest, the first for many months. So ended our operations in the Hejaz though our second in command, Lord Winterton, remained behind with Feisal and Lawrence and he accompanied the latter on the subsequent Arab march to Deraa and the capture of Damascus, as related in Seven Pillars of Wisdom which, among its many illustrations includes drawings of Lord Winterton and Colonel Buxton. Lord Winterton was a very tall man and his height was accentuated by his extreme leanness. He was also a very brave one. There was an occasion when he was standing up on a parapet observing with his glasses and in full view of the enemy. Bullets were spattering all round and the men behind him were imploring him to come down or he would get pipped to which he replied 'They'll not pip me, I'm too d—— d thin'!

A few days later Allenby launched his final and overwhelming offensive which was to put the Turks out of the war and cause them to sue for an armistice, and it is no exaggeration to say that he was helped by the fact that, because the Turks were misled into thinking that the whole of the Imperial Camel Brigade was present in the Hejaz, they substantially reinforced the Amman-Maan area, thus weakening their main front in Palestine.

It would, I think be helpful if I were to supplement the above account with some further details I have received from Laurence Moore, Captain Lyall and others, commencing with the text of the relevant Operations Order issued by the General Staff, Hejaz Operations, Savoy Hotel, Cairo, on the 16th July, 1918, and addressed as follows to Major R.V. Buxton, O.C., I.C.C.

Two Companies Imperial Camel Corps (Commander Maj. R. V. Buxton with sixteen officers, 300 other ranks, 400 camels, six Lewis guns) have been placed at the disposal of Hejaz Operations for the purpose of these operations on the Hejaz Railway:

(a) To seize Mudowra with the primary object of destroying the enemy's valuable water supply.

(b) To destroy the main railway bridge and tunnel at Kissela, 5 miles south of Amman, or if circumstances render (b) impracticable, which will be decided solely at the discretion of O.C., I.C.C. then

(c) To demolish the rail bridge north of Jurf ad Derwish and destroy the enemy's supply dumps and wells at Jurf station.

All operations will be night attacks. Precise plan to be decided by O.C., I.C.C. after personal reconnaissance of the positions. Stress is laid on the value of surprise, the Turks in the Hejaz being hitherto unaccustomed to attack by night. Artillery support during the operation against Mudowra will be provided by the Hejaz ten-pounder section. This section will not proceed east of the Railway but will return to Guweira. Bombing support by aeroplanes of the Hejaz Flight. Ground/air signal code to be agreed at Akaba. For the operation against Kissela, a detachment of armoured cars to be held in readiness to cover the retirement of the column to Bair in the event of pursuit by hostile cavalry from Amman. SUPPLIES: O.C. Troops, Hejaz to arrange dumps, at Rumm, 5 days rations for men and forage for animals, at El Jefer, 4 days rations and forage and at Bair, 14 days rations and forage. WATER: plentiful drinking water for men and camels at Rumm, Mudowra, Jefer, Bair, Wadi Dakhl. MEDICAL: A casualty hamla with cacolets for 12 sitting and lying cases to accompany column organised by Maj. Marshall M.C., R.A.M.C. Scheme for evacuation of casualties to be prepared by Maj. Marshall. AMMUNITION: 260 S.A.A. per man, 2000 rounds per Lewis gun will be carried. EXPLOSIVES: An explosive hamla with 7,500 lbs. of gun-cotton will accompany column from Akaba to Mudowra and return to Akaba. For the Kissela operation, a hamla with 6000 lbs. of gun-cotton will meet column at Bair. GUIDES: O.C. Northern Hejaz will arrange, through Sherif Feisal, guides from the Amran Howeitat to conduct the column to Rumm. A suitable Sherif, selected by Sherif Feisal (if available Sherif Hazaar or Sherif Fahad), with guides from the Abu Tayi will join column at Rumm and conduct from thence to Mudowra and then to El Jefer. Guides from Jefer to Kissela will be arranged, on his arrival, by Lt. Col. Lawrence. ATTACHED OFFICERS: Political Officer for liaison with Arabs: Maj. Marshall R.A.M.C. (in addition to duties as M.O.). Demolitions: Capt. Scott Higgins or Bimbashi Peake, L.A. Staff Officer as far as Jefer only: Maj. Stirling D.S.O., M.C.

The station at Mudowra was covered by three Redoubts, the Northern, Central and Southern and, apart from medical services under Major Marshall and H.Q. under Major Buxton, the assault column was divided into six parties of which two were to sever the telegraph line and blow up the rails a mile or so to the north and south of the station. Of the remainder one party under Captain Lyall, who was awarded the M.C. for his part in the action, was to attack the Southern Redoubt, another under Lieutenant W. T. Davies of No. 10 Company, who was also awarded the M.C., was to attack and capture the main station buildings and blockhouses, another under Captain Bell-Irving of No. 7 Company was to attack the Central Redoubt, and a small raiding party under a subaltern of No. 7 Company was to create a diversion in front of the strongly held Northern Redoubt while the other parties attacked from the rear.

The assault started with a demonstration from the west to confuse the enemy and signals from the demolition parties. Then at 4 a.m. assaults were launched against the station and Southern Redoubt. Davies and his party crawled round the stone buildings throwing Mills bombs through the windows before going in with their bayonets, and very soon captured the position. The Turkish trumpeter was shot just as he was raising the instrument to his lips to sound the alarm. (The trumpet was taken by Davies as a souvenir and used to call guests to dinner at Camel Corps reunions.) The attack on the Southern Redoubt was equally successful. Crouching under the sangars the assault party threw their bombs over into the Turks, many of whom were still asleep, before also going in with their bayonets. One of the casualties sustained by No. 10 Company during this attack was Lieutenant J. W. Jones who was killed. By first light the Central Redoubt had also been captured by Captain Bell-Irving and his party, but the Northern Redoubt was still putting up a stout resistance, and it was not subdued until it was bombed from the air, as described by Moore. Most of the Turkish gunners had been killed at their posts. In the meantime the Lewis gunners had fired up a captured heavy machine gun on the flat station roof and a Turkish patrol, coming from the south to investigate the failure of Mudowra to reply to any signals, was greeted with bursts of fire from their own guns. Before it had time to recover its wits some of the assault party grabbed their rifles, jumped on their camels, which had been off saddled, and literally galloped out bareback to round up the bewildered Turks and bring them in as prisoners.

While all this was going on Major Marshall had set up an aid post in what seemed to be an old Roman Temple. During the day messages had to be 'run' and Moore, who was in charge of signals 'borrowed' the Turkish Commandant's Arab stallion to speed things up a bit. Just before the attack on the Northern Redoubt some delay had been caused by the apparent inability on the part of two of the signallers, newly trained and a little inexperienced, to give the correct messages from the station, which was now being used by Buxton as his H.Q., for the aerial bombing raid to begin. One of Moore's signallers, Corporal Fox, volunteered to go over himself to see what was causing the hold-up. Although the intervening 300 yards or so was quite flat and swept by enemy machine gun fire he made the crossing unhurt and within seconds his messages were coming through and Moore was able to pass on the order 'Bomb Northern Redoubt'.

There is no doubt that the capture and destruction of Mudowra was a great achievement. Captain Gilman, who was in command of the Hejaz Armoured Car Battery, has related how Feisal was so delighted with the victory that he decided to give a special celebration for the Camel Corps at Jefer, where he and Lawrence were waiting to greet them on their return. A large bonfire of brushwood was collected and at the appointed time Feisal, Lawrence and all the British officers took up their positions on rugs and the 'orgy' began. It was a sort of war dance by the Arabs, who dashed through the flames rolling over and over round the fire to the accompaniment of rhythmic chanting and firing of rifles in the air, until finally they had worked themselves up into a frenzy. Of course, there was a great feast which continued for hours after Feisal had decided that it was time for him and his guests to retire from the scene. Gilman could hear from his tent the celebration going on into the small hours which, he was told, was a most exceptional occurrence and a great honour to the guests. Even Lawrence said that he had never before witnessed such a spectacle in Arabia, and it was really put on for the benefit of the British as the victors of an operation in which the Arabs had not themselves taken any part. Among his decorations Gilman, who had originally gone to France with the H.A.C. in September, 1914, was awarded the Order of el Nahda by Feisal's father, the old King Hussein, for his services during the Hejaz campaign.

All that remains is to direct anybody who may be interested to Book IX - Balancing for a Last Effort - of Lawrence's wonderful Seven Pillars of Wisdom, which was first published for general circulation by Jonathan Cape in 1935. This is the edition to which I am referring and which also contains on pages 544 and 582 illustrations of Buxton and Lord Winterton. Perhaps, however, I may be permitted to quote the following extract from Chapter CIV:

> I had reached this useful stage when there was a disturbance from the Toweiha tents. Shouting men ran towards me. I pulled myself together to appease a fight between the Arabs and the Camel Corps, but instead it was an appeal for help against a Shamrmar raid two hours since, away by the Snamirat. Eighty camels had been driven off. Not to seem wholly ungracious, I put on our spare camels the four or five of my men whose friends or relatives had suffered, and sent them off.

> Buxton and his men started in the mid-afternoon while I delayed till evening, seeing my men load our six thousand pounds of gun-cotton on the thirty Egyptian pack-camels. My disgusted bodyguard were for this ride to lead or drive the explosives' train.

> We had judged that Buxton would sleep just short of the

Hadi, so we rode thither; but saw no camp-fire, nor was the track trodden. We looked over the crest of the ridge, into a bitter north wind coming off Hermon into our flustered faces. The slopes beyond were black and silent, and to us town-dwellers, accustomed to the reek of smoke, or sweat, or the ferment of soil freshly dug, there was something searching, disquieting, almost dangerous, in the steely desert wind. So we turned back a few paces, and hid under the lip of the ridge to sleep comfortably in its cloistered air.

In the morning we looked out across fifty miles of blank country, and wondered at this missing our companions: but Daher shouted suddenly from the Hadi side, seeing their column winding up from the south-east. They had early lost the track and camped till dawn. My men jested with humour against Sheikh Saleh, their guide, as one who could lose his road between the Thlaithukhwat and Bair: just like one might say between the Marble Arch and Oxford Circus.

However, it was a perfect morning, with the sun hot on our backs, and the wind fresh in our faces. The Camel Corps strode splendidly past the frosted tips of the three peaks into the green depths of Dhirwa. They looked different from the stiff, respectful companies which had reached Akaba, for Buxton's supple brain and friendly observation had taken in the experience of irregular fighting, and revised their training rules for the new needs.

He had changed their column formation, breaking its formal subdivision of two hard companies: he had changed the order of march, so that, instead of their old immaculate lines, they came dotted, in groups which split up or drew together without delay upon each variation of road or ground surface. He had reduced the loads and rehung them, thereby lengthening the camel's pace and daily mileage. He had cut into their infantry system of clockwork halts every so often (to let the camels stale!) and grooming was less honoured. In the old days, they had prinked their animals, cosseting them like Pekinese, and each halt had been lightened by the noisy flapping massage of the beasts' stripped humps with the saddle-blanket; whereas now the spare time was spent in grazing.

Consequently, our Imperial Camel Corps had become rapid, elastic, enduring, silent; except when they mounted by numbers, for then the three-hundred he-camels would roar in concert, giving out a wave of sound audible miles across the night. Each march saw them more workmanlike, more at home on the animals, tougher, leaner, faster. They behaved like boys on holiday, and the easy mixing of officers and men made their atmosphere delightful. My camels were brought up to walk in Arab fashion, that bent-kneed gait with much swinging of the fetlock, the stride a little longer and a little quicker than the normal. Buxton's camels strolled along at their native pace, unaffected by the men on their backs, who were kept from direct contact with them by iron-shod boots and by their wood and steel Manchester-made saddles.

Consequently, though I started each stage alongside Buxton in the van, I forged steadily in front with my five attendants; especially when I rode my Baha, the immensely tall, large-boned, upstanding beast, who got her name from the bleat-voice forced on her by a bullet through the chin. She was very finely bred, but bad-tempered, half a wild camel, and had never patience for an ordinary walk. Instead, with high nose and wind-stirred hair, she would jig along in an uneasy dance, hateful to my Ageyl for it strained their tender loins, but to me not un-amusing.

In this fashion we would gain three miles on the British, look for a plot of grass or juicy thorns, lie in the warm freshness of air, and let our beasts graze while we were overtaken; and a beautiful sight the Camel Corps would be as it came up.

Through the mirage of heat which flickered over the shining flintstones of the ridge we would see, at first, only the knotted brown mass of the column, swaying in the haze. As it grew nearer the masses used to divide into little groups, which swung; parting and breaking into one another. At last, when close to us, we would distinguish the individual riders, like great water-birds breast-deep in the silver mirage, with Buxton's athletic, splendidly mounted figure leading his sunburnt, laughing, khaki men.

It was odd to see how diversely they rode. Some sat naturally, despite the clumsy saddle; some pushed out their hinder-parts, and leaned forward like Arab villagers; others lolled in the saddle as if they were Australians riding horses. My men, judging by the look, were inclined to scoff. I told them how from that three hundred I would pick forty fellows who would out-ride, out-fight and out-suffer any forty men in Feisal's army.

Many other tributes were paid by Lawrence to the Camel Corps and I am proud to think that it measured up to the high standards of one who, when he did not approve of anybody or anything, never hesitated to speak his mind.

23. The End Of The Imperial Camel Corps

The Hejaz operations brought to an end the activities of that truly extraordinary institution known as the Imperial Camel Corps, although it was not until the spring of 1919 that it was finally disbanded by which time, of course, the war had been over for several months.

The Australian and New Zealand companies had already been broken up when Colonel Buxton and his men went down to Akaba to join up with Lawrence, but remnants of the five British companies stayed on until the process of demobilisation was complete.

I should like to say once more that my story has been concerned almost exclusively with the 2nd Battalion, and it is only fair to pay my tribute to the Australians and New Zealanders who greatly distinguished themselves in many engagements at which no units of the 2nd Battalion were present. Their adventures have been recounted in other books besides Oliver Hogue's The Cameliers, including With the Cameliers in Palestine by John Robertson and The Fighting Cameliers by Frank Reid which were published in New Zealand and Australia respectively, but as far as I am aware, nothing had been recorded or rather published, officially or unofficially, of the part played by the British during those three eventful years until my own writings were published.

I am indeed grateful for all the assistance I have been given by some of the survivors from those far distant campaigns, and without which neither I nor anybody else could have completed the record. There has been no regimental history because there was no regiment. The Camel Corps never at any time had any headquarters or organisation in this country for the simple reason that all who served with it were only on detachment from their various regiments, to which they reverted automatically the moment their services for any reason came to an end, unless they were posted elsewhere.

It will, I hope, be understood that without an official record to fall back on it has been a difficult task to try and reconstruct, after so long an interval, the story as it unfolded and the background against which it has to be set. In fact there was more than one background. A glance at the map will show the vast area over which the operations of the Camel Corps extended – from Sollum and Siwa in the west to Baharia, Kharga and Dahkla in the south, Beersheba, Jaffa, Jerusalem and Jericho in the north and finally Amman, Akaba, Mudowra and Azrak in the east.

The engagements of the Camel Corps are shown on its War Memorial in Thames Embankment Gardens as Romani – Baharia – Mazar – Dahkla – Maghara – El Arish – Maghdaba – Rafa – Hassana – Gaza 1 – Gaza 2 – Sana Redoubt – Beersheba – Bir Khuweilfe – Hill 265 – Amman – Jordan Valley – Mudowra – and it also records the names of all those who were killed or died of wounds or disease as follows:

1st Battalion (Australian)	7 officers	96 other ranks
2nd Battalion (British)	14 officers	86 other ranks
3rd Battalions (Australian and New Zealand)		
	9 officers	76 other ranks
4th Battalion (Australian)	1 officer	43 other ranks
M. G. Section	1 officer	5 other ranks
Hong Kong and Singapore Battery (Indian)	1 officer	8 other ranks

Which makes a total of 33 officers and 314 other ranks.

And there must, I suppose, have been at least as many who were wounded but survived.

I cannot speak for the others but, in the 2nd Battalion, in addition to Colonel Buxton who received the D.S.O., at least eight and possibly ten officers were awarded the M.C., and a number of D.C.M.s and M.M.s were also awarded to various N.C.O.s and other ranks including, in addition to Sergeant Hobbins and Corporal Freeman of No. 10 Company both of whom received the D.C.M., Sergeant-Major Guppy of No. 8 Company who also received the D.C.M., Sergeant Bolt also of No. 8 Company who received the D.C.M. and Bar in addition to his Italian decoration and Sergeant R. Coombe, Lance Corporal W. Murray and Private R. Mills, all of No. 7 Company who with Sergeant Morgan and

Private Robinson, both attached to Battalion H.Q., also received the D.C.M.

I am only too regretfully aware of the fact that there must be many omissions from my story and particularly the parts of this book which relate to the experiences of others. The Battalion was a very loosely knit organisation and, unlike in France, each company often found itself operating entirely on its own, or perhaps with one other, hundreds of miles away from the rest and with very little knowledge of what they were doing. Nonetheless we had all come from Yeomanry regiments and there was a tremendous esprit de corps so much so that, whether or not we earned our appellation in the 'poem' I have quoted as the 'Curse of Egypt' we would certainly have regarded it as a great compliment if we had, and at any rate I can truthfully say of the Camel Corps that, for better or worse, its like will never be seen again!

The last chapter came to a close two or three years later with the unveiling of the War Memorial in a quiet and secluded part of the Embankment Gardens. The ceremony, which was intensely impressive, was performed by General Sir Philip Chetwode, that great soldier who won so much renown in the Palestine campaign, and under whose overall command the Imperial Camel Corps had so often served. The very simple dedication service was conducted by the Bishop of London and a guard of honour was supplied by the Grenadier Guards.

General Chetwode, in the act of unveiling, referred to the little known and almost unrecognised services rendered by the Imperial Camel Corps in the sun-bleached wastes of the Libyan and Sinai deserts and the Hejaz and, in dedicating the Memorial to those who had made the great sacrifice, either killed in battle or the victims of cholera, malaria and dysentery, he remarked that they had come from nearly every part of the Empire and, therefore, no place could be more fitting for the creation of a monument to their memory than this little garden in the heart of its great capital, a city which was not England's alone but which was shared by every British subject as his capital city also.

Wing Commander Ashlin was one of the cameliers who were able to attend and he has described the unveiling in the following terms:

The simple ceremony and the General's address brought back vividly to the minds of those who had been there, the scorching days in the desert, weary forced marches, lack of sleep, food and especially water, sweating smelly camels and the remembrance of those gallant men whose memory was being honoured on that bright cold November day. The clear notes of the Last Post, sounding out above the noise of traffic in that ultra civilised metropolis, gave the final touch to a scene which those of us who were present will never forget.

I do not think that there is anything more to say.

24. Home Again - Marriage - Oxford

Returning to my personal story, our voyage through the Mediterranean was relatively uneventful. The ship was a converted Union Castle liner, I think the Glamorgan Castle, and was full to overflowing with sick and wounded. Our beds were so close together that there was hardly room to walk between and being mid-August it was, of course, stiflingly hot. But at any rate a hospital ship has one enormous advantage over a troop ship because, so far from having to observe a black-out we were, during the hours of darkness, a blaze of light from stem to stern, and the portholes were kept wide open in those calm seas. I was particularly lucky as my bed was in a corner and right under a porthole, and I do not remember suffering any inconvenience whatsoever from the heat. Apart from the overcrowding the ship was very comfortable, and the food superb, although this may have to some extent been by way of contrast to what had been dished out to us at the hospital. My arm was still in a splint but with regular attention and a rigorous course of massage was becoming better every day and in fact I had no more trouble with it.

There was one exciting incident. Sometime in the morning a German submarine surfaced about two miles away and proceeded for the next hour or so along a course exactly parallel to our own. We were all a little jumpy because we had been told that several hospital ships had been torpedoed recently on account of alleged (by the Germans) breaches of the Geneva Convention or of whatever rules had been imposed by the Germans if a hospital ship was to preserve its immunity. Frequently, for instance, the submarine would send a boarding party to search the ship and if it was carrying anybody or anything who or which did not conform exactly to the functions of a hospital ship the submarine would order its evacuation and give barely sufficient time for the boats to be lowered and filled before it was torpedoed. I suppose that the Germans were strictly within their rights, but it was understood that they interpreted them very strictly. However, on this occasion anyway, nothing happened, no boarding party was sent and after some time the submarine slowly submerged and we never saw it or any of its companions again.

It took us about a week to reach Marseilles and I remember the voyage as a very pleasant interlude.

We spent a day in Marseilles before embarking on the hospital train which was to take us across France to one of the Channel ports. Not unnaturally the conditions here were not nearly so comfortable as on the ship and the crowding was even worse. There were about forty officers in our coach, some of them still stretcher cases and others suffering from a variety of wounds and sickness including dysentery. There was one tiny compartment at the end of the coach which served us as a wash place and loo, and as the entire drainage system packed up on the first of the three days we spent in the train the atmosphere was indescribable.

Further along the train there was a coach filled with shell-shock cases and I am afraid that some of these poor devils were virtually insane. Although the coach was padded there seemed to be something wrong with the supervision arrangements. At any rate on the second day one of the kitchen-hands happened to be looking out of a window in the direction of the coach when he saw a man jump from the train and disappear beneath the wheels. The alarm was raised and the train brought to a standstill about half a mile further on. There then ensued what I can only describe as a tragicomedy. It seems that under French law the victim of a murder, suicide or other unnatural death cannot be removed until an inquest, or at any rate a preliminary police investigation, has been held on the spot. Unfortunately the train was passing at the time through a very secluded, and I remember very beautiful, part of the countryside, and it was difficult to obtain the presence of an official of any kind. However, the chef-du-train was adamant, and quite rightly so in view of the trouble he would have been in, that the law must be observed and the train could not proceed until the enquiry had taken place. Eventually some uniformed personage arrived on the scene, the body, or what was left of it, was inspected, statements were taken from the kitchen hand who had witnessed the occurrence and various other people, and last but not least the body was gathered up and deposited in a receptacle of some kind which was committed to the charge of the chef-du-train, with instructions to unload it at the next large town through which we passed.

212

All this caused a delay of nearly three hours and the unbelievable part of it was that we were occupying the main line, that the final push which was to topple the German armies for good and all had just started in the north, or was about to do so, and that behind us there had piled up several trains crammed with troops and guns and ammunition and so forth on their way to the front. The fury and the shouting and the general chaos, of which we were the delighted witnesses, were indescribable. A lot of hair must have been torn out that day.

Our progress, which had been slow enough as it was, became even slower as we entered every available siding to make way for the endless stream of military traffic. But the weather was lovely, the country was beautiful, and despite the discomfort of the train, most of us quite enjoyed the experience and were quite sorry when on the third evening we reached our destination at Le Havre.

We sailed that night in deteriorating weather and by the time we reached Southampton on the following morning it was raining cats and dogs and bitterly cold. I wonder why it is nearly always like this when one returns to England after a long sojourn abroad, and particularly when one has been in a warm climate. We shivered miserably in our light clothing and suffered from an acute feeling of anti-climax. The harbour was swarming with American troopships and the quays with American troops in their unfamiliar uniforms, and we stared at them as if they were visitors from another planet.

However, there was very little delay and we were soon in London.

I should mention here that we all of us wore little labels which had been provided by the medical authorities in Alexandria and Basra, and which were supposed to, and in fact did with one exception, indicate either the hospital, or type of hospital, to which we had been allocated. After all we were a mixed bag and suffering from a variety of complaints. The exception was myself and none of the doctors or nurses either in Egypt or on the ship or train had been able to throw any light on the letters P.G., which I proudly bore and nothing else on my label. Apparently they had never been seen before and caused quite an amount of interest, so much so that I was invariably addressed by everybody not by my name but by these mysterious initials. The mystery was intensified when we reached Waterloo because we had hardly drawn up at the platform when the door of the coach was thrown open by an officer who enquired as to which of us was carrying this particular label, and when I had been pointed out to him with a whoop of joy by my travelling companions, announced that I was to go with him before anybody else left the coach. It all seemed rather sinister to me, but I had no alternative and it is curious to reflect that from that moment I never saw one of those companions again.

My 'escort' led me to a small car and my apprehension was increased when I discovered that it was padded! He was singularly uncommunicative during the short journey but I was able to extract from him the information that we were on our way to No. 11 Palace Green, which at any rate solved the problem of the initials. On our arrival I was firmly ushered up the steps of what was obviously a considerable mansion, where I was greeted by a nurse who led me to an extremely well-appointed and comfortable bedroom, looking out on an immense garden. Expect for my brief and occasional visits on leave to Cairo I had not been provided with anything like this since I had left England two and a half years before and I felt singularly honoured. The nurse left me with instructions to unpack my bag (all my heavy stuff was in transit from Egypt) and get straight into bed. She returned a few moments later and enquired in a sepulchral tone whether I had got a revolver and when I told her in an equally serious tone that I never travelled without one she said that I must hand it over, and thus deprived me of my only weapon of defence in this extraordinary place. I made some fatuous remark as to whether she thought I was going to shoot her or myself, but was not surprised when this did not even draw a smile.

Soon afterwards I was brought a most delicious dinner, which was followed by a visit from the matron, who was nice but evaded all my questions as to what sort of hospital it was and why I was there and so forth.

On the following morning, I was provided, in bed, with an equally delicious breakfast, and was told I could have a bath provided that I did not speak to any other of the patients should I happen to come across one as this was strictly against the rules. I was by now becoming completely bewildered, but endeavoured to accept all these strange goings on as philosophically as I could.

In the middle of the morning there was a knock at the door and in came a procession consisting of the matron, a sister, a nurse and a most distinguished-looking gentleman with red tabs, who introduced himself as Colonel somebody or other of the R.A.M.C. I was told to get out of bed and sit on a chair in the middle of the room, after which no word was spoken but the entire party revolved slowly round my chair several times keeping their eyes steadily fixed on mine so that I had to swivel about all the time in order to maintain contact. Suddenly the colonel darted forward and gave me a paralysing blow just below the knee, which almost sent my leg up to the ceiling. This violent reaction seemed to disappoint them a little and I had the feeling that they also might be beginning to wonder what I was doing there. After various other attentions the party left, still without a word, and I was left to my own devices.

I was there for a fortnight and apart from massage for my arm I do not remember receiving any other treatment. As time went on I began to discover that No. 11 Palace Green was a hospital for severe cases of shell shock and what I suppose would now be called battle fatigue, and I longed to know what there was on my medical record which had resulted in my being sent there. I had, of course, attended several medical boards before I left Alexandria, but I was under the impression that they were concerned chiefly with the condition of my arm and my suspected jaundice. I never found the answer.

One extraordinary coincidence was that in the previous year my eldest brother, Peter, had spent a couple of months in the same hospital, but, of course, his was exactly the sort of case for which the hospital was designed.

It was a wonderful place and I could not have wished for anything more comfortable. All the 'inmates' had separate rooms where they slept and had their meals. But nobody was allowed to speak to anyone else and when we sat out in the garden no two chairs were set anywhere near each other.

I did, however, once get the chance of speaking to my next-door neighbour, who used to keep me awake at night by intoning for hours on end a dismal dirge about plum and apple jam, punctuated at intervals by an appalling yell. I asked him why he did this and he said that it was to try and prevent himself from going to sleep because if he did he invariably had the same dream, which ended in a fearful nightmare. He had been on the Salonika front and one moonlight night his battalion had made an attack on the Bulgarian trenches. They had almost reached their objective, though not without heavy casualties, when at the range of a few yards a Bulgarian soldier stood up in his trench and apparently he and my neighbour fired at each other simultaneously, the Bulgarian being killed and my neighbour unhurt. I asked why all this was so dreadful in view of the happy result and he said, 'The trouble is that in my dream the Bulgarian always gets me'. I hope that the poor man recovered.

After I had been there a week it became apparent that I was having a recurrence of the camel mange with which I had been infected during the Jerusalem campaign. I cannot imagine what the effect would have been on those in charge of this somehow very respectable institution if I had disclosed my shameful condition in addition to which I was, of course, highly contagious. Certainly I would have been summarily ejected and sent to an isolation hospital. At the same time the irritation was so acute that I had great difficulty in keeping it to myself, so to speak. At the first opportunity I had to get out for an hour or two I went to a chemist in High Street, Kensington, to whom I shall be eternally grateful, and explained my dilemma. He provided me with the hardest nail brush he could lay his hands on and a large pot of a rather evil-smelling ointment and told me first of all to scrub the 'affected parts' until they were bleeding profusely and then rub in as much of the ointment as my skin would absorb. I followed his instructions to the letter, and within two days was completely cured.

In the meantime I was gradually resuming contact with various relations and friends. I saw my father, who was still working in the city, several times and my mother came up from Devonshire and spent a fortnight at the De Vere Hotel. I remember going to several matinees with her including Chu-Chin-Chow with Oscar Asche and Lily Brayton, The Boy with W. H. Berry, The Bing Boys or The Bing Boys on Broadway with George Robey and Violet Lorraine, and As You Were with Alice Delysia, Leon Morton, Lennox Pawle and Jack Buchanan and also a marvellous drop curtain painted by H. M. Bateman. I also lunched one day at Claridge's with my brother and his wife, and explained how it was that I had been prevented from attending their wedding.

After a fortnight I left Palace Green and went to its convalescent home at a house belonging to Lord Knutsford at the top of Campden Hill, where I remained for another fortnight, at the end of which time I was granted three weeks' leave and joyfully proceeded to my home in Devonshire, where within a matter of days I received a telegram from the War Office ordering me, at the expiration of my leave, to report for duty to my regiment in Dublin of all places. This was the second line which, shortly after I had left them in January, 1916, had, much to their disgust, been deprived of their horses and issued with bicycles instead! They had hardly recovered from the shock when they were dispatched to Ireland, future reinforcements for the first line in Palestine being provided by the third line which was still in England.

As it turned out I was unable to report to Dublin or anywhere else. I had not yet finished with Egypt or, more strictly, Egypt had not yet finished with me. A week before I was due to leave home I was attacked by the Sixth Plague – 'And the Lord said unto Moses and unto Aaron, Take to you handfuls of ashes of the furnace, and let Moses sprinkle it towards the heaven in the sight of Pharaoh. And it shall become small dust in all the land of Egypt, and shall be a boil breaking forth with blains upon man and upon beast throughout all the land of Egypt.' I started with one boil or blain and within two days I had five, the forerunners of nearly fifty of these horribly painful things which were constantly recurring over the next two years. Some eventually came to a head and broke on their own, others had to be lanced and it soon became apparent that my blood was badly infected either from the septicaemia in my arm or the various bites I had received from the insect world, or a prolonged diet of chlorinated water, bully beef and tinned fruit, or a combination of all three. Anyway, a medical board was quickly convened, my instructions were cancelled and it was ordained that I should go to hospital. But here I had a wonderful piece of good fortune. The big push in France had now commenced in earnest and all the hospitals had been cleared as far as possible for the expected heavy casualties. As a special concession, therefore, I was allowed to stay at home under the supervision of our own doctor, who had to send in a report at regular intervals to the nearest military hospital.

I was still at home when the Armistice came on the 11th November, and in the following month I went to London, where I shortly afterwards became engaged to Rosemary Ilbert whose father, Arthur, was the son of a former rector of Thurlestone, the Rev. Peregrine Ilbert, and had been a close neighbour of my father in China during their bachelor days.

But Egypt, or rather Palestine, had yet another card to play. I was still in London when I became very ill indeed. The outbreak of Spanish Influenza, which was supposed to have killed more people than had died fighting, was at its height and it was virtually impossible to get hold of a nurse or for that matter a doctor. However, my father eventually secured one and he not unnaturally assumed that I was an influenza victim, and treated me, if I remember rightly, with very little more than aspirin to bring down my temperature from the 104-105 to which it climbed every night. Nothing much happened except that I got worse and worse and things began to look a bit serious. I had told the doctor of my similar attack in Alexandria, which had been diagnosed as jaundice, and by good fortune he was able to get hold of a doctor in the Indian Medical Service who came along and gave me various tests, which showed conclusively that I had malaria, and it seemed to have been purely accidental that the tests in Alexandria had been negative. After giving me 135 grains of quinine in six days, which produced a blinding headache and for a time made me stone deaf, the fever at last subsided and I began to mend. When I was well enough I returned to Devonshire, and after another outbreak of boils I was sent to hospital in Plymouth, and from there to another hospital - for tropical diseases - at Somerville College, Oxford (the only time I have stayed in a Ladies' College). A fortnight later I was discharged and demobilised nearly nine months after failing to destroy that blasted or rather unblasted bridge.

Rosemary and I were married in April and in the following March our son, Michael, was born. There had been a lot of discussion with my father as to what I was going to do and eventually it was decided rather against my will, because I wanted to start earning my living straight away, that I should go to Oxford and read law. Both my wife and I held out against this for some time, but eventually we were persuaded by the gift of a motor-car, and I need hardly say that we had a wonderful time at Oxford and never for a moment regretted the decision. I managed to find quite a nice little house in North Oxford at a fairly reasonable rent and there we repaired at the end of April, when Michael was six weeks old.

I had intended going to New College if they would have me and in fact I got as far as an interview with the Warden, the Rev. W. A. Spooner, about whose endearing habit of what the Concise

Oxford Dictionary describes as 'accidentally transposing initial letters etc. of two or more words - e.g. receipt of a blushing crow' hundreds of anecdotes have been related. He was extremely nice and had, of course, known my brother Jack before the war. There would have been a place for me but I came up against the realisation that New College was really another Winchester, and it would in some ways have been like going back to the same school after an interval of four years, during which an awful lot of things had happened. Coming away from the college I ran into Pat Brain, who had entertained us for the cricket week at his home Cwrt-y-rala in 1913, and had also been best man at my wedding, and he suggested that I should join him at Oriel where he had already been for a couple of terms. With his help I managed to secure a place, although I do not think that any rooms would have been available in College itself. However in view of my married state this was of no consequence and all was well.

Oxford was a curious place in those days. There were two classes of undergraduates, the young men who had served during the war and the younger men who had come straight up from their various public schools, and there was a wide gulf, not simply of age but of experience, between them. The younger men were finding for the first time in their lives a relative degree of freedom from control, whereas the older ones were in a sense taking a backward step. For example I was had up twice by the proctors, the first time for having a drink at the George after 9 p.m. and the second time for accosting a female in the High St. after 10 p.m. If I remember rightly I was fined two pounds for the first offence, but let off the second after it was explained that the female in question happened to be my wife.

After four years of war there was a tremendous recurrence of every sort of sporting activity and I remember such famous names as F. W. Gilligan, M. Howell, G. T. S. Stevens, R. H. Bettington and D. R. Jardine (to whom I had taught the rudiments of Winchester football six years before) at cricket, V. H. Neser, Lawton, Campbell, the Price and Waldock brothers and later G. P. S. Macpherson and the all-Scottish International three-quarter line at rugger, Cyril Tolley and Roger Wethered at golf, and Raikes, who stroked the Oxford boat and had not so long before been awarded the D.S.O. and, I believe, the M.C. as well. This was the era of the Ashton brothers from Winchester, who for some years dominated the Cambridge scene at cricket, soccer and hockey. Hubert Ashton's century against Armstrong's Australians in 1922 was something to remember although I did not have the privilege of seeing it.

Unfortunately, for obvious economic reasons, I could only afford to spend two years at Oxford instead of four and had to work very hard to obtain my law degree. My tutor was W. T. S. Stallybrass who was the Bursar of Brasenose and was later to become Vice Chancellor of the university. He was a great teacher and a man of caustic wit. I remember that I was paired with Alan Stonex, a young man of considerable athletic prowess and also a brilliant scholar, though not always a very hard-working one, for our regular tutorials. On one occasion when he had put in an essay on the subject of vicarious liability, for which he had made no preparation whatever and in consequence been forced to waffle, his paper was marked by Stallybrass as 'prolix, pretentious and prone to verbosity', a cutting but probably a very accurate description.

The car with which my father had presented me was a Calthorpe, and by way of being a sports model although I cannot remember having been able to exceed a speed of fifty m.p.h. It was not, I fear, a very good car and it was perpetually going wrong. Still we had the greatest fun with it and on the night we finished our final examinations I drove it from Oxford to the village of Kidlington where some of us were having a celebration dinner with Toby Stokoe, a golf blue and my companion on the front seat, standing up the whole way with his right leg between the spokes of the steering wheel. How we should have got back I do not know as the lights were not working, but fortunately the foreman at the garage in North Oxford where I kept the car observed or perhaps heard us going by and pursued us in his own car. Not only that but he remained at Kidlington until we had finished our celebrations and followed close behind us all the way home, so that I could drive by the light of his head lamps. I had a vague idea that they were my own but he explained it all to me in simple terms when we got back to the garage. He was that sort of man and it was that sort of evening. When I first had the car it was a nice shade of grey, but after a year I had it painted a bright canary yellow and it became quite a feature of the Oxford landscape.

However, all good things come to an end and after getting

my degree in June, 1922, I left Oxford, bought a small house at Weybridge, sold the car and became articled to a firm of solicitors in London with whom I remained for the next forty-five years. In 1923 our second son, Tony, was born, and in 1925 our daughter, Presiley.

25. War Again

The last few years had been very happy ones, but after Hitler's advent to power in 1933 it became increasingly obvious that we were only living on borrowed time. Even our holidays were overshadowed and I can remember buying a paper and reading about the murder of Dolfuss, the Austrian Chancellor. However, Munich gave a breathing space for better or worse and in the following spring I decided to take a chance and pay a long-deferred visit to Canada, with which my firm had many business associations.

I booked passages for my wife and myself on the Empress of Australia but, only a very short time before we were due to sail, she was taken over lock, stock and barrel for the official visit to Canada of the King and Queen. The royal party had originally intended to travel on H.M.S. Renown, or one of the other battle-cruisers, but the international situation had by now become so critical that she could not be spared. Arrangements were made for passengers who had booked on the Empress to be transferred to the Duchess of Richmond, and as a matter of fact we had a very pleasant and comfortable voyage. The sea was relatively calm the whole way and I particularly remember one evening when we were somewhere off the coast of Newfoundland and gradually became enveloped in a dense and icy fog. The Captain decided to stop the ship and the sea was so still that if you dropped any floatable object, such as an empty cigarette carton, over the side it would be in exactly the same spot an hour later. We retired to bed and about 6 a.m. were woken up by the engines being restarted and the usual slight throbbing throughout the ship. I drew the curtains and we looked out on to a magnificent sight. The fog had completely disappeared, a brilliant sun was shining from a cloudless sky, the sea was almost as blue as the Mediterranean and last but not least we were surrounded by icebergs, some of which we were slowly passing at a distance of only a few hundred yards. They were of all shapes and sizes, some with flat tops, others with a succession of crags and pinnacles, and there must have been thirty or forty within view at the same time. In the early morning sunshine they were indescribably beautiful. I do not know whether the story that nine tenths of every iceberg are submerged is true or not, but if so some of them must have been enormous. We hoped that we would catch sight of a stranded polar bear or seal, but even with the help of powerful binoculars we could see no sign of life.

There had been some grumbling the night before when the Captain had stopped the ship but those who had complained the loudest were quite conspicuous for their silence that morning. Indeed the mere thought of steaming through an ice-field in pitch darkness and in a dense fog (there was, of course, no radar at that time) was enough to keep anybody quiet! Apart from this and the lovely two days we spent sailing through the lower reaches of the St. Lawrence the voyage was uneventful, and we finally reached Montreal a day late on the 28th May.

Speaking for myself I had a relatively quiet war. The previous year I had joined the Officers' Emergency Reserve, but owing to my service with the Berkshire Yeomanry in the first war had been classified as 'Cavalry' and as there was, I believe, only one cavalry regiment, that is to say one equipped with horses, in existence it is hardly surprising that I was not called up. However, I took to riding again in a mild sort of way and waited on events.

In April, 1940, I went to Paris on a business trip and was amazed by what I saw or rather did not see. Calais was empty and deserted and there was no sign of any activity at all, military or otherwise. On arrival in Paris I got the impression that the whole of the French army was on leave. The hotels, restaurants and theatres were full and the food was as superb as ever. There was a black-out at night but, apart from this and the presence of uniforms everywhere, there was no sense of urgency whatever and hardly even a suggestion that there might be a war on.

This was, of course, the peak of the phoney war so rudely to be shaken only four weeks later by the invasion of France and on the 14th June by the occupation of Paris itself. My last night there I dined with a friend at his lovely flat near the Place de l'Opera. Little did either of us realise that within two months he would be flying for his life, and under dreadful conditions, along the road to Bordeaux, from where he eventually got a ship to England. Yet curiously enough during all this time dramatic and tragic events were happening in Norway, but they were making hardly any impression at all although I read an account in a French paper one morning of the exploits of H.M.S. Warspite and her attendant destroyers at Narvik and a description of the British navy as truly 'formidable'.

Shortly after Dunkirk there came the announcement of the creation of the Local Defence Volunteers, afterwards known as the Home Guard, and I helped to recruit and eventually take charge of the Chobham section, whose chief function consisted at the time of guarding the Post Office during the hours of darkness. We built a marvellous contraption of sandbags in the street and, armed with six rifles and a miscellaneous collection of pistols, shotguns, pikes and other supposedly lethal weapons, which had to be handed over every time the guard was changed, we prepared to meet the assault of any enemy force which might suddenly and miraculously emerge from round the corner on the road to Woking, notwithstanding the fact that one shell from the smallest calibre gun in existence would have blown our little collection of bags, lovingly filled with sand from Chobham Common by various ladies in the neighbourhood, to smithereens together with the unfortunate members of the Home Guard who might happen to be behind them. Plans were also laid for the ringing of the church bells in the event of the code word coming through that the Germans had landed. I must admit that after a time I became a little tired of being on duty half the night either from 8 p.m. to 1 a.m. or 1 a.m. to 6 a.m. and then having to spend the day at my office in London, so I thought I would try the War Office again who obligingly transferred me from Cavalry to Infantry, and before July was out instructed me to report to a battalion of the Royal Berkshire Regiment then at Hereford, in the guise of a second-lieutenant though it is only fair to say that I got a second pip within a month and a third some weeks later.

I was, of course, quite rightly regarded by my fellow officers, most of whom had recently graduated from the O.C.T.U. at Sandhurst, as a bit of an antique and it was not long before I was dispatched to Aldershot on an officers' training course. This was definitely hard work, but it had the advantage of enabling me to go home at week ends.

On the very first occasion when this happened I was reclining in the drawing room enjoying my first drink of the evening when our parlour maid, who somehow or other was still with us, came and enquired whether the ringing of the church bells had any particular significance because she could hear not only the Chobham bells about a mile away, but also those of other churches at varying distances. There was also, she said, a sound of banging in the distance. The date was the 7th September and there was no doubt about it. This must be invasion. We tore upstairs to the landing and looked out of the window which faced towards London and could see a lurid glow all along the line of the river and we could hear quite distinctly the explosion of the bombs, which as it turned out were raining down on dockland, and the fire from the A.A. batteries. I felt there was nothing for me to do except report to the Home Guard C.O. who had taken over from me and was a great friend of mine. I ran him to earth in the village, which was in a state of great excitement, but as the supply of weapons was limited to those I have already mentioned and the entire Home Guard, some thirty to forty strong, had turned out, the situation was a little confused. However, the C.O. informed me that he had succeeded in acquiring a few more rifles which he had been keeping safely at home, pending an emergency, and suggested that perhaps we should go and get them. This seemed to me a good idea and so was the whisky and soda which he offered me directly we got to the house, and which was repeated before we left. We quickly arranged that his wife, who would otherwise have been alone, should stay the night at Halebourne and returned to the village with the rifles.

But there had been no invasion and no hostilities. On page 276 of Vol. II of The Second World War, Sir Winston Churchill describes the events of that night as follows:

> There was however at that time no machinery at General Headquarters, Home Forces, by which the existing eight hours' notice for readiness could be brought to 'readiness for immediate action' by intermediate stages. The code-word 'Cromwell', which meant 'invasion imminent', was therefore issued by Home Forces at 8 p.m., September 7, to the Eastern and Southern Commands, implying action stations for the forward coastal divisions. It was also sent to all formations in the London area and to the IV and VII Corps

225

in G.H.Q. Reserve. It was repeated for information to all other commands in the United Kingdom. On this, in some parts of the country, the Home Guard commanders, acting on their own initiative, called out the Home Guard by ringing the church bells. This led to rumours of enemy parachutist landings, and also that German E-boats were approaching the coast. Neither I nor the Chiefs of Staff were aware that the decisive code-word 'Cromwell' had been used, and the next morning instructions were given to devise intermediate stages by which vigilance could be increased on future occasions without declaring an invasion imminent. Even on receipt of the code-word 'Cromwell' the Home Guard were not to be called out except for special tasks; and also church bells were to be rung only by order of a Home Guard who had himself seen as many as twenty-five parachutists landing, and not because other bells had been heard or for any other reason. As may be imagined, this incident caused a great deal of talk and stir, but no mention of it was made in the newspapers or in Parliament. It served as a useful tonic and rehearsal for all concerned.

But at any rate it had been a very exciting night!

Soon after my return to the battalion it was sent to Norfolk as part of East Coast defence, and in November I was attached to brigade H.Q., where the brigadier formed the rather misguided idea that in due course I might qualify for appointment as staff-captain to the brigade. However, the War Office intervened again and I was dispatched to Shrewsbury as a staff-captain at H.Q. North Wales District, part of Western Command, where I remained until August, 1942, when I was promoted to major and sent to H.Q. Northern Command at York and there I remained for the rest of the war.

Our eldest son, Michael, was called up in May or June, 1940 and also obtained a commission in the Royal Berkshire Regiment, with whom he served in Yorkshire and Northern Ireland before being posted to India where he remained until 1945. He has since made a considerable name for himself as an interior designer and decorator. Our second son, Tony, was at Sherborne when the war broke out and incidentally became caught up in a very severe raid one afternoon when dozens of bombs were rained down on the town and school. I remember his telling me that when he emerged from the classroom, where he had been working, he had the greatest difficulty in the dust and smoke in getting back to his house, where he found a large bomb crater just outside the front door and that his study had virtually disappeared. From Sherborne he went for a year to Trinity College, Oxford, before joining the Grenadier Guards. Soon after getting his commission he was sent to North Africa and was eventually posted to the 6th Battalion, part of 201 Guards Brigade, with whom he also served in Italy, where he was killed or rather died of wounds near Mount Cammino in December, 1943, four months after his twentieth birthday. A few days before he left England my wife and I gave a small dinner party at the Savoy for him and three other Guards officers of about the same age, who were shortly going overseas as well. Of those four young men, two were killed or died of wounds and one was very severely wounded. I do not know what happened to the other apart from the fact that he was awarded the M.C. In the course of both wars there must have been many dinner parties just like that one.

But apart from Tony the member of the family who seemed closest to the war was my wife. For some reason Chobham and the surrounding district, although twenty-five miles from London and affording no particular military objective, had more than its fair share of bombing, which may have been due to the relative proximity of Aldershot. At any rate from September, 1940, until the end of the war there were a good many incidents. Quite early on a bomb exploded in our front garden damaging the gardener's cottage, and on one occasion a land mine fell in the field opposite, but fortunately failed to explode, as my wife had been warned that if it did our house would be severely damaged if not destroyed. It was a relief when a bomb disposal squad from, I believe, the Navy removed it. On another occasion after she had driven me back to Aldershot there was a very nasty raid and a bomb exploded in the road just behind her. Driving a car on a dark night in the country with dimmed lights and an air raid going on was a frightening and lonely experience which my wife had to endure more than once, but then she had all her life been a very courageous person, and in her younger days a well-known and quite fearless skier and one of the first women to pass her tests and qualify as a judge. I think that most people who regularly went to Murren during the winters immediately preceding the first war and are still around would remember the name of Rosemary Ilbert. In 1920, the year after we were married, I went to Switzerland with her, the only time I have ever been, and she certainly frightened the life out of me. However steep the descent she in variably took it straight and within minutes all that was visible to the rest of us, struggling along as best we could in the rear, was her small figure half a mile beyond and below us and still going like a bomb.

However, I am digressing. In addition to being a member of the Red Cross my wife was taking in various members of the services as paying guests, some with and some without families, and with very little help from outside she had a pretty hard time one way and another. And then on the 15th June, 1944, the seemingly inevitable occurred. My daughter was at home at the time with a broken leg and she was lying that evening on a sofa in the drawing room when my wife came in and said that she had just heard the sound of a rather odd aircraft approaching the house but that the engines had cut out. Very fortunately my daughter had been listening to the news and she struggled off the sofa on to the floor and, gripping her astonished mother by the legs, proceeded to propel her to the door. They had only just got through when one of the first V.1's to arrive in England exploded with a massive roar in the garden a few yards away from the house, half the roof caved in, one of the main walls was split from top to bottom, all the windows were blown in and most of the ceilings came down. The floor of the hall where they were sheltering was covered inches deep in rubble and dust and glass and it was a miracle that neither of them was hurt. The drawing room, which had large plate glass windows, was a shambles, curtains and upholstery being ripped to pieces, ornaments smashed, furniture, including the grand piano, cut and scored by flying glass, and part of the ceiling lying on the floor. It had been a narrow escape. Meanwhile the orchard was on fire, but this was put out by a party of soldiers, who happened to be passing by in a truck. There were several people in the house all of whom escaped injury with the exception of a baby, who was in one of the rooms upstairs and sustained a slight cut on the face, and a man who rushed out of the front door immediately after the explosion and was hit by a lump of clay the size of a football, which sailed over the top of the house and fell on his head! Meanwhile the parrot, which had been blown across the kitchen, cage and all, was screaming its head off though quite unhurt.

Air raid wardens arrived with commendable promptitude and within an hour everybody had been evacuated to other homes, the house being left in charge of a policeman. And then the almost unbelievable happened. Three hours later a second V.1 arrived and exploded exactly fifteen yards from the crater made by the first, both having fallen on the same fence. I say almost unbelievable because, whether or not it came from the same projector, the second one had come in on a very low trajectory with its engine running full blast, while the first had drifted down like a falling leaf from a considerable height after its engine had cut out. The odds against this happening must have been millions to one. The unfortunate policeman had hardly recovered from the shock and the increased confusion of debris inside the house, when he heard someone in the kitchen. As the house was supposed to be empty he dashed in only to find the parrot, which was now convulsed with rage and fear, perched on the dresser, swearing like a trooper and regarding out of a jaundiced and malevolent eye the remains of its cage, which for the second time that night had been blown right across the kitchen. For years after the war it included in its repertoire, which was vast and lurid, a vivid presentation of what it sounds like when a bomb comes down and destroys one's home.

The second bomb had completed the work of the first and the mess was indescribable. One noticeable feature was that the doorway in the hall, where my wife and daughter had crouched for protection, now consisted of a jagged piece of wood attached to a hinge. Providence was certainly on their side that night.

The news was conveyed to me at York through military channels the following morning and I was assured that, although the house had been very severely damaged, nobody had been hurt. I was instantly granted leave and went to stay in the house where my wife had been evacuated. My daughter was staying with friends, but she was pretty badly shocked and it was necessary that she should get away as early as possible so, a couple of days after my arrival, I went with her by train to Devonshire, where she stayed for several weeks at Thurlestone with an aunt of mine.

Somehow or other we succeeded in procuring the necessary licence and labour for the rebuilding of Halebourne, and about eight months after the bombing we were able to re-occupy the house. Soon after the war my daughter was married to Henry Lumley-Savile who was also in the Grenadier Guards and had been a friend of Tony's, and as Michael was working and living in London and the house was far too big for the two of us, we decided to sell it and move to something smaller. No doubt that was the right decision, but it was a painful one to take. In the whole of our married life there was never anything quite like Halebourne.

Afterword

One evening in Spring 1967 I was standing for the second time, after an interval of forty-nine years, on the bank of the River Jordan at the spot, near Jericho, where tradition has it that Jesus was baptised.

My wife and I were on a visit to the Middle East and we had flown into Amman that morning from Beirut. From there we had gone by road to see the ruins of the ancient Hellenistic Roman City of Jerash, which lies across the river Jabbok (now Zerka) in a remote valley among the mountains of Gilead, and we were on our way to Jerusalem where we were to spend the night.

The Jordan Valley looked much the same except that the river, which was as muddy as ever, seemed to have shrunk, and large sections of the marshy area to the east, through which we had picked our way so laboriously on the march to Amman, had been drained and converted into what looked like extremely rich and fertile farmland.

Musellabeh lies about ten miles to the north of Jericho and I was unable to distinguish it from the surrounding hills. We were also some distance to the south of the Wadi Auja, through which we had approached the river for our advance on the bridge.

Our hotel in Jerusalem was at the top of the Mount of Olives and after dinner that evening we walked down to Gethsemane. We spent the whole of the next day on a tour of the Old City where we visited most of the holy places, including the Wailing Wall which, according to our excellent Jordanian guide, no Jew would ever see again. Nothing could have been more peaceful and, apart from a few Jordanian officers coming and going by the Citadel, which was a key point in the Jordanian defences, and, of course, out of bounds to sightseers, there was no sign of any military activity, and it is still almost impossible to believe that exactly six weeks later the whole of Jerusalem was in the hands of the Israelis, not one of whom had we seen.

That evening we returned to Amman, and it was odd to reflect that a journey which lasted for less than three hours had taken me longer than four days and nights on the last occasion when I made it though admittedly under very different conditions.

June, 1967

Epilogue: Lawrence - An Appreciation

What is there to say about Lawrence that has not been said already? He was a legend during his lifetime and has remained one since his death. I do not believe that any other man could have achieved what he so brilliantly succeeded in doing when, in the face of every conceivable difficulty, he built up and for two years co-ordinated and controlled a force of Arab guerillas, made up from dozens of different tribes many of which had for generations been enemies with blood feuds going back to God knows when.

Not only that. His tremendous qualities of intellect, endurance and sheer physical courage, his determination and ability, though built on frail lines, to take his share and more than his share in the hardships imposed on him and his Arab companions by the conditions under which they lived and fought in that stark, relentless desert, almost made him a god in their eyes. Sensitive to a degree, reserved, aloof, introspective, impatient sometimes to the point of rudeness, vain sometimes to the point of arrogance, though seeking no personal glory and persistent in his refusal of all honours, basically unsure of himself and of a deeply melancholy disposition, I have never ceased to wonder how he managed first to become and then to remain for so long the venerated leader of those fierce and savage desert warriors with whom, one would think, he could never have had anything in common, but in whose company he learnt to live and endure and suffer as though he had himself been born and bred in the harsh environment from which they sprang.

Of course, like all great men, he had his detractors both before and after his publication of Seven Pillars. No doubt some of these were genuinely disturbed by his flamboyance, but others were actuated by nothing more or less than jealousy of the tremendous world wide publicity which he received, particularly after the famous lectures given after the war by the American reporter Lowell Thomas, who has pointed out that he did not 'invent' the Lawrence legend, nor (as was stated at the time in an English newspaper) go to Arabia in

233

search of a myth that would sell in America, but because he had been introduced to Lawrence in Jerusalem and told by Allenby himself that it would be an excellent idea if he were to visit Arabia and then tell the world what had been happening in that remote desert.

But the cruelest attack of all came from the pen of Richard Aldington, who as late as 1955, twenty years after Lawrence's death, wrote and published a book called Lawrence of Arabia, which in the words of the Oxford Companion to English Literature was a 'bitter denigration of T. E. Lawrence and his career'. Why the bitterness I wonder and for that matter why wait for twenty years? Aldington was a novelist, biographer and poet, whose chief work was probably Death of Hero, published in 1929, and based presumably on his own experiences with the army in France during the war. I have no idea whether Aldington ever met Lawrence or what triggered off this attack on his memory after all that time, but it may be that he was incensed by the limelight afforded to Lawrence, both before and after his death, as compared with the relative obscurity in which so many of his friends had fought and died in France. But although it is opportunity which makes the man I do not think that Aldington would have made much more success as a guerrilla leader in Arabia than Lawrence would have achieved as a regimental officer in France.

Seven Pillars, apart from the sheer excitement of the narrative, is not a very easy book to read and it may be that at times Lawrence drew a little on his imagination. Whether he did so, and if so to what extent, in his account of the flogging and other dreadful experiences which he was forced to endure at the hands of the Turkish Bey, nobody will ever know because there were none to witness that dreadful scourging and humiliation of the body and spirit, but that the encounter did indeed take place and inflict a permanent and ineradicable scar on Lawrence cannot be doubted for a moment.

The incident was portrayed in the film Lawrence of Arabia directed by David Lean, and with Peter O'Toole taking the name part, as well as certain other incidents, the authenticity of which I am inclined to question. Although O'Toole gave a virtuoso performance there was a certain unreality about it, because he seemed to tower over all the other actors, whereas Lawrence was a very small and slightly built man. Nor was he anything like the sadistic creature he was sometimes made out to be. I suppose that most men have a streak of sadism in them which may manifest itself in times of stress, and especially of war, but whatever cruelty, if any, Lawrence may have on occasion perpetrated on the enemy was as nothing compared with the suffering which he inflicted on himself.

No - this was indeed a great man, and although the suggestion has been made by some of his critics that Allenby, who was venerated by the British who served under him in Palestine just as Lawrence was by his Arabs, did not like him and could not get on with him, I can only say that this is not borne out by the tributes which Allenby paid to his memory after his death and which made it abundantly clear that he held him in the highest admiration, affection and esteem.

I have no personal knowledge of Lawrence in the sense that, so far as I am aware I never met him either in Palestine, or when I was at Oxford and he was a Fellow of All Souls, but let me repeat some words of Laurence Moore who, as already recounted, not only knew him but for a time became his close companion in the desert campaign.

> And then his untimely death. And after that his detractors with their criticisms and condemnation and their claim that there was no military value in his performance. They accused him of being theatrical. Yes, looking back, the whole campaign was slightly theatrical. It had to be to impress the Arabs to say nothing of the Turks. He has also been accused of being a charlatan and poseur but I can affirm that he was neither, but a genuine performer, and I can say this as one who for one Act at least, and in a very minor role, appeared on stage with him, and that whenever we of the Imperial Camel Corps who still survive meet together to reminisce about the past, those of us who took part in the campaign are proud to recall that at one time, and a long time ago, we had the honour to serve with Lawrence in Arabia.

It was not until after I had written the preceding paragraphs that I saw a copy of the new enlarged edition of Lowell Thomas's book With Lawrence in Arabia, which was originally published in 1924. The importance, to me at any rate, of the new edition, which was published in the U.S.A. in 1967, lies in the Foreword and also in the Epilogue which contains a report on the men around Lawrence and, although it had not been my intention to become involved too deeply in the attacks which have been made on Lawrence ever since his death, but which have only reached their climax in recent years, I feel that I cannot altogether escape it, and I am more than grateful to Lowell Thomas for allowing me to make use of some of the material which his book contains.

At the same time I have made no alterations to the words which I have already written and which, at any rate so far as the film is concerned, appear to coincide very closely with the views expressed by many of those, including the late Sir Basil Liddell Hart, who were closely acquainted with Lawrence and are far better qualified, therefore, to judge than myself, and it is significant that while they unanimously agree that the film was a brilliant technical achievement, and the photography superb, they also affirm in no uncertain terms that the story which it told and the delineation of the principal characters, such as Allenby and Lawrence, which it portrayed, bore scarcely any resemblance to the real facts.

I suppose that there has never been such a controversial motion picture and that the reason for this is that there has never been quite such a controversial figure as Lawrence himself. Nonetheless I am convinced that, when the final history is written, the attacks on his reputation and achievements will be forgotten, and he will be acclaimed as one of the greatest figures of his age.

Lowell Thomas has stated in his book that in his opinion the main reasons for these attacks are threefold, (1) because some of the British officers of the so-called Mesopotamian group believed that they should have had the support that went to Lawrence, and resented his efforts on behalf of the Hejaz Arabs, (2) because of the bitter Near and Middle Eastern clash of interest between the British and the French Empires, and (3) because of the simple fact that Lawrence was in truth a great man.

The last of these may appear to be a little fanciful but Lowell Thomas relates how on the eve of the publication of Richard Aldington's book he told Lord Beaverbrook, who was passing through New York on his way back to London, that he had received information to the effect that a British novelist was about to bring out a smear book on Lawrence and that his friends were concerned, to which Beaverbrook replied, 'Don't worry. It will simply add to Lawrence's stature. Every great man is subject to attack. There are no exceptions. The one who will suffer will be the author of the book'.

As to the second reason there can be no doubt whatever that such a clash existed, and it must be admitted that Lawrence can hardly have endeared himself to the French by his continuing and outspoken hostility towards them, while the French in their turn regarded him also as an enemy and as the man chiefly responsible for spoiling their plans of a Middle Eastern Empire. Incidentally it has to be remembered that Richard Aldington was an ardent Francophile, who had lived in France for years, and it is easy to understand the influence which his French friends brought to bear on him, and which may have been a principal factor in the cruel attack which he made on Lawrence.

As for the Mesopotamian group there is undoubtedly truth in the statement that criticism of Lawrence originally came from those who were involved in the Mesopotamian campaign, but Lowell Thomas goes out of his way to point out that there were exceptions to the general rule and that some of these were to remain Lawrence's lifelong friends.

Inevitably there was another group from which Lawrence might have expected very little sympathy or understanding, the Zionists, and it is worthy of note that this included a very senior member of Allenby's staff, who after the war said of Lawrence, 'He owes everything he has ever had to Allenby. He was created by Allenby, and his reputation, such as it is, is of Allenby's creation.'

And yet Chaim Weizmann, the great Zionist leader and 'father of modern Israel' said this, 'There was a lasting friendship between us. I frequently had occasion to ask his advice . . . Lawrence readily gave not only this but his personal help in furthering both the Zionist aspirations and an understanding with the Arabs . . . a very great service on his part to the cause of Zionism.... I remember with gratitude his help in furthering the cause of the Jewish people'.

It stands to reason that the controversy, for so long as it continues, will lie between those who were more or less Lawrence's contemporaries, including the men who accompanied him on the long and bitter desert marches which he and others have described

237

so well, who fought by his side, who knew and understood him and the tasks which he had set himself to perform, who for one reason or another became associated with him both during and after the war, who marvelled at his achievements, or who were simply his friends, on the one hand, and the increasing number of people who never knew him, who were perhaps not even born when he led and inspired his Arabs throughout the vicissitudes and privations of that amazing war, and whose writings are based on the so-called fresh documentary evidence which they have succeeded in bringing to light, on the other hand.

To illustrate what the first of these groups thought about Lawrence here are a few of the quotations given by Lowell Thomas from men whose views can hardly be described as other than worthy of respect, and all of whom are dead.

Lord Wavell (who had been a major on Allenby's staff):

> 'His name will live in history. He had many fairy godmothers at his cradle, with gifts of fearlessness, of understanding, of a love of learning, of craftsmanship, of humour, of Spartan endurance, of frugality, of selflessness.'

Lord Lloyd (who went on special missions to the Hejaz):

> 'On the long night marches we had wonderful talks . . . his brain is like quicksilver and his humour unquenchable . . . I have got very fond of him, and respect his indomitable courage, self sacrifice and enterprise. Alone he has conquered this country.'

Colonel W. F. Stirling (who was Chief of Staff to Colonel P. C. Joyce, who was in command of British co-operation with the Arabs):

> 'Lawrence was the greatest genius England has produced in the last two centuries.'

Liman von Sanders (the German General who commanded the Turkish and German armies in Gallipoli and later in Palestine):

> 'The desert revolt was a British success, because of the immense handicap it imposed on the Turks. With courage, endurance and skill Lawrence captured the support not only of the Arabs, but of Allenby.'

Lord Winterton (who remained behind with Lawrence after the Imperial Camel Corps Assault Column was withdrawn from the Hejaz):

'A noteworthy feature of the campaign was the personality of Lawrence. At intervals, attacks by men of lesser minds are made upon his reputation and claim to fame. These blandly ignore the regard for him felt by so many men of eminence who knew him and, in many cases, worked with him. They include Winston Churchill, Bernard Shaw, Allenby, Wavell, Trenchard, Storrs and others. They brush aside the admiration which we, who served with him, had for his genius and the great influence which he had over our Arab allies. I have worked directly under many eminent men. Of these, in my judgement, only Churchill exceeds Lawrence in stature....'

And finally Sir Winston Churchill himself (who in 1921 was Colonial Secretary and succeeded after several attempts in persuading Lawrence to join his newly created Middle East Department as adviser on Arab affairs. It was this Department which brought about the offer of the throne of Iraq to Feisal, who in the previous year had been driven out of Syria by the French)

'He was a dweller on the mountain tops, where the air was cold, crisp and rarefied.... His name will live in history, in English letters, in the annals of war, in the traditions of the Royal Air Force, in the legends of Arabia. I was under his spell and deemed myself his friend. I account him one of the greatest beings alive in our time.'

Before bringing this chapter to a close I feel that I must make some reference to the book The Secret Lives of Lawrence of Arabia by Phillip Knightley and Colin Simpson, which has been published recently.

The authors have certainly carried out a wonderful task of investigation and, although they have succeeded in bringing to light certain documentary evidence, part of which on the face of it would not appear to rebound to Lawrence's credit, I detect that they are by no means wholly unsympathetic towards him or unmindful of the almost insoluble problems which confronted him towards the end of and immediately after the war.

There are just four comments which I, as a staunch supporter and admirer of Lawrence, would like to make on the story which they have unfolded.

1. Lawrence did not create a policy entirely on his own. He was, after all, acting under orders from higher authority with whom, it is hardly necessary to add, he frequently disagreed. I am not, of course, referring to Allenby, with whom he succeeded in establishing a firm and lasting relationship based on mutual respect, but to his superiors in London.

2. The authors confirm that one of his main motivations throughout the Revolt, apart from patriotism, was hatred of the French and their ambitions to create for themselves an empire in the Middle East. I have already mentioned the fact that the French were equally bitter in their attitude towards Lawrence. There was not only a constant clash of personalities but also an issue, which became increasingly aggravated with the approach of final victory and the complete destruction of the Turkish Empire, and which involved nothing more or less than the political reorganisation after the war of the vast territories which had been wrested from Turkish domination. It is easy to say that there was nothing in the extension of either the British or the French interests in the Middle East which was likely to help or at any rate cement the cause of Arab independence, and it may well be that the Arabs had been promised, in return for their assistance, a far greater degree of autonomy than they were ever likely to achieve in the foreseeable future, but the plan which Lawrence had gradually been evolving in his mind, and for which he fought so hard during the Paris Peace Conference, would have gone a long way towards meeting Arab aspirations. However, the plan was overruled and in the result the French were given the protectorate over Syria and the Lebanon, both of which Feisal had rightly or wrongly imagined were to be handed to him.

But the blame for this deception, if deception there was, lay not so much with Lawrence as with the British Government. It originated with the famous - or infamous - Sykes-Picot agreement, a secret Anglo-French arrangement which was concluded in 1916 and provided that after the war Britain, France and Russia (which had been a party to the negotiations) should have well defined spheres of influence over various parts of the vast territories which Turkey would be compelled to relinquish following the break up of the Ottoman Empire. These included Palestine, the whole of Mesopotamia (now Iraq) except for its northern district of Mosul, and what is now Jordan for the British, Syria including the Lebanon, and Mosul for the French, and the Caucasus for the Russians. It is doubtful whether Lawrence knew anything about this agreement at the time and in fact it was not until Russia for its own reasons let the cat out of the bag at the end of 1917 that its existence was revealed to the world. Whether or not it would ever have been disclosed to the Arabs until it was too late to retract is a matter for speculation, and the only accusation which can be levelled against Lawrence is that after it came to his knowledge, as it was obviously bound to do, he continued to persuade Feisal that it was the firm intention of the British that the Arabs should be granted their independence. By then, however, Lawrence had been placed in an almost impossible position and in any case he was determined to do his utmost to wreck the Sykes-Picot agreement which he detested from the start and which cut right across his own grandiose plan for the establishment, admittedly under British protection, of a semi-independent Arab state which would include in addition to Northern Arabia the whole of Mesopotamia, Jordan and Syria, with the possible exception of the Lebanon which might have to go to the French.

3. What the original intention of Lawrence and, for that matter the British Government as well, may have been as regards Palestine it is difficult to determine but, with the announcement in November, 1917, by Mr Balfour, the Foreign Secretary, of his famous Declaration that H.M. Government viewed with favour the establishment in Palestine of a national home for the Jewish people, any hope which Feisal may have entertained, whether justifiably or not, that Palestine was to come within the area of Arab independence must have been shattered overnight.

Feisal was indeed, as the authors point out, desperately short of money after the war and it was Lawrence's idea that arrangements should be made for him to be financed on a large scale by international Jewry. According to what Lawrence said at the Peace Conference, Feisal who, not unnaturally, took the view that he was entitled to make his own choice as to who should be his financial advisers, and preferred to obtain the assistance of British or American Zionists in this capacity, had stated that the Zionists would be acceptable to the Arabs 'on terms'. What these were to be is not exactly clear but even as early as June, 1918, there had been a meeting between Feisal and Dr Chaim Weizmann who, according to his own account, told him that, if he wanted to build up a strong and prosperous Arab Kingdom, it was the Jews and only the Jews who would be able to help him. They would be his neighbours and would not represent any danger to him as they were not and never would be a great power. The authors go on to say that at a subsequent meeting in London between Feisal, Weizmann and Lawrence just before the Peace Conference, Weizmann explained that, in accordance with the Zionist programme, the Conference should recognise the national and historical right of the Jews to Palestine, that Britain should be the Trustee power, that the Jews should have an adequate share in government and that the country should be developed so as to create room for 4,000,000 or 5,000,000 Jews without encroaching on the ownership rights of the Arab peasantry. In return the Jews would be prepared to render Feisal every assistance in brains and money in order to help revive his country. An agreement was actually signed along these lines, Feisal making a reservation about the Arabs obtaining their independence as demanded in a memorandum he had submitted to the Foreign Office.

Now it may well be that, so far as Lawrence was concerned, his chief motivation was to set in motion a series of events which would have had the result of pushing the French out of Syria because, with a Zionist centre established in Jerusalem and the willingness and ability of the Zionists, in return for concessions, to provide Feisal with all the financial assistance he so badly needed, no help would be required from the French, and there would be no need, therefore, to grant them any concessionary rights over Syria. Nonetheless the position of Feisal would have been considerably strengthened by the addition of Syria to his Kingdom and I cannot see why the suggestion should be made that Lawrence was acting with a cynical disregard for Feisal's interests. The complete independence of the Arabs might or might not be achieved in the course of time but, for the immediate future, Lawrence was able to see that the establishment of a Zionist state in Palestine was not necessarily inimical to the interests of the Arabs as a whole. Quite the contrary in fact, because the union between the Zionists and Arabia, the latter supplying the land and the former the money, would have brought considerable benefits to both.

To the question, therefore, posed by the authors as to what the shape of the Middle East would have been today had such a scheme succeeded I would unhesitatingly reply, 'It might have been much better and it could not possibly have been any worse'.

4. A discussion of Lawrence's private life is really outside the scope of this book and I propose to say very little on the subject. Like all great men he had his share, and perhaps more than his share, of human foibles but whether or not he had homosexual tendencies seems to me to be as entirely irrelevant as it is still unproven. As far as the incident of his capture at Deraa and his debasement by the Turkish Bey are concerned I am, as I have already stated, prepared to concede that Lawrence's account of this may not be strictly accurate in detail, although I for one am convinced that in substance it is true, and I do not think that the discovery that the Bey was known in Turkey as an aggressive heterosexual or that, had he ever exhibited any homosexual leanings, he would never have been admitted to, or at any rate, lasted as a member of the first nationalist parliament at Ankara, with its puritanical overtones, really contributes very much to an assessment of Lawrence's sexual proclivities. All we do know, as the authors' researches seem to have made clear, is that whatever may have been the exact experience which Lawrence suffered on that dreadful occasion, he was never able to heal the wound which it had inflicted on his psyche and which, I think, goes far to explain what happened, or is supposed to have happened, to him later on.

Robert Graves has pointed out that Lawrence is on record as having stated that, long before the war, he had fallen in love with a woman in Damascus who, throughout the desert campaign, was never for a minute absent from his waking thoughts and who provided a disproportionate share of the motive for the Arabian adventure. He has gone on to say that in Lawrence's dedication to Seven Pillars of Wisdom she is addressed as S.A., which has been mistaken for her initials, or those of Sheikh Achmed, a close Arab friend, or even of a country - Saudi Arabia - but which in fact, according to hints subsequently dropped by Lawrence, stood for 'Son Altesse', the language of the troubadour for the lady who gave him inspiration to write his poems, and devotion to whom sustained him through perils and hardships when he went on crusade. Fact or fantasy? I doubt if we shall ever know, but it is all part of the romance and mystique which will forever be associated with that enigmatic, tortured, but somehow noble figure 'Lawrence of Arabia'.

LEONAUR

ALSO FROM LEONAUR
AVAILABLE IN SOFTCOVER OR HARDCOVER WITH DUST JACKET

EW2 EYEWITNESS TO WAR SERIES
CAPTAIN OF THE 95th (Rifles) *by Jonathan Leach*

An officer of Wellington's Sharpshooters during the
Peninsular, South of France and Waterloo Campaigns
of the Napoleonic Wars.

SOFTCOVER : **ISBN 1-84677-001-7**
HARDCOVER : **ISBN 1-84677-016-5**

WFI THE WARFARE FICTION SERIES
NAPOLEONIC WAR STORIES
by Sir Arthur Quiller-Couch

Tales of soldiers, spies, battles & Sieges from the
Peninsular & Waterloo campaigns

SOFTCOVER : **ISBN 1-84677-003-3**
HARDCOVER : **ISBN 1-84677-014-9**

EWI EYEWITNESS TO WAR SERIES
RIFLEMAN COSTELLO *by Edward Costello*

The adventures of a soldier of the 95th (Rifles) in the Peninsular
& Waterloo Campaigns of the Napoleonic wars.

SOFTCOVER : **ISBN 1-84677-000-9**
HARDCOVER : **ISBN 1-84677-018-1**

MCI THE MILITARY COMMANDERS SERIES
**JOURNALS OF ROBERT ROGERS OF THE
RANGERS** *by Robert Rogers*

The exploits of Rogers & the Rangers in his own words
during 1755-1761 in the French & Indian War.

SOFTCOVER : **ISBN 1-84677-002-5**
HARDCOVER : **ISBN 1-84677-010-6**

www.ingramcontent.com/pod-product-compliance
Lightning Source LLC
Chambersburg PA
CBHW030357100426
42812CB00028B/2745/J